LOCAL LABOUR MARKETS AND WAGE STRUCTURES

EDITOR
Derek Robinson

Gower Press

First published in Britain by Gower Press Limited
140 Great Portland Street, London W1N 5TA
1970

ISBN 0 7161 0052 5

Printed in Britain

Contents

Illustrations

Notes on contributors

W M CONBOY served his "time" in engineering and spent thirteen years in the industry on the shop floor and then in the drawing office. He maintains that the the deciding factor in the decision to leave industry and enter Oxford as an adult student was the fear that otherwise he would be known in the history of engineering as the only draughtsman whose block capitals could not be read.

After taking his degree in Politics, Philosophy and Economics he joined the staff of the Oxford University Institute of Economics and Statistics, specialising in labour economics. His present appointment is with the Extra-mural Delegacy at Oxford where he lectures to "both sides" of industry on Industrial Relations.

He is at present working with a colleague at the Delegacy on a research project for the CIR on the impact of the TV series "Representing the Union," the results of which are expected to be published later this year.

Besides his many lecturing commitments he says he most enjoys "looking around" firms - and asking "why?"

DAN GOWLER. After working fourteen years in industry, he received a Mature Student's State Scholarship to Queens' College, Cambridge. Here he read Economics and Social Anthropology and then took up a post at the Centre for Business Research, Manchester Business School. Following three years' field work examining the function of wage payment systems, he took up a lectureship in Industrial Anthropology in the Manchester Business School. He is the author of several papers in the general field of labour economics.

KAREN LEGGE read Modern History at St Hugh's College, Oxford, and also obtained a Diploma in Social and Administrative Studies, after which she became a Research Associate, and later Research Fellow at the Centre for Business Research, Manchester Business School. During this time she carried out intensive field studies on the functioning of wage payment systems and labour turnover in labour-intensive firms employing female workers. She is the author of several articles on these topics, and is now investigating the personnel function in a number of enterprises.

DONALD MACKAY, who is very particular about the way his name is spelt and pronounced, is a Senior Lecturer in Applied Economics in the Department of Social and Economic Research at Glasgow University. He is author of "Geographical Mobility and the Brain Drain" (Allen and Unwin, 1970) and of a number of papers on labour and regional economics. His interest in engineering dates from a three-year period of employment as a systems analyst in that industry. An academic appointment followed because, he claims, there were no systems to analyse. He is currently completing a study of the labour market policies pursued by engineering plants entitled "Labour Markets in Theory and Practice." It will be published in 1971.

E J ROBERTSON read philosophy at United College, St Andrews. After national service in the Air Force, he joined Esso Standard to sell oil - mainly in East Africa. He worked for five years there in several marketing roles, including that of retail co-ordinator Uganda.
   On his return to UK he was appointed lecturer in the Department of Sociology, University of Strathclyde, where he became interested, inter alia, in problems

of collective bargaining. This interest resulted in his taking up a post as Central Personnel Executive for the Avon Rubber Company, and subsequently as Director of Research for the Engineering Employers' Federation, London. He is Editor of the Federation's Research Series and its Industrial Relations Research Bulletin. He has lectured extensively in the UK and in Europe; he is at present Chairman of the Labour Statistics Panel of the CBI.

DEREK ROBINSON is Senior Research Officer, Oxford University Institute of Economics and Statistics, and Fellow and Tutor, Magdalen College, Oxford. After a period as a clerk in the civil service, he spent two years at Ruskin College and a further two years at Lincoln College, Oxford, reading PPE. Following a year at the Extra-mural Department, University of Sheffield, he joined the Institute where for the past ten years he has been engaged on labour economics research. During this time he has been attached as Economic Adviser to the National Board for Prices and Incomes (1967-9) and as Senior Economic Adviser, Department of Employment and Productivity (1968-70). He was visiting Professor of Economics at the University of California at Berkeley in 1968. He has worked as a consultant to OECD (Publications: "Non-wage Incomes and Prices Policy"; "Wage Drift, Fringe Benefits and Manpower Distribution"; "Workers' Negotiated Savings Plans for Capital Formation") and to the Organisation of American States. He often lectures to trade union and management groups. He is Chairman of the working party on manpower utilisation in the Distributive Trades EDC.

Dedication

This book is dedicated to Professor Clark Kerr to whom we all owe and acknowledge a great debt.

Preface

Three groups of academics at Glasgow, Manchester
and Oxford are working on problems of wage structures,
wage systems and local labour markets. We started
our work from various and different premises and
used different techniques. We tend to look at the same
problems from somewhat different positions; the
Manchester group, for example, are social anthro-
pologists while the others are economists. We knew
from our meetings and discussions that we were
coming to similar conclusions even though we were
using different sources of data and different
disciplines. For some time we have therefore had a
mutual interest in each other's work. There is one
belief we have in common which is vital to our work.
We all believe that analysis and examination of wages
and the associated problems should begin at plant or
company level. In this sense, we are all committed
to a micro-approach to these problems at least as a
starting point. Our work is showing that there is such
a diversity of behaviour between different firms in the
same local labour market that generalisations based
on aggregate data and analysis are unlikely to provide
a useful foundation on which to build. In addition, we
were all interested in applying academic research to
practical problems and believed that we should try to
relate our findings to the real world. We were therefore very interested when the Engineering Employers'
Federation suggested holding a seminar at which we
would present papers on wage structures and local
labour markets.

This book is based on the papers we presented in
March 1970. They have been rewritten slightly so
that each chapter can stand in its own right while the

13

collection of chapters will present a unified treatment
of various problems. Inevitably there is some degree
of overlap between some of the chapters; this is
inevitable when researchers present their findings. In
order to explain the findings of each piece of work it
is necessary to sketch in the background assumptions
and quote the preliminary results even though someone
else might also present some of them elsewhere in the
book. Such overlapping is, however, of interest and
has not been edited out because the similar findings
come from analysis of different material from different
sources.

We are all continuing our research in these areas
and are fully aware that the material presented here
is not the last words on the subject. We will all
probably publish further results later but we all agree
that there is benefit in presenting our results and
thoughts to date in this way, as we believe that the
interrelationships of the different approaches can be
brought out better in a book such as this than by three
quite separate works. Also we believe that having
set out our basic positions in this book we can use this
text to build on later, and the speed of publishing
means that we can produce our results before they
get out of date.

1 Local labour markets and plant wage structures: an introduction

by E J Robertson

One of the principal objects of the Conference at which the chapters in this book were first presented was to consider the results of various academic research programmes, in order to throw some light on a number of practical areas of industrial relations work; I am confident that there is something in this material of direct interest to all concerned with the everyday problems of managing industrial conflict. The approaches of our academic experts are not unduly theoretical, and fitting academic arguments to practical problems has been given prime consideration.

This introductory chapter poses certain questions and considers possible answers in the light of what the main contributors have to say. These questions are:

1   What are local labour markets?

2   Why analyse these labour markets?

3   What approaches are there to such analyses?

4   What explanations do these analyses afford in explaining the behaviour of employers and employees?

5   Does labour market analysis throw light upon current problems in industrial relations in the UK?

1.1 LOCAL LABOUR MARKETS : WHAT ARE THEY ?

Labour markets are the mechanisms, principally institutional, which employers (as buyers of labour) and workers and their representatives (as sellers of labour) can affect the deployment and utilisation of manpower.

As a bald definition, this may appear to be a statement of the obvious; but it needs some qualifications to put into context the arguments which follow.

The first is that, apparently, people find it abhorrent to speak of buying and selling labour in industry: "Labour is not a commodity" (ILO Convention). While appreciating the idealism rejecting this economic fact, and appreciating the need to consider other factors beside the crudely economic in industrial and personnel relations, the first axiom to establish, for present purposes, is that labour markets exist primarily as mechanisms for the buying and selling of manpower. In fairness, economists have always held that what is bought and sold is not men but their labour services. These services are a factor, like machinery and materials, in the production process. There is a market for such services out of which arises a price; the worker sells his services without selling himself.

We shall consider how these operations affect the industrial relations world. In particular, consideration will be given to an analysis of the influence of labour market pressures on wages levels, wage systems and wage structures at the factory level in industry, as well as the ways in which labour market pressures can influence such factors as labour turnover, industrial conflict, training problems, and so on.

1.2 LABOUR MARKET ANALYSIS : WHY ?

Many of us spend much of our working time thinking and talking about labour markets and their problems. Moreover, even if industrial relations practitioners do not customarily use economic of sociological theory and, of necessity, have no time to investigate the operations of a local labour market (especially when disrupted by a dispute or work stoppage), nevertheless we do talk about labour markets.

George Brown once said he could not define a "restrictive practice," but he knew when he saw one. Although industrial relations specialists cannot isolate and define a "labour market problem," it is comforting to think that we know one when we see one.

1.3 APPROACHES TO LABOUR MARKET ANALYSIS
At the risk of oversimplifying the opinions of many notable commentators, I want to review some alternative approaches to the analysis of industrial relations problems, as suggested by the perceived constraints imposed by the operations of labour markets. And here arise some of the qualifications to the basic statement that labour markets are mechanisms for the buying and selling of manpower.

But first let us examine more closely the concept of "the labour market" itself. There is a distinction to be drawn between external labour markets and internal labour markets. In brief, the external labour market is the one in which the company, together with other companies employing similar grades of labour, is drawing on the labour force as a whole, at the national level, and (most significantly perhaps) at the local level. The actions of managements in all the companies and of the government and the trade unions, together determine who gets employed where, and on what terms and conditions.

The internal labour market is in many respects far more complex, and in its influence on the make-up of wages and wage structures at the factory level, is more important. The internal labour market refers to the interaction of forces related to wage systems, the factory technology, the actions of management and

17

work force and so on that determine the utilisation and deployment of manpower within the firm itself, given its existing work force. This obviously is of crucial interest at the present time, with emphasis increasingly put on factory level productivity bargaining.

Thus two broad areas of analysis are involved that, while necessarily somewhat interdependent, can be considered separately. Roughly speaking, the operation of the external labour market has traditionally been the subject of labour economics, while that of the internal labour market has occupied industrial psychologists, sociologists and management scientists. Before attempting to bring these approaches together, some of the shortcomings of existing approaches to problem solving in these areas must be outlined.

The classic economic theories of labour markets are of interest in various crucial respects, some of which accord with reality, and some of which manifestly do not. There is a great deal of insight into the operations of (external) labour markets in a key statement from Adam Smith's "Wealth of Nations," written at the end of the eighteenth century. What he says about the regulation of terms and conditions of employment seems sound common sense; but what he also says is that the local labour market operates most freely under certain circumstances, that is, given certain assumptions. It is important that to a large extent our troubles in industrial relations often arise because these conditions, of the free operation of the market, do not prevail in real life. Adam Smith said:

> The whole of the advantages and disadvantages of the different employments of labour ... must in the same neighbourhood be either perfectly equal or continually tending to equality. If, in the same neighbourhood, there was any employment evidently either more or less advantageous than the rest, so many people would crowd into it in the one case, and so many people would desert it in

the other, that its advantages would soon return to the level of the other employments. This at least would be the case in a society where things were left to follow their natural course, where there was perfect liberty, and where every man was perfectly free both to choose what occupation he thought proper, and to change it as often as he thought proper. Every man's interest would prompt him to seek the advantageous and to shun the disadvantageous employment.

Many of the characteristics of the economic world assumed away by Smith actually appear in our existing complex industrial society, in which the prevailing conditions or "advantages and disadvantages" of employment are far from "continually tending to equality," and in which his perfectly self-regulatory mechanism is very unlikely. The extent to which people can know in advance of "the whole of the advantages and disadvantages" of all jobs in the neighbourhood, to which they could move, is of course not only partly theoretical (since some aspects of a job cannot be ascertained until it has been tried) but also probably very small (if the actual evidence of the relative lack of knowledge about other jobs is anything to go by). The extent to which people are free to change to any "more advantageous job" "as often as (they) think proper" is of course diminished by what can be called the "inconvenience factors" of training, retraining and the sheer trouble of moving jobs too often. Often, people clearly prefer job security against the theoretical idea of always looking for an advantageous change. And whether vacancies always exist for more advantageous jobs primarily depends on the state of product markets in those companies, and not (as Smith assumed) necessarily on the cost of employing extra labour. Workpeople do not change jobs solely in response to relative improvements in terms and conditions.

19

The obverse side of all this again seems obvious:
that in a situation where a firm wishes to attract
labour in a locality where there is probably little
unemployment, the extent of success merely by
making the terms and conditions of employment more
attractive by comparison with the other companies in
the area, is limited. Other devices are necessary in
any case, even where there is concentration on inter-
firm competition for labour - for example, advertise-
ment of some sort - and prior analysis of what other
companies are offering is also involved.

That the supply of labour to the market (the firms in
the local, external, labour market) is imperfectly
responsive to the price offered is verified by much
empirical research. I will quote just one example of
research into this phenomenon. Seventy-five jobs in a
local labour market of forty firms were examined:
The large majority showed enormous spreads of
average hourly earnings between the different firms
for the same job, and tests were used to ascertain the
linkage between wage increases offered and changes
in numbers employed. There was again a large spread,
between firms, of average percentage increases in
earnings through time, for the same jobs, and in
some cases the larger increases were matched by
increases in the number employed by the firm. But
other firms were able to increase the men employed
in the same occupation, by the same number, while
giving much lower wage increases. Sometimes the
firms giving the biggest increases did not augment
the numbers employed at all. The influence at the
bargaining table of the concept of "going rates" may
be great; but empirical economic research indicates
perhaps a degree of unreality in that concept in
relation to the actual operation of local labour markets.

Keynes wrote somewhat condescendingly in his
"General Theory of Employment, Interest and Money":
    The ideas of economists ... are more powerful

than is commonly understood. Indeed the world is ruled by little else. Practical men, who believe themselves to be quite exempt from any intellectual influence, are usually the slaves of some defunct economist.

An example of what Keynes intended is that our thinking on labour markets is often conditioned by visions such as Adam Smith's: workpeople moving on to greener pastures when they cannot get what they want in their existing jobs, and companies being able to get and keep all the employees they want merely by observing the so-called going rates and conditions for the locality. It is quite impracticable to rely purely on market mechanisms to recruit and retain labour, yet the evidence of some firms giving in unquestioningly to "comparability claims," despite national agreements, and of bargainers on both sides talking of a "going rate" when in fact a large spread of rates exist in a locality for a job, suggests there is a grain of truth in Keynes' allegation.

On the face of things, the "comparability claim" is a rational argument: in classic economic theory, the operation of the labour market is made more perfect by the interchange of knowledge about market conditions, and by the willingness of sellers (the workers) to move freely to get better conditions.

In practice, however, comparability claims are often decided on faulty analysis by the employer, especially if he believes a threatened strike would be damaging, or one is already in progress. Long-term evaluative analysis, to work out the full cost of avoiding a strike, might indicate that the strike has to be taken despite the short term product market disadvantages entailed. In my experience, however, such analysis is rarely made. We do not know the full economic consequences of strikes, or the full economic consequences of attempting to avoid them.

21

A "comparability claim" is saying, it seems: "If you do not pay what (we say) they are paying down the road, we will go and work down the road; yes, all 1000 of us." This is nonsense, until at least it has been ascertained (a) exactly what they are paying down the road, (b) whether it is really likely that you will lose labour by not paying the going rates, and (c) whether it really would be more expensive to take a strike. When it gets to the stage that comparability with general European conditions is a factor in a claim, clearly the whole argument becomes ridiculous. If they cannot get what they want, are they really going to pack and go to Dusseldorf?

ws ?

The comparability claim is a convenient one for the unions, especially when backed by a strike or strike threat. In principle, it is also a convenient one for the employers, when they realise that the prima facie threat of "upping-and-leaving" is bogus and the use of the strike indicates yet another slogging match. But this does not solve the problem of how to get value for money increases paid out, in terms of manpower effort called forth; nor does it solve the problem of what really makes the local labour market tick, in terms of who works where, for how much, and how changes in this can be achieved.

1.4   INTERNAL LABOUR MARKETS

The operations of a company, in a local labour market, are inseparable from the whole set of circumstances of the company itself. Its demand for labour, and its fluctuations which often affect labour relations attitudes and actions, are derived primarily from the production needs engendered by market demand. That is straightforward and evidenced by a strike proneness of some industries traceable partly to job insecurity due to seasonal lay-offs. Certainly, only in a minority of cases is it true that the decision as to how many men to employ is taken mainly on the grounds of the price

22

of employing them. In general, the demand for labour is primarily responsive to product market needs, and much less wage-level responsive than traditional economic thinking supposes.

Among the circumstances internal to the firm, however, more interesting is the supply side of the market. A company can decide how many employees it needs and their working hours, within certain standard constraints. The major question - and answers are numerous and often contradictory - is: "What determines, and what can alter favourably, the supply of manpower effort offered by the available workforce?"

The balance of the demand for manpower effort and the supply of manpower effort within the company is regulated by what we shall call the mechanisms of the internal labour market, and it is in this context that much of the discussion will take place. A number of crucial similarities between "internal labour markets" and "external (local) labour markets" will become apparent.

Perhaps the most important lesson that can be carried over from the analysis of external labour markets to that of internal labour markets (and this is a basic assumption), is that the price of manpower (level of wages and so on), in itself does not explain all the behaviour of the market. It is not irrelevant nor insignificant; equally it is not the whole of the story. Again, as with external labour markets, the interesting areas of behaviour, that throw light on the everyday industrial relations difficulties, are those which indicate a breakdown, total or partial, of the money mechanisms as a regulator of the balance of the supply of and the demand for manpower effort. A few examples will illustrate this important point.

1   Productivity bargaining is an attempt to overcome the constraints of external markets, that is, short-age of labour and need to get increased production,

23

by offering inducements to increase the internal supply of manpower effort. The important thing is not that improvement is paid for, but that payment in itself is not enough. To produce extra manpower effort requires detailed planning, close cooperation with the unions, supervision of necessary changes by management and the maintenance of appropriate controls. If offering the money would suffice all would be much simpler, but the internal labour market does not work on money alone.

2 Another example is the necessity for agreements and procedures for dilution. If the internal labour market worked by money alone it would be enough to offer the appropriate rate for the skilled job, and expect to fill it without difficulty. Not so in the real world, as many an employer can testify.

3 Again, piecework systems assume that the monetary incentive is sufficient to evince maximum manpower effort. But I am sure that any employer would be ill-advised to rely solely on money bonuses to operate a successful payments-by-results system. Without involving the technicalities of wage payment systems, the appropriateness of the incentive system to the type of production, the quality of the work study controls, the attitudes and degree of cooperation of the trade unions and so on, are all now considered at least as important as the fact that monetary incentives are offered, when manpower effort must be increased.

1.5 EXPLAINING WORK PLACE BEHAVIOUR
The level of earnings offered is not in itself sufficient to explain how demand and supply of manpower effort balance on the internal market. What is then?

24

As printed before, alternative explanations are numerous, confusing and somewhat contradictory. The test to apply to any theory answering the question of the determinants of the internal labour market is this: "If this explanation is a good one, plausible as it is, does it lead to any guide or set out guidelines as to how companies, employers of labour, can improve industrial relations and increase their manpower utilisation?" That seems to me to be the crux of the issue.

When and if an employer cannot get consistently from his labour force the levels of output that he requires, a host of explanations are possible. Are they not being paid enough, for example? Or are they paid too much, so that it is not worthwhile their trying for more? Is job security too great and the dole queues too short? Or perhaps the dole queues are too long, "swollen with the idle layabouts who are sapping moral fibre"? Are the trade unions too powerful, obstructing the progress of industry? Or are they not powerful enough to take a more decisive part in bargaining for the best balance in the labour market, by making better utilisation necessary for expensive manpower?

To take an alternative tack: perhaps workers' jobs are so boring and unsatisfying that they have become complacent? Or perhaps they are complacent because jobs are too satisfying? Could jobs be made "richer" by extension of the concepts of job enlargement applied to managerial jobs? Or would less special-isation in manual jobs result in lower production levels? These may seem inappropriate arguments, and some evangelists of the human relations school have perhaps overreached themselves in trying to provide industrial relations panaceas.

Then how do we explain the imperfections of monetary mechanisms, as exemplified by problems of recruitment, retention, high turnover, strikes and stoppages, wage drift and wage claims, restrictive practices and rejected productivity agreements? How are we to consider systematically the various factors, social, economic, technical, political and psychological that can be brought to bear on the problems of labour markets?

Common to all the main contributions is that, granted full employment, the responses of companies and the effects on their operations of shortages of labour have a considerable bearing on industrial relations problems. In market theory, a shortage situation is an advantage to sellers, and a relative disadvantage to buyers. The buyers in the labour market are employers of labour, the managements of companies. How to overcome these disadvantages is the job of industrial relations specialists like those in companies, and in Employers' Associations and Federations.

As a result of many pressures, Incomes Policy, productivity bargaining, the Donovan Report, the CIR and so on, we are moving towards a decentralisation of collective bargaining. National bargaining has not been abolished yet, but the emphasis on factory-level bargaining as laid down in national agreements is with us now and will probably remain.

Without being alarmist, or even critical of this trend, I want to indicate some of the destabilising pressures that could arise under plant bargaining. The experience of the United States, where collective bargaining in industry started out on a general plant-bargaining road in the 1930s, suggests that trade union pressure, in the medium term, often seeks, from a plant-bargaining base, both company-wide bargaining (in multi-plant) companies, and ultimately industry-wide bargaining, in order to serve best the union membership. In Britain, we are already experiencing claims for parity of rates between motor plants in different parts of the country, while unions value negotiations for national, industry-wide minima.

In the USA, even those diminishing industries where collective bargaining is still substantially de-centralised, the pressure of pattern bargaining is strongly felt.

The more organised a trade unions movement is, and the more its officials learn to cope with plant bargaining, the better equipped they are to set out strategies for getting the same increases all round regardless of the productivity increases in each company, by playing off one comprehensively plant-bargaining employer against another. This happens in the USA; it could happen here if we are not sufficiently prepared to withstand these pressures. And I suggest that a necessary part of preparing for specifically plant-bargaining, though under union pressure, is to become more aware of the labour market operations involving our member companies, and to assist them in coping with the difficulties that undoubtedly will arise.

2 External and internal labour markets

by Derek Robinson

2.1 EXTERNAL LABOUR MARKETS

We probably know what is meant by a "labour market"
though we can neither see nor define one very easily.
A labour market concerns the activities of hiring
certain labour to perform certain jobs, and the process
of determining how much shall be paid to whom in
return for performing what tasks. In addition the way
in which wages move and the mobility of workers
between different jobs and employers falls within the
meaning of the term "labour market." To use the
term "labour market" does not imply that labour is
exactly as any other commodity; rather it refers to
activities affecting employment activities in the
economy. We can consider various types of labour
market. Sometimes we refer to the whole economy as
when we assert that the cause of the rate of inflation is
the low level of unemployment or the tightness of the
aggregate labour market. At other times we refer to
the labour market for the industry, as when we discuss
the supply of certain skilled workers.

However, for most practical purposes, most
employers think the local labour market the most
important in which they have to operate, simply
because they expect generally to recruit most
additions to their labour force from nearby. They
know that geographical mobility of labour, involving
the movement of home, accounts for only a few job
changes, particularly for manual workers, and that
when recruiting employees they must look primarily

to those already living within the locality. Moreover, employers believe their ability to retain labour is threatened by other local employers rather than by employers elsewhere, even though the latter may be in the same trade, and the local competitors are not. The entry of a new firm into a local labour market does not alter this; although the firm may at the moment be outside the local labour market it is the action of coming into it that raises manpower problems for other employers.

In conditions of high employment, implying a shortage of labour for some employers, the tactics of recruitment and retention of labour are often seen, in some ways, as the tactics of competition, with employers in the same locality competing more intensely between themselves than with employers elsewhere.

A local labour market is the geographical area containing those actual or potential members of the labour force that a firm might induce to enter its employ under certain conditions, and other employers with which the firm is in competition for labour (Robinson 1968). This brings out the two aspects of the market: the supply represented by the workers who might be available to the firm, and the demand represented by the firm and other firms seeking to employ that labour. In reality, it is often extremely difficult to specify the boundaries of the local labour market as fringe members come and go, and the boundaries can be extended. Provision of transport, for instance, may increase the number of workers who are now possible employees. Two firms, situated close to each other, might regard themselves as having quite different local labour markets with only slight overlap. While this may seem conceptually appropriate, it is not a workable definition. A concession to practicality is to decide that a certain area, say a town, is a local labour market, and that firms

29

within the area will be compared with each other while those outside will not. There is inevitably some arbitrariness about this, and we musk seek to temper this with commonsense based on discussions with those in the area. The ideal, if information was available, would be to discover the firms between which labour moved, so that the potentiàl catchment areas and their degree of overlap and the preferences of workers as expressed in their job changes could be brought together to produce an effective local labour market. However, in practice this is not possible. Applied research has very often to take such information and statistics as are available and make the best of them. Despite their limitations, it is often possible to undertake an analysis and draw conclusions which appear reliable.

A highly simplified approach to how economic forces operate in a labour market would say that the forces of supply and demand for different types of labour create a "rate for the job." The market determines the price for a certain kind of labour; if a firm pays less it will fail to attract and retain sufficient workers. Then it must either curtail production or increase wages sufficiently to compete with other employers. If it pays more than the "market rate" either it attracts more workers than it needs, reacting to this excess of supply by reducing wages to establish an equilibrium between supply and its own demand, or it continues to pay such higher wages and foregoes the profits that reduced wages would produce. But this is too simple, and other factors apply.

Firstly it is widely accepted that wages alone are insufficient to explain the rewards to labour. There are many additional rewards bracketed as "fringe benefits." It is difficult to define fringe benefits accurately and I have discussed this point elsewhere (Robinson 1968). Here they can be regarded as payments, current or deferred, which while arising out of the employment performance are not made because of it but by virtue of some other related event such as retirement, sickness or death. Or they may be forms of reward arising from employment performance but not made in cash, for example the use of a car, subsidised housing, or free meals. Sometimes these are seen as "perquisites" rather than fringe benefits but for our purposes they constitute rewards over and above the direct money payment. To quantify the "worth" of fringe benefits is often extremely difficult, and the value to the recipient need not be the same as the cost to the firm.

There are also "other attractions" which, while again not easily quantifiable are often assumed effective in recruiting or retaining labour. The work environment, the general conditions of the factory (whether noisy or dirty), whether employees have close contact with other people, and if they do whether they get on with the others, the type and personality of the supervisors, all affect the attraction of the firm as a place of employment.

The total reward to labour is a "package" of the three elements of money, fringe benefits and other attractions. Various firms will offer packages containing various mixtures, and different individuals will prefer different mixtures and their choice may change through time. Thus, even assuming a "perfect market" where the total packages of different firms competing for the same labour cost the firms the same in total, we should find the specifically wage content differed from firm to firm. In fact it would probably not be possible to work out the precise cost of the various packages of attraction; to allocate the cost of particular fringe benefits to different types of labour, and more especially the cost of the different "other attractions," would be impossible. Even if it were not, there are other factors. For, even regarding only the conditions in the labour market for

31

a specific occupation - for instance fitters, in one industry, in one town - merely to concentrate on the rewards to labour is misleading. We must also regard the disadvantages of some of the employment opportunities offered. Work in some firms would be harded, heavier, more skilled, less pleasant, and so on, than in others.

In these situations the total package of attractions might differ to offset the disadvantages of the work. In the terminology of Alfred Marshall we should look at the net advantages of an occupation:

> Every occupation involves other disadvantages besides the fatigue of the work required in it, and every occupation offers other advantages besides the receipt of money wages. The true reward which an occupation offers to labour has to be calculated by deducting the money value of all its disadvantages from that of all its advantages; and we may describe this true reward as the net advantages of the occupation (Marshall 1966).

He was referring to the relative advantages of one trade or occupation against another, but the approach equally well explains the relative attraction for an employee of employment at one firm rather than another.

This approach provides a comprehensive conceptual framework within which the workings of a particular labour market can be analysed. Thus, within a specific local labour market where, expectedly, labour would be mobile between different employers, the balance of net advantages between different firms for the same occupation might be theoretically equal. However, this conceptual framework is not necessarily a realistic tool of analysis. For example, if the wages plus quantifiable fringe benefits provided by different firms for the same employees are not equal, the other advantages and disadvantages might be

32

thought to balance out the observed differences. We could then "explain" any differences by saying that the other conditions were the cause. But this is merely to accept the explanation provided by the concept and not to test it. To test the approach we would need to quantify the balance of net advantages as seen by each individual worker, clearly not a realistic proposition. By the time the process was completed the relative wages would have changed.

Effectively, therefore, we must either accept this explanation or compare such quantifiable aspects of the net advantages, or total package, as we can, and decide whether the differences are explained by such advantages and disadvantages as might exist. This is in some ways theoretically unsatisfactory, but the economist seeking to explain the world as he finds it cannot accept the restrictions of a theory which, no matter how elegant, is incapable in practice of direct application in quantifiable terms.

The conceptual framework explains therefore how an individual worker chooses his occupation or firm at which to work, that he does so by maximising net advantages. But as individuals have different views or interpretations of net advantages, variously evaluating the features of particular employments, it is not possible to say that the net advantages of all the firms will tend to become equal. All we can say is that individuals will, or rather should, choose so that the selected employment offers the highest net advantages to them. And the conceptual explanation being essentially subjective to each individual, no objective or externally quantifiable criteria can be stated to judge whether the market is working according to theory. This makes the theory difficult to validate and of very little practical use without analysis of the preferences of a number of different people.

If all people in a certain category chose the same package of attractions or had the same views on the

advantages and disadvantages of different employments
generalisation would become possible. Strong
assertions from theory are impossible, but experience
suggests that some people will act in the same way in
similar conditions. We cannot tell how many, nor
whether they do so because they have evaluated the
advantages and disadvantages of employments
similarly or because they have evaluated the various
components differently but to the same overall effects,
or whether they have not evaluated the whole package
at all but are instead influenced only by some part.
Thus, while being unable to show empirically that
people behave rationally, we can draw some conclusions
about their behaviour sometimes. We know that
sometimes people react strongly to monetary inventive;
we also know that in other situations they do not.

Whether people do or can put a money value on the
various advantages and disadvantages of different
employments is debatable. Most people do not approach
employment decisions in this way and, if they did,
could not make very realistic valuations. To put a
price on advantages or disadvantages it is probably
necessary to have experienced them though, even
without experience it might be possible to value them
or the image they have for an individual, so producing
a list of preferences of different employments. The
worker choosing employment he has not experienced
previously may find that he changes the valuation
placed on various items. He might then reassess his
preferences so that the job is no longer his first
choice. For example, he might reduce the value of
some advantages or increase the value of some disadvantages and decide that some other job provides
higher net advantages. This is one way of explaining
labour turnover. However, there is still the problem
that as an explanation it holds only if we believe that
it holds. As a framework for practical policy making
it is either true or it is valueless in many situations.

It is valuable because some observed relationships lead to practical conclusions on how parts of the labour market behave.

Additional complications arise because the assumptions that relatively low wage firms will go out of business, either being unable to recruit and retain sufficient labour, or being unable to increase their prices; or, conversely, that high wage firms will reduce wages to increase their profits imply sharp competition between the firms in the product market. This may not be true; firms who are competing in the same labour markets for the same type of workers may be in different product markets. Again, the link between the wages or total reward to labour and the profitability, or ability of the firm to pay, is the productivity of labour and the importance of various costs in the total cost structure. Thus, when comparing different firms, even within the same broad category of industry as engineering, they are not necessarily product competitors nor is an individual worker in a specific occupation "worth" the same to each firm. Therefore the expected similarity of wages or total package in different firms might not occur.

Despite tendencies towards uniformity and certain institutional constraints imposed by collective bargaining, we still cannot assert that if wages of the same occupation are unequal then the individuals are of unequal ability or efficiency, nor that if workers are equal they have equal ability or efficiency.

Moreover, in reality, labour is far less mobile than in economic theory. Workers seldom change their places of work in response to small or even moderate differences in wages or package content. An explanation is that the disadvantage of changing jobs is greater than the expected increase in reward and therefore the net advantages of the current job are

greater than those of alternatives. But this regards
the "other attractions" or advantages and disadvantages
as always sufficient to explain differences in the
observed quantifiable rewards to workers in different
jobs. Trade unions reduce the realism of mobility as
a pressure towards equalisation of total rewards from
different jobs. For example, in theory, if the relative
rewards of different jobs got out of line, labour should
move from one to the other. In practice, the unions
would doubtless argue the case of comparability saying
not that workers will change their employment without
a correction in wages but that what has happened elsewhere is relevant here. Behind this argument lies the
threat that if the firm did not match the changes
elsewhere labour would leave, but this would seldom
occur. Trade unions as organisations bargaining with
individual employers remove external labour market
mobility as a major economic adjustment focusing
attention on internal arguments which, while seeking
outside evidence of what is happening, look to obtain
increases in rewards while also retaining present
employment. Despite exceptions, this is broadly what
happens. Security with an existing employer is more
highly regarded than the advantages to be gained by
frequent job changes, and many of these are the result
of people seeking higher money rewards, or better
fringe benefits, as well as the opportunity to obtain
better working conditions.

2.2 LOCAL LABOUR MARKET SURVEYS

Economic theory seeks to explain how workers choose
particular employments, both the choice of occupation
and place of employment or firm. We shall concentrate
on the second choice, assuming the occupation. The
wages of members of the same occupation or grade in
different firms in a locality will be examined to see
how the local labour market works in terms of economic
pressures tending to equate the money reward.

Details were obtained of "standard" hourly earnings, excluding all overtime and shift premiums, of a number of firms in three areas as reported to the Engineering Employers' Associations. Possibly total or gross earnings might change the picture somewhat as, for example, overtime pay led to greater similarity between firms, but of course inclusion of overtime might exaggerate any differences. Which earning figures to choose is always a problem that becomes more involved when assessing the importance of wages in influencing the allocation of labour between firms. It appears that the figures looked at by workers considering alternative jobs are gross pay including overtime. Enquiries about overtime opportunities are made when details of a job are sought, and newspaper advertisements indicate that employers use this when recruiting labour: phrases such as "overtime available" or "weekend work opportunities" are common. Moreover, workers might leave a firm if they believe that they are not getting their "fair" share of available overtime. But while overtime and total gross pay may be the major aspect of the money reward comparing gross pay figures involves complications. If workers have to work longer hours in one firm to match the gross pay in another a straight comparison is misleading. The use of standard hourly earnings avoids this difficulty. In addition, employers and Employers' Associations regard standard hourly earnings as the most appropriate for comparisons. Details of gross pay were therefore not available.

There are other reservations to such comparisons and surveys. The wages of men in the same occupation in the same industry being equal, does not imply that they are all equally efficient or skilled. Fitters in different firms may be performing quite different work in terms of skill content. The pace as well as difficulty of work may be different. Some workers may be on piecework and others on time rates. There may

37

be enough differences in the fringe benefits and physical surroundings of the firms to be significant. Not all these factors have been considered, nor have their productivity or profitability. Details of the first are scarce; and, although profit figures are published, to apportion them realistically among multi-plant companies is practically impossible.

There are thus a number of reservations, but not such as to invalidate the comparison of standard hourly earnings. The statistics do provide some factual and useful evidence. They are produced by the firms themselves for purposes of comparison which they obviously believe of value for their operations in a local labour market.

To preserve confidentiality the markets are called LM1, LM2 and LM3. Figures are available only for workers in the engineering industry. This is not the whole of the local labour market and in LM2 and LM3 other industries might be more important in terms of total number employed. Yet, though we are, in two cases at least, looking at only part of the local labour market, it is reasonable to assume that the operation of economic forces and the effects of such institutional pressures as trade unions, shop stewards' meetings and local employers' association behaviour and pressures are much more likely to be similar within a single industry in a town than between all its industries. Thus, our selection of evidence will tend to make the wages examined seem more uniform than would be the case across the board. The direction, but not the extent, of any distortions is known. For example, on a different project, the starting rates of maintenance electricians in various firms in twenty industries in the same district were examined. Throughout the industries they ranged, in 1966, from £12 to £21.19, a difference of 76.6 per cent. The widest range of starting rates in a single industry was only 37.7 per cent, from £13.50 to £18.10½. Including more

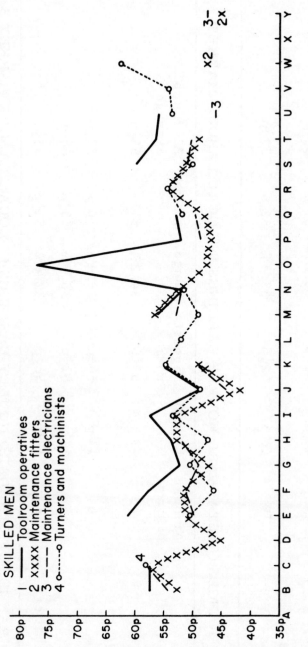

FIGURE 2:1   LOCAL LABOUR MARKET 2
Average standard hourly earnings
(November 1967)

	Number of firms	Lowest firm	Highest firm	Range	Median firm	All firms average
Toolmakers	18	49 p	77 p	59.0%	56 p	$57\frac{1}{2}$p
Maintenance fitters	20	41 p	$57\frac{1}{2}$p	39.4%	$50\frac{1}{2}$p	51 p
Maintenance electricians	17	44 p	$57\frac{1}{2}$p	30.2%	50 p	51 p
Turners and machinists	17	46 p	$62\frac{1}{2}$p	35.1%	52 p	$57\frac{1}{2}$p

TABLE 2.1 RANGES OF STANDARD HOURLY EARNINGS IN LOCAL LABOUR MARKET 2

	Number of firms	Lowest firm	Highest firm	Range	Median	All firms average
Fitters	6	43 p	$57\frac{1}{2}$p	34.2%	51 p	$55\frac{1}{2}$p
Turners and machinists	6	43 p	$56\frac{1}{2}$p	18.4%	50 p	$52\frac{1}{2}$p
Setters	6	44 p	$61\frac{1}{2}$p	38.7%	$53\frac{1}{2}$p	56 p
Maintenance fitters	6	$42\frac{1}{2}$p	$56\frac{1}{2}$p	32.6%	$51\frac{1}{2}$p	$53\frac{1}{2}$p

TABLE 2.2 RANGES OF STANDARD HOURLY EARNINGS IN LOCAL LABOUR MARKET 3

industries increases the overall range and the diversity.

Figure 2:1 shows the average standard hourly earnings of adult males in four grades of skilled workers in twenty-five firms in the same locality, LM2, for a pay week in November 1967. The ranges of average standard hourly earnings between the firms are expressed in Table 2.1 as a percentage of the lowest ranking figure.

Figure 2:2 shows the same sort of information for four occupations in LM3, and the ranges of standard hourly earnings are shown in Table 2.2.

In these two local labour markets a range of about 30 per cent between the lowest paying and the highest paying firm is fairly typical. The figures indicate that a firm is not necessarily high paying for all its occupations. Thus, firm D in LM3 is generally the highest although firm F pays its fitters more. In LM2, firm O pays its fitters more but its maintenance fitters are paid less than the average of all local firms, $47\frac{1}{2}$p against 57p.

Figure 2:3 gives details of eight skilled occupations in thirteen firms in LM1. This contains forty firms, information being collected for some ninety-eight male manual occupations. This clearly provides a much more detailed coverage than do the other two localities. The figures are also for four years, allowing some examination of the movement in wages through time.

Table 2.3 gives details of the range of standard hourly earnings for certain occupations at different dates. It is not always possible to calculate a weighted average as details of numbers employed in each occupation are not always given. But obviously there is a very wide range indeed for many occupations. The inter-quartile ranges are also shown.

If the firms are ranked as in a league table the firm coming exactly in the middle is the median, the one

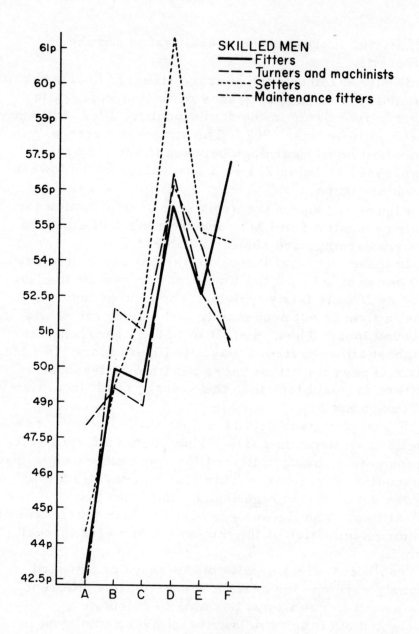

FIGURE 2:2 LOCAL LABOUR MARKET 3
Average standard hourly earnings
(January 1968)

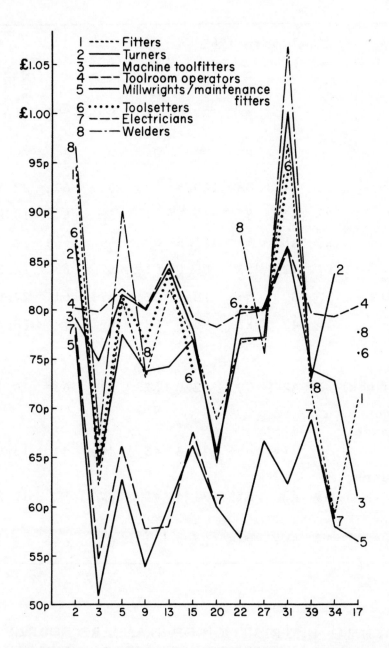

FIGURE 2:3 STANDARD HOURLY EARNINGS OF 8
OCCUPATIONS IN 13 FIRMS IN LM1
(9 October 1968)

43

	Number	Lowest p	Highest p	Range %	Median p	Q1 p	Q3 p	Inter-Q range %
7 April 1965								
Fitters	23	39	82	109.4	62	54	$67\frac{1}{2}$	22.1
Turners	24	$53\frac{1}{2}$	83	55.5	61	58	$60\frac{1}{2}$	10.9
Millers	23	$48\frac{1}{2}$	83	71.5	62	59	$66\frac{1}{2}$	12.1
Grinders	27	$42\frac{1}{2}$	83	96.0	$61\frac{1}{2}$	59	$66\frac{1}{2}$	12.2
Hardeners	17	39	$65\frac{1}{2}$	78.4	$52\frac{1}{2}$	$47\frac{1}{2}$	$61\frac{1}{2}$	27.0
Welders	18	42	82	95.0	69	55	$74\frac{1}{2}$	28.5
Machine tool fitters (maintenance)	22	38	69	82.0	62	57	$63\frac{1}{2}$	10.1
Millwrights/ maintenance fitters	35	$37\frac{1}{2}$	$55\frac{1}{2}$	47.3	48	44	51	13.9
Electricians II	32	33	57	74.4	49	47	52	10.2
Toolroom operators	32	$55\frac{1}{2}$	74	23.8	64	63	$64\frac{1}{2}$	2.6

TABLE 2.3 DISTRIBUTION OF STANDARD HOURLY EARNINGS FOR SELECTED OCCUPATIONS LM1

Number	Lowest	Highest	Range	Median	Q1	Q3	Inter-Q range
	p	p	%	p	p	p	%
22	41	$92\frac{1}{2}$	124.2	73	$62\frac{1}{2}$	76	18.3
23	51	91	79.0	71	66	75	19.3
25	$50\frac{1}{2}$	91	79.8	74	65	$76\frac{1}{2}$	15.8
26	59	$92\frac{1}{2}$	57.4	$73\frac{1}{2}$	64	76	17.0
20	$45\frac{1}{2}$	$83\frac{1}{2}$	83.5	64	$55\frac{1}{2}$	$63\frac{1}{2}$	12.3
13	62	99	60.3	$76\frac{1}{2}$	$69\frac{1}{2}$	$85\frac{1}{2}$	20.7
27	51	$79\frac{1}{2}$	55.5	73	69	$75\frac{1}{2}$	9.1
33	41	$77\frac{1}{2}$	87.9	$57\frac{1}{2}$	$50\frac{1}{2}$	61	18.8
28	$36\frac{1}{2}$	$78\frac{1}{2}$	113.7	61	$54\frac{1}{2}$	83	46.6
29	$51\frac{1}{2}$	82	59.7	75	74	76	2.8

8 November 1967

Amounts have been rounded to the nearest $\frac{1}{2}$p: the percentages may therefore appear slightly out as they have been calculated on precise figures.

Inter-quartile range is Q3 - Q1 as a percentage of the median.

	Less than 25%	25.0% - 29.9%	30.0% - 34.9%	35.0% - 39.9%	40.0% - 44.9%	45.0% - 49.9%	50.0% - 54.9%	55.0% - 59.9%
11 Aug 1965	1	1	3	7	5	10	9	4
17 Apr 1969	2	1		1		2	5	4

TABLE 2.4 RANGE OF STANDARD HOURLY EARNINGS
Employed in at least 10 firms in LM1

coming exactly one quarter down from the top is the
higher quartile and the one three quarters down from
the top is the lower quartile.   The inter-quartile range
is the spread between the two quartiles.   One half of
the firms will fall inside the inter-quartile range and
one half outside it; it is therefore another measure of
dispersion or spread but concentrating on the middle
half of the distribution avoids the extreme cases which
are picked out only if we look at the range.   Thus if
there is one very high or very low firm exerting very
strong influence on the range this will be disregarded
in the inter-quartile range.

The firms are not always the same as some dropped
out or occasionally did not provide details for certain
occupations.   Indeed, some evidence suggests that
firms paying either unusually high or low wages for
certain occupations excluded them from surveys or
merged them into composite groupings.   These figures
were collected by the Association for circulation to
member firms and so it is understandable that the
more extreme wage levels were not reported.   There
is some conflict for firms which collectively subscribe
to this sort of information collection for later

60.0% - 64.9%	65.0% - 69.9%	70.0% - 74.9%	75.0% - 79.9%	80.0% - 84.9%	85.0% - 89.9%	90.0% - 94.9%	95.0% - 99.9%	100% or more	Number of Occupations
3	6	3	3	2	4		3	12	76
5	1	4	5	3	4	2	3	9	51

OF OCCUPATIONS

circulation among them. They want to know what other local firms pay as they are in competition for labour, but conversely all belong to an Employers' Association which has certain rules or conventions regarding acceptable or tolerable behaviour.

The wide range of standard hourly earnings in local firms is brought out in Table 2.4. This shows the distribution of the ranges for all the occupations present in at least ten firms in LM1: that is, for each occupation the difference between the standard hourly earnings in the highest and lowest paying firms is expressed as a percentage of the lowest standard hourly earnings for that occupation. Of the seventy-six occupations in at least ten firms in August 1965, forty-nine had a spread of at least 50 per cent between the lowest and highest paying firms and twelve had a spread of more than 100 per cent. The numbers of occupations covered changed in 1969 so that direct comparison with the seventy-seven occupations is not possible. However, for the fifty-one occupations with appropriate details only six had a range of less than 50 per cent and nine had a range of more than 100 per cent.

47

This very considerable variation in standard hourly earnings found on analysis leads to endorsement of the view expressed by Professor Clark Kerr:

> It is a certain sign that the local market has not been left to its own devices when rates are equalized for comparable work and workers; it is a sure sign of intervention by the state or the union. The market can make the massive change of reducing occupational differentials or raising money wages in an inflationary situation, but it cannot equalize money wages in the local labour market. (Kerr 1969, emphasis in original.)

Differences in wages for the same occupation are therefore to be expected; if they do not occur it is because some institutional authority has imposed uniformity either by law or by collective bargaining deliberately designed to equate wages in various firms in the same area. Such pressures need not necessarily come from trade unions aiming to establish "the rate for the job"; employers' associations too may seek to prevent spiralling of wage settlements as evidenced by this clause in an Association's constitution.

> No member shall give any general increase in wages, or make any general concession to his workmen without first reporting to and obtaining the approval of the Executive Committee.

Of course, such a rule is not always observed.
For employers and trade unions the local labour market is widely held to be very important in determining the degree of competition for labour and the levels of, and rate of change of, wages. "The going rate in the town or district" is referred to very frequently. It is commonly held that the working of competitive forces within a local labour market is often such as to leave the employer with little choice but to increase wages as do other employers or suffer

48

the consequences of a loss of labour.

2.3 CHANGES IN WAGES THROUGH TIME

Strictly speaking, traditional economic theory does
not require that all firms pay identical wages. It is
the balance of "net advantages" to individual workers
of equal ability and efficiency which provides the
incentive or motivation for job selection and changes.
Thus, the relatively wide spread of standard hourly
earnings between firms in the same industry in the
same town is not unduly surprising. Possibly economic
forces work on the changes in wages so that these are
more uniform. Wage changes being widely different,
there would be presumably a change in the relative
attractiveness of different jobs leading to workers
moving to those now more attractive. On this view,
differences in wage levels can exist in being offset by
other attractions or by fewer disadvantages. But if
the relative wage levels between different jobs change,
new preferences, based on revised lists of "net
advantages" emerge, unless there are some corresponding changes in the non-wage components in the
package of attraction.

In LM1 wage levels were followed through time, a
series of surveys carried out by the Association from
October 1964. The response to the first survey in
October 1964 was less satisfactory as more firms
later provided more details. We will therefore take
April 1965 as the base date for calculating the percentage change in standard hourly wages for certain
occupations.

Table 2.5 shows the distribution of the percentage
increases in wages from April 1965 to June 1967 for
occupations which occur in at least ten firms. There
is a fairly wide spread of increases. In some cases
about half the increases fall within two class
intervals; for example, with turners, millers and
grinders, a little over half are within the range 10.0

49

Occupation	Minus	0.0–4.9	5.0–9.9	10.0–14.9	15.0–19.9	20.0–24.9	25.0–29.9	30.0–34.9	35.0–39.9	Over 40	Total
1 Fitters	1		3	5	6	1	2		1		19
2 Turners		2	1	7	6	3	1			1	21
3 Millers			3	6	6	5				1	21
4 Grinders		2	2	7	6	2	2		1	1	23
15 Hardeners			3	3	4	3				1	14
18 Welders	1		2	2	2	2			2	1	12
22 Maintenance fitters machine tool	1		1	7	8	3	1	1			22
28 Tool setters	1		1	5	6					2	15
32 Millwrights maintenance fitters		2	7	7	10	2	1		1	1	31
34 Electrician II	2		3	8	3	7	1		1		25
35 Plumbers/ pipe fitters				3	5	4			1		13
37 Toolroom operators				5	15	4					24

TABLE 2.5   DISTRIBUTION OF PERCENTAGE INCREASES IN STANDARD HOURLY EARNINGS BETWEEN APRIL 1965 AND JUNE 1967

per cent to 19. 9 per cent. While this suggests fairly
similar increases, these increases took place over a
period of only two years and two months, the degree
of similarity therefore not perhaps being as marked
as one might expect. Also of course between a half
and a third of the increases fell outside even this
broad range of 10 per cent.

Figures 2:4 and 2:5 show the movement of standard
hourly earnings through time of welders and fitters in
a selection of firms in LM1. Clearly the rankings and
relative wage levels between firms change, though not
dramatically every few months. But there are very
considerable differences in the increases received by
workers in different firms over shortish periods of
time and preliminary analysis suggests that these are
not necessarily or even frequently evened out over a
longer period.

2. 4   INTERNAL LABOUR MARKETS

As well as external or local labour markets there are
also internal labour markets. Indeed, every plant
can be regarded as an internal labour market. Labour
is supplied and demanded within the firm in various
ways without direct access to the external market.
With overtime, for example, a plant by increasing
the hours worked by existing employees is turning to
its internal labour market for an increased supply of
labour as opposed to recruiting additional workers
from the external market. There may also be agreements whereby vacancies in certain grades or occupations
must first be offered to members of other grades or
occupations before "outsiders" can be recruited.
While those employed yesterday have some prefer-
ential treatment in the employment relationship today,
whether in security or seniority or promotion, there
is an internal labour market.

Conditions in the internal labour market provide a set
of rules which influences the behaviour of employers

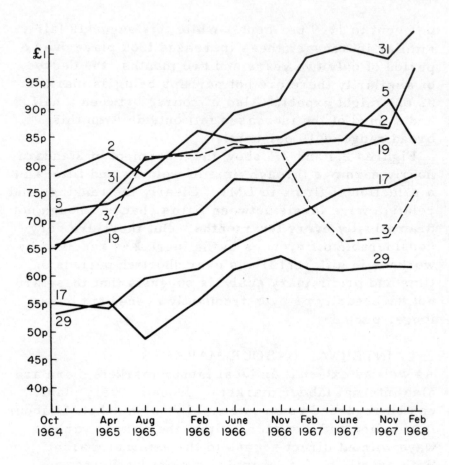

FIGURE 2:4 STANDARD HOURLY EARNINGS OF
WELDERS THROUGH TIME IN 7 FIRMS
IN LM1

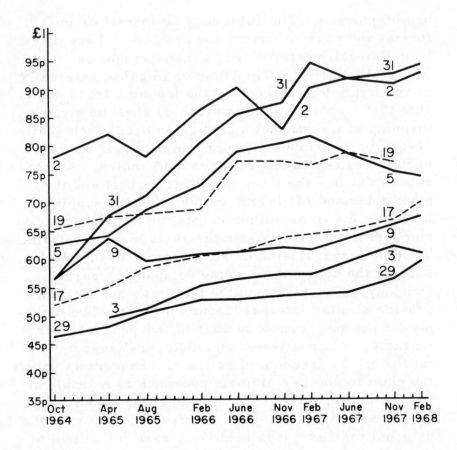

FIGURE 2:5 STANDARD HOURLY EARNINGS OF
FITTERS THROUGH TIME IN 8 FIRMS
IN LM1

and employees. The rules may be formal or informal and part of custom and practice. They may
be unilaterally determined by management or
bilaterally agreed. They may be imposed externally
on the firm, for instance by the law or a trade union
rule that a specific type of machine shall be given a
manning scale, or that a particular occupation shall
always be a member of a particular union, or that
certain craftsmen shall always have mates. All these
rules influence the internal labour market and the
plant's demand for labour or the effective supply of
labour to the firm, either in total or in relation to the
numbers employed. Again the rules may be determined
by some managerial authority external to the plant
such as the board of a holding company or parent
company. The plant and the firm may not therefore
provide similar internal labour markets. The multi-
plant firm may form a number of independent internal
markets. Alternatively, an employers' association
may limit the freedom of action of management within
the plant to obtain a uniform approach to a problem.

Here an important feature of internal labour
markets is in providing the points of contact with the
external market. It is relatively rare for a firm to
recruit all its workers from outside directly into every
occupation it has. Generally it recruits into certain
occupations only; there are certain "ports of entry"
(Kerr 1954) into the local labour market and other
grades or occupations are filled by internal training
or promotion. Similarly, firms differ in the extent
to which they provide opportunities for additional
training and promotion. Figure 2:6 illustrates
different kinds of internal labour market. This is
highly simplified, the internal labour market being in
fact much more complicated and difficult to interpret,
but is sufficient for present purposes.

A vertical block represents an internal labour market,
that is, a plant, which will be assumed the same as the

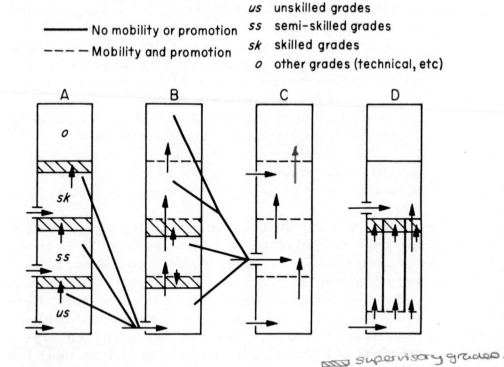

A   B   C   D

o

sk

ss

us

ᔕᔕᔕ supervisory grades.

FIGURE 2:6   TYPES OF INTERNAL LABOUR
             MARKET

firm. Main skill groups have been taken in place of
specific occupations. An arrow from outside pointing
into a skill group shows that the firm recruits that
type of labour at that level. Solid unbroken lines
between skill groups show that labour does not move
from one group to the other, while dotted lines with
vertical arrows connecting them indicate that
workers can expect to be promoted from one skill
group to the other. The shaded areas represent the
supervisory or chargehand grades and the arrows
indicate the areas of recruitment of these grades.
   Firm A represents a highly compartmentalised
internal market with the different occupations self-

contained. Recruitment is direct into each grade and there is no mobility between them. Promotion is limited to the supervisory levels for each occupation. Alternatively, firm B represents the other extreme which is a very open type of internal market. For manual workers, excepting craftsmen, there is a single port of entry into the unskilled grade. This is rather similar in principle to the situation in traditional steel mills, workers being recruited in unskilled labourers' grades and progressing by seniority and experience to become first hand smelters.

Firm C illustrates very high earning opportunities for semi-skilled workers so that workers from other industries may leave their skilled occupations to earn very high wages. Thus, its recruitment area is much wider than for other firms paying lower wages. Here economic forces operate, not to produce uniformity of earnings in the local market, but to attract large numbers of men who put money very high on their list of preferences of the various advantages of different employments. At the same time, the firm may have to pay high wages to offset the disadvantages of the work, say, monotonous repetitive work tasks. This can be fitted into a net advantages type of approach, the difference being that in this case money is the attraction whereas in most cases the disadvantages of the work are much less clearly established. It does not follow that a general case is valid just because some extreme example appears to illustrate it.

Firm D shows how the firm can compartmentalise its internal market for certain grades but not necessarily for all. In this case workers enter as un - skilled and are allocated to one of three sections within which there is considerable upward mobility, but for only one into the skilled category.

Different promotion prospects to supervisory or chargehand grades have been illustrated for two firms and excluded from the others for simplicity.

A comparison of the types of internal labour market emphasises that, even though there is fairly detailed job classification for purposes of comparison, the same occupation in two different firms sometimes means two quite different things. Firm A may be recruiting an unskilled worker who might be content to stay unskilled, but firm B someone who is expecting and expected to be upgraded in time. When firm B recruits an unskilled worker it is gaining a skilled worker of ten or twenty years hence. It therefore seeks a completely different type of unskilled worker; it wants men with potential ability and sufficiently well motivated to enter as unskilled workers and spend some time in relatively low grade and possible low paid work, because they are taking a long term view of the prospects over their full working life. In these circumstances, it is not possible to say whether the wages of unskilled men in the two firms will be the same, or, if different, which will be the higher.

Because firm B offers better career prospects, the internal labour market being geared to internal upward occupational mobility, entrants will accept lower wages in the early days. Unskilled workers might therefore receive less in firm B than in firm A. Alternatively, being in some ways better types of worker, able to become more highly skilled, they will require higher wages now to induce them to work as unskilled grades. There is, therefore, no clear a priori reason for thinking that a relationship exists to explain any differences in pay. As a result of examining the internal labour markets of the two firms we certainly can conclude that they are not basically competing in the same external labour markets for certain grades of labour and should not necessarily expect the uniformity in relative wages that would exist on an external market if all the firms had the same kind of

		Firm																
		303		304		101		702		703		704		206		405		201
Occupations		A	N	A	N	A	N	A	N	A	N	A	N	A	N	A	N	A N
Miscellaneous	01	–	1	6		3	8	7		35	1	4	9			1	1	
Turners	02	6	4	11		2	2	2		2	5	1				1	6	
Machinists	03	2	3	3		18	2			5	3					8	8	
Burners	04									2		1						
Fitters	05		1	11				19		8		4				20	1	
Chargehands	06			1		6	4	1				2			1			
Grinders	07															2	4	
Welders	08	1		1				1	4	13								
Miscellaneous	31	1	1	1		1	4			13	1			1	1			4
Electricians	32			1		2		3		1		3	1		1			2 2
Millwrights	33	1		1		4				1		3	1					3 9
Toolroom	34	3	1			1	1	1				2	1	1		2		
Setters	35	1		1		1	1			5		14		1	31			1 2
Chargehands	36					1				1		2						
Inspectors	37	6				4	3			5		4				3	2	
Building trade	38					1		2		1		4		1		1		3
All		21	11	37	0	32	39	41	1	65	13	70	12	5	33	40	22	6 20

TABLE 2.6 APPRENTICESHIP OF SKILLED WORKERS IN FOURTEEN

Notes: A = Apprenticed
    N = Not apprenticed
   NK = Not known

Figures exclude 121 employees for whom the information was not

	207 A	207 N	103 A	103 N	103 NK	104 A	104 N	104 NK	105 A	105 N	105 NK	403 A	403 N	403 NK	All firms A	N	Total	% A	% N
	3	2	3	-		-	3	-				11	-	4	69	29	98	70	30
						2	-	-				9	2	-	36	20	56	64	36
	1		-	-	-	1	1	-	3	-	-	8	1	10	37	36	73	51	49
												-	-	-	2	1	3	67	33
	1					6	3	-	1	-	2	11	-	5	80	6	86	93	7
	13											-	-	3	10	18	28	36	64
												-	1	-	2	5	7	29	71
						-	1	-				1	2	-	20	4	24	83	17
	12	1	1	-		1	3	-				23	-	6	47	24	71	66	34
	7	1	-	-		-	1	-				3	-	2	20	10	30	67	33
	2	-	2	1		1	1	-				3	1	-	18	15	33	55	45
3	45	2	3	1		3	1	-	-	-	1	5	1	1	32	54	86	37	63
	27	2	4	2		6	8	-				6	5	2	38	78	116	33	67
	4											1	-	2	4	5	9	44	56
	10	1	1	1		1	1	-				1	-	4	25	17	42	60	40
	2	1	4	-								2	-	1	13	9	22	59	41
6	126	11	18	5		21	23	-	4	-	3	84	13	40	453	331	784	58	42

FIRMS

available

internal market.

Referred to orthodox economic theory, the efficiency earnings can be different not just because of varying ability and efficiency in current performance and employment, but because of potential abilities required as job mobility leads to promotion. Consideration of the internal labour market means that we have to cease looking at members of specific occupations purely in an external sense; some are in an occupation at any one time en route to some other occupation while others are not. The internal market therefore strongly influences the quality of labour required, emphasising the point that labour is not homogenous. Introducing the time or career element into the analysis means that comparison of only the monetary element of the reward to labour at a specific point in time is, in many cases, misleading as it is incomplete and shows only part of the picture.

The ability and efficiency of workers in different plants cannot be compared; the data are not available, firms are not very forthcoming and measurement and comparison would be very difficult. But some conclusions regarding the meaning of various occupational terms in different firms are possible. Table 2.6, based on detailed surveys by the Institute, shows the proportion of skilled male workers who have served an apprenticeship. Classification into skilled grades was carried out by the firms concerned and checked to ensure uniformity. This does not mean that different definitions or qualifications necessarily indicate varying ability, but that within internal labour markets responses to shortages of skilled men and to the problems of the supply of skilled occupations do vary. Some firms were able to increase the supply of skilled men from within the internal market without the delay of taking on more apprentices. Some firms show considerable internal upward mobility, meaning that recourse to external labour markets is reduced

60

or takes place at semi-skilled level. Interestingly firms coded in the 700 range are in an area where it is widely held that only time-served craftsmen may do skilled work. Unpublished academic research elsewhere shows that in some cases semi-skilled workers are transferred to the toolroom and, if able to perform the work after a trial period of four to six weeks, are regarded as skilled workers.

Firm	Minutes per week	Standard hourly earnings p	Value of breaks £
92	178	60.31	1.7890
8	145	73.63	1.7797
9	175	68.02	1.9837
10	60	76.67	0.7667
13	130	84.16	1.8239
15	90	75.83	1.1375
17	115	69.90	1.3396
18	160	74.71	1.4916
20	60	63.85	0.6385
43	115	80.00	1.5332
39	75	70.15	0.8771
31	175	89.80	2.6188
33	115	69.47	1.3317
36	165	51.25	1.4093
2	180	91.77	2.7531
22	105	77.50	1.3563
5	160	79.26	2.1140
27	90	75.21	1.1281
37	125	86.25	1.7969

TABLE 2.7   PAID BREAKS FOR FITTERS FOR A STANDARD WEEK

Table 2.7 illustrates the difference in conditions existing in internal labour markets for firms in the same industry in the same town, showing the paid breaks allowed to workers during a week, included the time allowance for late clocking on, where this occurred. The total time allowed ranges from 180 to 60 minutes or, in terms of money based on the standard hourly earnings of fitters in the firms, from £2.75 to £0.64. The Spearman ranking coefficient of total amount of paid time allowed and the standard hourly earnings of fitters in each of the 19 plants was + 0.0088, which is for practical purposes no relationship. This suggests that generally the length of paid breaks granted bears no relation to the wages of the plant. For example, while the firm granting the longest paid breaks was also the highest paying firm, that with the second longest breaks (178 minutes) was next to the lowest paying. The lowest paying firm came fifth in respect of paid breaks: 165 minutes.

The relationship between internal and external labour markets is seen very clearly in productivity bargaining. Where a productivity bargain provides for ending job demarcations or permits members of different crafts or trades to do work previously monopolised by one, the firm essentially increases the effective supply of labour to itself while decreasing demand for labour from the external labour market. At the same time it raises wages. It eases its labour shortages without increasing the total employed, and sometimes might reduce its workforce, at least probably those employed in certain categories. There is a close interrelationship between supply and demand determined by the conditions in the internal labour market. What is difficult for many orthodox economists to understand is why the firm should increase wages at the time that it is reducing its demand for workers, higher wages being normally associated with a desire to employ more people.

The answer lies in the distinction between the
internal and external labour markets. Without the
higher wages, to increase the effective supply or
reduce demand would not be possible as unions or
workers would not agree to the changed working conditions within the internal labour market that cause
the higher wages. The increased wages become
necessary for internal labour market reasons just as
the changes in supply and demand are internal changes.
The internal market in effect isolates itself from the
external market. Possibly other internal labour
markets will try to emulate them or individual workers
seek employment there, but the institutional
arrangements surrounding the internal market
prevents this potential inflow from yielding the re-
duction in wages expected in situations where potential
supply exceeds demand. These arrangements prevent
potential supply from becoming actual supply.

2.5   CONCLUSIONS

Orthodox economic theory concerning relative wages
of members of the same occupation in the same locality
does not provide a clearly applicable framework of
analysis for applied research. The assessment of
"net advantages" is subjective, differing with the
individual. It is therefore not clear whether wide
disparities in wages between different firms in the
local labour market supports or denies economic
theory, which is to this extent indeterminate. Our
findings could represent the working of economic
forces. However, this is in some ways unsatisfactory
for practical purposes.

Disparity in pay between firms may mean that
workers were either of different abilities and
efficiencies or that they valued the non-wage elements
of their rewards differently. The non-wage elements
in the reward can be regarded as a makeweight,
always sufficient to offset the observed differences in

wages and fringe benefits. If this is the explanation, then clearly the workers must place very considerable emphasis on the non-wage elements. All the evidence suggests that fringe benefits tend not to reduce the differences in direct standard hourly earnings between firms as, generally speaking, firms with good fringe benefits also tend to pay relatively higher wages. It is the "other attractions" that must therefore carry the burden of equating net advantages. If so, they must be very powerful indeed to overcome the wage differences.

This explanation, despite its apparent comprehensiveness, is perhaps for practical purposes a trap. It is more useful to change the emphasis so that, while money wages are one of the features of attraction influencing the worker's choice of employment, it is for many only one feature. It seems a rather blunt instrument for obtaining a reallocation of labour through external labour market mobility. With mobility between firms and between occupations, wages do not move to produce equality of money reward, and in practice few workers turn to the external labour market to maximise their wage levels. Probably in most cases, pressures on the internal labour market induce movements in wages, based on considerations of what has happened elsewhere, or is believed to have happened. But this external comparability is imprecise and from an economic viewpoint insensitive, there not being any marked uniformity in the increases given by the different firms.

It is probably more helpful to emphasise the economic distortions in relative money wages than to stress the other attractions. That wages tend to be the same for a given occupation in a local labour market is widely believed, and people refer constantly to "the going rate." Similarly, certain increases are given "in order to stay in line" with other firms. The evidence does not support this reasoning but in fact shows that firms do not do what they often say they do; they do not give the

same increases as other local firms. The pressure
of economic forces as reflected in money wages is
therefore much weaker than is often believed. The
answer that net advantages must be equal or workers
would change their jobs, which conditions of high
employment permit, does not really explain the world
as we find it.

Wage differences may however reflect differences
in ability and efficiency, something no doubt impossible
to test. Discussion with employers and workers
suggests that it is not the higher paying firms who
employ the more able workers. For example, in two
plants in the same town belonging to the same company
the pace of work and skill content were higher in the
lower paying plant. In other cases the higher paying
firm employs men of higher skills though they are
classed in the same occupation.

All the evidence suggests that there are factors
operating within individual plants which effectively
isolate it partially from the external economic forces
operating in the local labour market. Conditions in
the internal labour market can apparently lead to
relatively high wages, or in other situations create
conditions in which rather low wages exist without
undue difficulty in recruitment or retention. There
are forces within an internal labour market emanating
from workers, trade unions and management. Regarding
these as institutional forces, though they may express
themselves through informal groups, then often they
seem more powerful than straight economic forces.

Trade unions and shop stewards possess bargaining
rights and powers and so perhaps economic forces
express themselves through institutional arrangements
becoming changed in the process. Thus, external
comparability may provoke a wage claim at plant level
and may be put forward as the reason for increasing
wages, but it does not follow that without the increase
there would be an outward movement of labour. Yet

65

this is the way economic forces ought to express themselves. Instead, there is sustained pressure in collective bargaining to change the package of reward at the current place of employment. This can be seen as a rejection of the working of economic forces through external markets or as anticipatory action to prevent the loss of labour or failure to recruit additional labour that would otherwise occur. There is little evidence to suggest that the latter is a correct interpretation of the likely chain of events. Instead, there can be substantial differences in wage levels and wage increases and firms can still recruit or retain labour. But the pressures of the internal labour market may be such that failure to grant an increase on the belief that wages elsewhere are rising would lead to a stoppage or other effective loss of labour. Collective bargaining is here, so it appears, effecting an economic change by creating artificially some of the features of economic markets. But these features are artificially created by institutional factors and do not lead to this result. There is far greater freedom, in principle, with institutional factors, than there is in principle, with economic forces. Institutional pressures can be contained or can be much greater than expected, even though economic conditions might suggest a different degree of pressure.

What is important therefore is the conditions within the internal market. External forces are also important but are in practice often subordinated to internal or institutional pressures. It may be that economic forces set limits within which the internal market can act, but these limits are wide. To develop a satisfactory and realistic plant level manpower and wages policy it is therefore necessary to understand the workings of the specific internal labour market and to assess the importance of the institutional and economic forces. The balance between them changes through time and from plant to plant, but in the great majority

of cases and for most occupations the internal
labour market will exert a stronger influence than the
external market.

REFERENCES

Kerr, C (1954) "The balkanization of labor markets,"
in "Labor Mobility and Economic Opportunity" edited
by E W Bakke, M I T Press

Kerr, C (1969) "Marshall, Marx and Modern Times:
the Multidimensional Society," Cambridge University
Press

Marshall, A (1966) "Principles of Economics" eighth
edition, Macmillan

Robinson, D (1968) "Wage Drift, Fringe Benefits and
Manpower Distribution," OECD

3 Wages and labour turnover

by D I Mackay

3.1 INTRODUCTION

The competitive theory of labour market behaviour
assumes that employees, in choosing between alternative employments, act as rational economic men
and pick the job which on balance they consider most
advantageous. This classical view of labour market
behaviour is that described in The Wealth of Nations,
and was reviewed and quoted in Chapter 1. Of the many
aspects of economic theory propounded by Adam Smith,
those relating to labour market behaviour have suffered
least by the passage of time. The theory has survived
virtually unaltered because it provides many predictions
which accord with reality. Individuals do take many
elements into account when choosing employment.
Again, if offered jobs with the same earnings they are
likely to take the job where non-monetary factors are
most advantageous. Yet the assumptions of the competitive model may not hold. The working of the market
may be disturbed or even suspended by inadequate job
knowledge, by barriers to labour mobility and by the
existence of institutions such as trade unions or
employers associations.

Such imperfections are stressed in most empirical
investigations of labour mobility such as those reported
in Myers (1954), Myers and Maclaurin (1943) and
Reynolds (1951). To simplify we might summarise
their findings: Manual workers - this is the appropriate
group for our purposes as the data used subsequently
relates to manual employees only - have limited job
horizons; they know little about the wage and non-
wage conditions of different employments; those in

work are often not interested in considering potential alternatives and job search is often limited and haphazard, conducted within a narrow area and strongly influenced by friends and relations. Thus, some labour mobility in a market is "wasted," in not resulting in the equalisation of net advantages. Instead it may impose costs on both employees and employers without corresponding benefits to either. It has been suggested that:

> The greater part of labour turnover consists of a continuous and fruitless inter-change of workers between firms which involves the waste of national and private resources and does not, in general, offer any immediate benefit even to the workers concerned, since they are usually moving into jobs which other workers have been eager to leave. (Long 1951, p12)

The contrary view is that, although imperfections in knowledge exist, they are not as serious as is commonly supposed, and that these informal methods of filling manual job vacancies may be effective in communicating job information. Competitive pressures may be strong despite the apparent disorganisation of the labour market. "Potential mobility is the ultimate sanction for the inter-relation of wage-rates" (Hicks 1963, p 79). An employer cannot ignore the actions of his competitors. If an employer "steps out of line," and does not match the wages of rivals, he will lose labour. Alternatively, by raising his wage level he can recruit additional labour, at least until his competitors respond to losses of labour by raising theirs. Thus, it is suggested the competition for labour will prevent wide wage differences from emerging between plants in the same labour market.

Yet studies which compare the wages of different employers have found substantial disparities in plant wage levels within the same labour market as the

rule rather than the exception; see Dunlop (1957),
Lester (1946) and Reynolds (1951). Much of this
evidence is collected at one particular moment in
time, so possibly differences are temporary and
might gradually disappear with competitive pressures.
On the other hand, Derek Robinson (1967, 1968) has
suggested that employers know little in detail about
competitors' wage levels so that wide differences in
plant wage levels exist and wage changes are un-
related. Because of this, "The labour market does
not work in the way generally supposed. It is far
more chaotic than even the sceptics have believed"
(Robinson 1967, pp 38-9).

Despite these findings, the traditional theory of
labour market behaviour survives. The confusion
between theory and empirical research derives from
the difficulty of assembling sufficient evidence to
"prove" or "disprove" the predictions to be drawn
from the assumptions of the competitive model.
Assume two employers, A and B, each employing the
same type of labour within the same labour market
area. A is a high wage plant and B a low wage unit.
If labour moves from B to A, it moves in the
"expected" direction. Does this mean that any
opposite movement of labour, from A to B, is incon-
sistent with rational, economic behaviour? Unfortunately, it is not so simple, for the theory does
not assume wages to be the only consideration relevant
to job choice. On the contrary, it stresses that many
other considerations may be important: non-pecuniary
factors such as the nature of the work, personal
relationships within the plant and the physical working
conditions, as well as pecuniary factors such as the
wage level. It is the balance of net advantages which
matters. Hence, labour migration from the high
wage plant, A, to the low wage plant, B, may imply
that the balance of net advantages is now in favour of
B. The work in A may be unpleasant, or dangerous,

these factors counterbalancing the higher wages.

This exemplifies the difficulty facing all applied research in this field. Labour market theory is so versatile and so many factors may be important in job choice that almost any set of observations can be rationalised. One cannot easily measure the non-pecuniary factors; they are extremely numerous and their importance varies from job to job, from individual to individual and, even, from one period to the next. Therefore, research has concentrated on examining whether labour market behaviour is explained by observed differences in earnings between industries, plants or jobs. This study is no exception We proceed by the simplifying assumption that non-pecuniary factors are unimportant. Subsequently, this unreal assumption can be relaxed, but it is impossible to quantify the many influences other than wages which influence the behaviour of employees, and discussion of them is always unsatisfactory. However, this is not, in itself, sufficient grounds for dismissing any investigation of labour market problems.

3.2 METHOD OF INQUIRY
This chapter now considers two aspects of labour market behaviour. First, we look at the relationship between wage earnings in different plants within the same labour market area. The basic objective is to discover whether the level of earnings is the same in all plants. Do fitters employed in engineering plant A earn the same as fitters in plant B? Or are there wide differences and, if so, do they persist? Can we, in other words, identify plants which are normally high wage or low wage units? Having described the main features of wage relationship between plants (termed, for convenience, the inter-plant wage structure), our second concern is any systematic relationship between plant earnings and labour turnover.

71

These questions are investigated via a study of sixty-four engineering plants over the period 1959 - 66. Most were in Birmingham and Glasgow, (twenty-five in Birmingham and twenty-seven in Glasgow) and this chapter is exclusively concerned with these two conurbations. The remainaing plants were drawn from North Lanarkshire and two smaller labour market areas which shall be called "New Town" and "Small Town." Certain information relating to these areas is utilised in Chapter 5. These areas were selected because they experienced substantial differences in labour market conditions over 1959 - 66. Of the major conurbations outside London, Birmingham had labour market conditions which were "tightest." Male unemployment rarely exceeded 3 per cent of the insured labour force and fell as low as 0.5 per cent. The unemployment rate for females was even lower. Glasgow is a contrast where engineering employment was contracting and where unemployment for both sexes substantially exceeded the British average over the entire period investigated.

The investigation of labour turnover is based on computer analysis of the case study plants' personnel records. Each year, over 1959 - 66, is subdivided into four quarters giving thirty-two quarters in all. These quarters being January - March, April - June, July - September and October - December. For each plant, the stock of manual employees at the beginning of each quarter is known, as is the number of persons leaving and joining during the quarter. Quarterly turnover rates are obtained by expressing these gross flows as a percentage of the appropriate stock. For each plant, quarterly turnover rates have been calculated on this basis for male and female employees plus, for male employees, turnover rates for the three main manual occupational groups: skilled, semi-skilled and unskilled. The great bulk of all female manual employees are semi-skilled operatives so that no analysis by occupation groups is necessary. Male occupation groups are based upon the Department of Employment and Productivity's classification of Occupations. As the "reason for leaving" was also obtainable from plant records, further distinctions can be drawn between all leavers (total separations) and those leaving voluntarily (voluntary quits).

Data on wage earnings was obtained from earnings' returns made by the plants to the Department of Employment and Productivity and to the local associations of the Engineering Employers' Federation. Some plants were not members of the Federation and others were not included in the sample from which DEP earnings' returns are collected. In addition, two plants in Glasgow and four in Birmingham would not permit disclosure of their earnings' returns. Two types of earnings' returns are collected by the DEP. The first, the WE returns, shows the total wage bill of the plant and the number of manual employees distinguished by sex. The returns relate to a given working week in April and October of each year and are available over the entire period 1959 - 66. No distinction is made by occupational groups and only average male and female earnings including overtime can be calculated. In the following text, a distinction is made between gross earnings, earnings including overtime payments, and standard earnings, earnings for a standard working week excluding all payments made in respect of overtime working. These deficiencies are offset by the occupational earnings' returns made to the DEP and the EEF. The EEF returns are made annually and show earnings by male occupational groups in a given working week. They are available for Glasgow plants for each year over 1959 - 66, save 1963. These returns could not be obtained for Birmingham plants but the second set of earnings' returns made to the DEP provide details by occupational groups being modelled on those of the

73

EEF. DEP occupational earnings' returns are available
on a bi-annual basis for 1963 - 66. Both sets of
occupational earnings' returns distinguish between
skilled and unskilled males, those of the DEP
providing additional information for semi-skilled
workers. For skilled males, details are also provided for fitters, turners, toolroom workers, etc. It
is possible to calculate gross earnings by occupations
and earnings for a standard working week excluding
all payments in respect of overtime working.

The information has certain deficiencies, the most
important being the inability to distinguish the spread
of individual earnings within the plant or within a given
occupational group. Averages obscure existing
variations between the earnings of individuals of the
same skill. The distribution of earnings, like all
income distributions, tends to be positively skewed,
those at the top of the distribution being probably
long-service employees. This may affect labour
turnover but be concealed by plant or occupational
averages. The new recruit is likely to find that his
earnings lie below the plant average for his skill and
this may lead to frustration and, consequently, to
labour turnover. These considerations are, however,
discussed in detail in Chapter 7. Here, it is noted
that our data is an improvement on that generally
available to the researcher. Investigation of the
relationship between wage earnings and labour turnover has generally been micro-economic. Yet employment conditions vary substantially from one local
labour market to the next and, manual labour being
reluctant to move great distances the local labour
market is the appropriate (and micro-economic)
framework to discover how labour turnover responds
to wages. Reluctance of labour to undertake geographical shifts is described in UK Social Survey
(1966), Wedderburn (1965) and Wilcock (1957).

3.3 INTER-PLANT WAGE STRUCTURE

If one's views on the inter-plant wage structure were derived from discussions with plant managers, then the competitive theory of labour markets would stand unchallenged. Such discussions are studded with references to "the market level of wages," "the going rate" and "paying the prevailing rate." Some managers believe there is only one level of earnings for each occupational group in the local labour market. More often, "the market level" and "the going rate" are not used literally but to describe the competitive pressures in the market. It is recognised that earnings levels may, and do, vary from plant to plant. Nonetheless, managers do not believe that wage differences are substantial. Moreover, they stress the difficulties in the recruitment and retention of labour if wage increases do not match those of nearby rivals. Earnings are seen as the key and sometimes almost the only element in determining labour turnover, and managers emphasise the sensitivity of turnover to large wage differences and to shifts in the inter-plant wage structure.

Few plant managers cannot illustrate their argument by "examples" of the competitive pressures. Some held that wage increases elsewhere had to be matched in response to shopfloor pressure and to prevent labour turnover. Others suggested that labour turnover increased because of an initial failure to respond to rival wage increases. While no manager could produce evidence for the latter argument, some examples are probably well founded. A plant cannot ignore the actions of other units which draw on similar types of labour. We do, however, dispute the popular myth that the manager is an automaton responding purely to economic pressures. Market pressures may, indeed, limit management's freedom of action but these limits are much wider than commonly supposed.

We begin investigating the inter-plant wage structure with Tables 3.1 and 3.2. Occupational earnings' returns provided for the EEF by fourteen Glasgow plants form the basis of Table 3.1. DEP earnings' returns by thirteen Birmingham units were used to compile Table 3.2. These were the number of plants providing occupational earnings' returns for the base and terminal years in Table 3.1 and Table 3.2. Different earnings' returns being used, the occupational groups analysed vary between the two areas. Again, for Birmingham, occupational earnings data was not available before 1963, but in Glasgow date back to 1959. Otherwise, the same methods applied to Tables 3.1 and 3.2. Both tables are based on standard earnings and hence exclude all overtime payments. The measures of dispersion shown are therefore obtained from an analysis of earnings for a standard working week. The inclusion of overtime payments to give gross earnings would not substantially affect the results obtained. To illustrate this, the coefficient of variation of plant gross earnings is shown in brackets below the coefficient of variation of plant standard earnings.

Three measures of the dispersion or "spread" of plant earnings are utilised. The range of occupational earnings between the lowest and the highest wage-paying plant in each occupation, and the inter-quartile range, both measure the absolute spread of earnings and are therefore rather crude measures of dispersion. The coefficient of variation measures relative dispersion based on all available observations and indicates whether the spread became relatively more or less important over time.

Clearly, at any given moment, there are very substantial differences between plant earnings' levels. For example, in 1959, standard weekly earnings for fitters in Glasgow ranged between an average of £9.30 in the lowest wage unit and £15.60 in the highest For

	Fitters	Turners	Unskilled	All workers
1959				
Standard weekly earnings (£)				
Range, lowest to highest	9.3 to 15.6	9.4 to 15.9	7.8 to 12.9	9.1 to 15.3
Inter-quartile range (Q3 - Q1)	2.3	1.6	2.2	2.1
Coefficient of variation	14.4 (18.3)	14.2 (15.4)	15.4 (16.5)	14.6 (13.8)
1966				
Range, lowest to highest	12.7 to 22.8	14.6 to 22.5	10.2 to 15.3	13.8 to 22.0
Inter-quartile range (Q3-Q1)	2.5	4.7	1.7	3.0
Coefficient of variation	14.1 (13.2)	13.2 (11.1)	12.2 (14.3)	13.8 (12.1)

TABLE 3.1 INTER-PLANT EARNINGS DIFFERENTIALS (STANDARD WEEKLY EARNINGS), GLASGOW PLANTS, JUNE 1959 and OCTOBER 1966

Source: EEF Occupational Earnings' Returns

	Toolroom	Semi-skilled	Unskilled	All workers
1963				
Standard weekly earnings (£)				
Range, lowest to highest	13.0 to 24.1	11.6 to 20.7	7.7 to 13.6	11.9 to 20.3
Inter-quartile range (Q3 - Q1)	7.6	5.3	1.4	5.1
Coefficient of variation	20.1 (19.7)	17.8 (16.7)	13.0 (18.2)	16.3 (14.5)
1966				
Range, lowest to highest	14.1 to 23.5	14.3 to 25.4	9.9 to 17.4	15.1 to 25.7
Inter-quartile range (Q3-Q1)	9.3	7.0	4.2	6.5
Coefficient of variation	22.7 (17.6)	19.9 (15.8)	16.0 (12.1)	17.5 (12.8)

TABLE 3.2 INTER-PLANT EARNINGS DIFFERENTIALS (STANDARD WEEKLY EARNINGS), BIRMINGHAM PLANTS, JUNE 1963 and JUNE 1966

Source: DEP Occupational Earnings' Returns

all groups shown and for all periods, the absolute
range in standard earnings is extremely large.
Approximately, in the highest wage plant they are
usually some 60 - 80 per cent above those in the
lowest wage establishment. For gross earnings, the
absolute range between lowest and highest widens in
all cases in Birmingham and in all, save two, in
Glasgow.

Similar results could have been produced for any
other period for which earnings data is available.
Therefore, the substantial differences in plant earnings
are not simply a transitory phenomenon which disappears as the market adjusts towards equilibrium.
Such differences are the rule and not the exception.
Nor is this result due to extreme observations at either
end of the inter-plant wage structure. The inter-
quartile range, which ignores such extreme observations,
and the coefficient of variation, which includes all
observations, both indicate such substantial differences. In Glasgow, the coefficient of variation of
plant earnings is lower for all groups in 1966, but the
fall in the coefficient is small whether the base is
standard earnings or gross earnings. In Birmingham,
the position is more complicated. The coefficient of
variation of plant gross earnings falls between 1963
and 1966 for each group while the reverse is true for
standard earnings. Too much should not be made of
such contrasts. The important conclusion to be drawn
is that differences in plant earnings are large whether
measured in absolute or relative terms and that such
differences do not disappear with the passage of time.

Moreover, the spread between plant earnings seems
as large in both cities. In 1966, the coefficient of
variation of gross and standard earnings for skilled
toolroom workers in Birmingham is greater than that
for skilled turners or fitters in Glasgow. The same
is true for "all workers", while in the case of the
unskilled, the results depend on whether gross earnings

or standard earnings are used. It has been suggested that job choice will be more responsive to differences in earnings in markets with low levels of unemployment (Bowen 1960), OECD 1965, pp 101-4, Parnes 1954, pp 153-4, Wilkinson 1961), and so it might be expected that wage differences would narrow as employers compete more vigorously for labour. Tables 3.1 and 3.2 do not support this thesis. Wage differences are as large in Birmingham as in Glasgow despite much less unemployment in the former. This conclusion is based on comparing cross-sectional results for two markets, Birmingham and Glasgow, with different employment conditions. Examination of wage differences over time within these markets does not suggest that wage differentials are sensitive to changes in local employment conditions.

The large differences in plant earnings shown by Tables 3.1 and 3.2 could indicate a fairly stable hierarchy of high and low wage plants. Certain units may remain near the "top" of the inter-plant wage structure in most periods while other units may normally be low wage payers. Equally, plants could change positions in the wage hierarchy frequently so that over time no stable wage hierarchy would emerge. We can investigate these possibilities through Tables 3.3 and 3.4. They are based on standard earnings and include the same plants and occupational groups as in Tables 3.1 and 3.2. For each occupational group the plants were ranked according to their position in the inter-plant wage structure in the first and last periods for which data was available (June and October 1966 in Glasgow and June 1963 and June 1966 in Birmingham). From this, the Spearman rank correlation coefficient was calculated for each group. In Glasgow, the coefficients are affected by the definition of earnings adopted. So, the process was repeated for gross earnings, the resulting coefficients appearing in brackets at the bottom of each table.

80

Plant	Fitters		Turners		Unskilled		All workers	
number	1959	1966	1959	1966	1959	1966	1959	1966
G1	1	3	1	4	1	2	1	3
G2	2	5	3	7	3	5	3	6
G3	3	1	2	1	2	1	2	1
G4	4	8	7	10	12	13	4	8
G5	5	6	5	5	5	14	5	5
G6	6	7	8	8	7	8	7	7
G7	7	4	9	3	11	4	8	4
G8	8	2	4	2	6	6	6	2
G9	9	13	11	12	4	7	9	10
G10	10	10	6	6	9	11	10	9
G11	11	11	10	13	10	10	11	11
G12	12	14	13	11	8	12	12	14
G13	13	12	14	9	14	3	13	12
G14	14	9	12	14	13	9	14	13
Rank cor-relation	+0.72 (+0.39)		+0.74 (+0.34)		+0.33 (+0.33)		+0.85 (+0.48)	

Plant ranking

TABLE 3.3 RANKING OF PLANTS BY STANDARD
WEEKLY EARNINGS, GLASGOW PLANTS,
JUNE 1959 and OCTOBER 1966

Source: EEF Occupational Earnings Returns

F

Plant number	Plant ranking							
	Toolroom		Semi-skilled		Unskilled		All workers	
	1963	1966	1963	1966	1963	1966	1963	1966
B1	1	2	3	2	1	1	2	1
B2	2	1	1	1	2	2	1	2
B3	3	5	2	3	11	3	5	6
B4	4	4	5	5	8	7	4	5
B5	5	3	4	4	4	5	3	3
B6	6	6	-	-	10	6	6	4
B7	7	7	6	6	9	8	7	7
B8	8	8	8	12	6	13	9	11
B9	9	9	7	7	5	4	8	8
B10	10	12	10	8	3	10	10	10
B11	11	11	12	11	12	11	11	12
B12	12	10	11	9	7	12	12	9
B13	13	13	9	10	13	9	13	13
Rank correlation	+0.95 (+0.91)		+0.90 (+0.94)		+0.38 (+0.44)		+0.94 (+0.92)	

TABLE 3.4 RANKING OF PLANTS BY STANDARD
WEEKLY EARNINGS, BIRMINGHAM PLANTS,
JUNE 1963 and JUNE 1966

Source: DEP Occupational Earnings Returns

All the rank correlation coefficients are positive. For standard weekly earnings, the coefficients are significant at the 1 per cent level for both markets and for all groups except the unskilled. In other words, plants which had relatively high standard earnings in the first period also tended to be wage leaders in the second period and vice-versa. This held for a period exceeding seven years in Glasgow and for three years in Birmingham. It can be seen that the rank correlation coefficients are higher in Birmingham than in Glasgow. The differences are unlikely to be significant for it is to be expected that the coefficients will be higher the shorter the period considered. Therefore, in the long run the inter-plant wage structure shows considerable stability so that some units are commonly at the top of the wage league and others consistently near the bottom. It should, however, be observed that in the short run substantial movement can occur due to changes in overtime earnings. Although the use of gross earnings data has no effect on the stability of plant rankings in Birmingham, it produces a marked shift in Glasgow. There, the co-efficients remain positive for gross earnings but are much smaller than those for standard earnings and none are significant at the 5 per cent level. How do we explain this?

The contrast in the Glasgow results is due to major shifts in the ranking of two plants when gross earnings replaced standard earnings. These shifts resulted from large variations in overtime working between the two periods. They could indicate a fundamental change in "ability to pay" or, more plausibly, a temporary adjustment in overtime working for essentially short term reasons. For example, if Birmingham plants are ranked according to male gross earnings, as shown by the WE returns, the inter-plant wage structure is extremely stable over very long periods, although in intervening periods substantial shifts in plant rankings occur. It will be recalled that the WE returns do not disclose information for occupational groups. They do, however, provide gross earnings for males and females for two separate weeks in each year over 1959 - 66. This is particularly so with car assembly plants in which earnings occasionally change sharply due to overtime or short time working. Normally, however, these plants pay high wages, any sudden and large change in relative positions being usually reversed very quickly. A study of male gross earnings for Glasgow indicates a similar behaviour pattern. Over the long run, most plants occupy much the same position in the wage hierarchy, but at times substantial changes follow variations in overtime payments.

Most engineering plants in Britain work "systematic" overtime, which is accepted practice. If, however, the pressure on productive resources changes the initial reaction is usually to adjust the amount of overtime working. Hence, variations in overtime earnings are the chief cause of the short run changes in the inter-plant wage structure. Large changes in overtime earnings are, however, exceptional, so that even where gross earnings are considered, changes in rankings are usually reversed fairly quickly. The long run position is better reflected by standard earnings and here the wage hierarchy remains very stable over long periods.

To summarise: in any period there are wide and persistent differences in the levels of earnings in a local labour market. Such stability might point to competitive pressures, yet further examination reveals that changes in plant earnings over any period of time vary considerably from one unit to the next. For example, for the Glasgow plants included in Table 3. 3, standard earnings for fitters increased by a minimum of 22 per cent and a maximum of 83 per cent over June 1959 to October 1966. Similar wide

differences in the rate of change of earnings are
observable for all groups in Tables 3.3 and 3.4, and
these differences in wage levels are a predominant
feature of labour markets. Hence the inter-plant
wage structure retains a high degree of stability over
fairly long periods of time not because changes in
earnings are the same from unit to unit but because
the difference in earnings' levels are so sustained in
the base period that large differences in earnings'
changes can be accommodated with relatively little
effect on the wage hierarchy. There is no such thing
as a market level of wages or earnings.

3.4 WAGES AND LABOUR TURNOVER
Labour market theory assumes that labour mobility
and turnover are responsive to differences in net
advantages. Other things being equal, high wage plants
will attract and retain new recruits while low wage
plants will experience difficulty. It is difficult to
establish whether "other things" are, indeed, equal.
The differences in plant earnings in our labour market
areas could, then, reflect that non-pecuniary factors
were most favourable in low wage units. Low wage
plants may offer more interesting and varied employment, more congenial working conditions, better
industrial relations and so forth. On the other hand,
the wage differences observed may reflect real
differences in net advantages.

This is a difficult dilemma but some clues help us
see whether variations in earnings are offset by other
factors so that net advantages are equalised. Consider
the following example. Assume two plants, A and B,
which is in the "previous" period, period 1, had average
weekly earnings of £10 and £20 respectively. Now
suppose that earnings increase by £4 in plant A and
by £5 in plant B so that in the "present" time period,
period 2, average earnings are £14 in plant A and
£25 in plant B. If there was initial equilibrium, with

net advantages equalised, then labour turnover in the present period, 2, should respond to changes in earnings between 1 and 2, this factor disturbing the initial equilibrium. The percentage or relative change in earnings is greater in plant A, though absolutely greater in plant B. There, therefore, remains the problem of measuring the change in earnings. This could be handled by relating both percentage and absolute changes in earnings to the appropriate measures of labour turnover.

Probably neither measure of changes in earnings will be systematically related to labour turnover. There is abundant evidence that various imperfections exist which prevent employers and employees from adjusting instantaneously to changes in labour market conditions. This being so, the differences in earnings in a labour market must, to some extent, be "real " that is, they must reflect differences in net advantages. Accepting this, then the crucial influence on labour turnover may not be the change in plant earnings for this would not ignore the disequilibrium existing in the first instance. The crucial factor in shaping labour turnover in the present period may be the level of earnings in that period and not the change in earnings over some past period. In our example plant B, with average earnings of £25 in period 2 should attract and retain labour more easily than plant A with average earnings of only £14.

Labour turnover may, then, respond to any one of three earnings variables: the level of earnings, and percentage and absolute changes in earnings. To further complicate the issue, we can measure labour turnover in various ways. Here, we adopt four different measures: the rate of recruitment, the percentage change in employment, the total separation rate and the voluntary quit rate. The measures chosen do not, strictly speaking, amount to labour turnover as such but to certain aspects which form part of the whole process of labour turnover. The reader is asked, in the interests of brevity, to accept "labour turnover" as a generic term for the measurements used. Information on gross flows of labour into and out of plants or industries being scarce, studies of the relationship between earnings and labour mobility (or turnover) usually take the percentage change in employment as the dependent variable - see Long and Bourger (1953), Reddaway (1959) and Wilkinson (1961).

The change in employment depends, of course, on the difference between the rate of recruitment and the total separation rate, the former being a function of job openings as well as of earnings. Yet there is no evidence that job openings are necessarily more plentiful in establishments with high earnings and/or changes in earnings. Hence, if no systematic relationship emerges between earnings and recruitment this need not necessarily reflect that employees do not respond to differences in plant earnings. Similarly, if there is no relationship between earnings and changes in employment, this may merely indicate that plants with high wage levels and/or increases in earnings are not seeking to expand their labour forces.

The number of job openings sets an upper limit to the rate of recruitment and to changes in employment. This is not the case with the voluntary quits and total separations. The individual wishing to leave a plant can always do so although he can only find new work in those units which offer him employment. Thus, the quit rate may be responsive to changes or differences in earnings' levels, while the rate of recruitment and the percentage change in employment are not influenced by these variables. Possibly also the relationship between earnings and voluntary quits is stronger than that between earnings and total separation. This is because the latter group includes persons who cannot be said to make a choice between staying with or leaving a plant. Those who are not voluntary quits leave through management action (redundancy, unsuitability and misconduct) or through other events over which they have little control (retirement, sickness and death). This distinction between voluntary quits and total separations may not be crucial, for the behaviour of the separation rate may be dominated by the behaviour of the quit rate. Nonetheless, the distinction has to be borne in mind for analytical purposes.

The expected relationships between our dependent variables, the various measures of labour turnover, and our independent variables, the level of earnings and changes in earnings, can now be specified. Assuming that labour turnover is responsive to earnings a positive relationship should emerge between recruitment and changes in employment, on the one hand, and any of the wage variables on the other. The reverse holds for the voluntary quit rate and the total separation rate. Plants with high earnings or with large increases in earnings should have low quit rates and low separation rates and vice versa.

These propositions are tested for Glasgow males and for Birmingham males and females through the WE returns showing, by plant, average male and female gross earnings per week. Females in Glasgow are not considered because the great bulk of such employment in engineering is concentrated in a handful of plants. These earnings' returns were made twice a year throughout 1959 - 66 so that in sixteen periods data is available for these three groups. Average plant gross earnings were calculated for each plant and from this the percentage and absolute change in earnings between periods was obtained. The number of observations per quarter varies between a minimum of 15 and a maximum of 22 plants for Glasgow males. There are 12 - 14 and 11 - 12 observations for Birmingham males and Birmingham females respect-

88

ively. Each variable was correlated in turn with the
voluntary quit rate, the total separation rate, the
percentage change in employment and the rate of
recruitment by plants. Hence, we relate these
measures of labour turnover in period 2 to the level
of earnings in period 2 and to the increases (percentage
or absolute) in earnings in period 2 over period 1.

The detailed results show that in certain cases no
systematic relationships exist between the earnings
variables and labour turnover. For example, the
correlation coefficients between any of the earnings
variables and the rate of recruitment are as often
negative as positive for all three groups - Glasgow
males and Birmingham males and females. The lack
of any systematic relationship between plant earnings
and plant recruitment rates need not arise because
potential employees do not respond to wage signals.
More likely, establishments with high earnings, or
large increases in earnings, are not seeking large
number of new recruits. Much the same comments
apply when the percentage change in employment is
substituted for the rate of recruitment as the dependent
variable. In the case of both Birmingham males and
females, a negative relationship frequently emerges
between employment changes and any of the earnings
variables. For Glasgow males, the sign of the
correlation coefficients obtained is usually positive,
as expected, but the coefficients are extremely small
and are seldom significant at the 5 per cent level.

It only remains to consider whether the behaviour
of the quit rate and the separation rate is responsive
to earnings. For quits and for separations, a clear
negative relationship emerges when the level of plant
earnings is taken as the independent variable. The
relationship between these measures of labour turnover and changes in earnings is, however, much
less systematic in the case of both percentage and
absolute changes. We can discuss this by reference to
Table 3.5.

Quarter	Glasgow males		Birmingham males		Birmingham females	
	Quit rate	Separation rate	Quit rate	Separation rate	Quit rate	Separation rate
2	-0.19	-0.32	0.15	0.11	0.21	0.07
4	-0.54¤	-0.54¤	-0.05	0.01	-0.02	-0.15
6	-0.35	-0.29	-0.09	-0.12	-0.35	-0.27
8	-0.59*	-0.55¤	0.09	0.13	-0.35	-0.38
10	-0.35	-0.30	-0.07	-0.07	-0.39	-0.47
12	-0.48¤	-0.36	-0.26	-0.19	-0.31	0.17
14	-0.15	0.03	-0.33	-0.44	-0.67¤	-0.61¤
16	-0.18	-0.18	-0.23	-0.15	-0.37	-0.43
18	-0.54¤	-0.65*	-0.17	-0.19	-0.40	-0.52
20	-0.36	-0.46¤	-0.41	-0.38	-0.41	-0.51
22	0.00	-0.02	-0.28	-0.33	-0.75*	-0.79*
24	-0.57¤	-0.49¤	-0.22	-0.18	-0.70¤	-0.65¤
26	-0.41	-0.40	-0.37	-0.40	0.49	-0.61¤
28	-0.32	-0.30	-0.24	-0.26	-0.68¤	-0.67¤
30	-0.54¤	-0.46¤	-0.26	-0.38	-0.38	-0.28
32	-0.39	-0.52¤	-0.48	-0.43	-0.50	-0.40

TABLE 3.5 CORRELATION COEFFICIENTS: LEVEL OF GROSS EARNINGS WITH (a) VOLUNTARY QUIT RATE AND (b) TOTAL SEPARATION RATE, BY PLANTS: GLASGOW MALES AND BIRMINGHAM MALES AND FEMALES.

Notes: * Significant at the 1 per cent level   ¤ Significant at the 5 per cent level
Source: Wage data from DEP returns

The table shows the coefficients obtained from correlating the level of gross earnings with the quit rate and the separation rate by plants.

For Glasgow males and for Birmingham males and females, the voluntary quit rate and the total separation rate are inversely related to the level of gross earnings. To simplify the discussion, we shall concentrate on the relationship between the voluntary quit rate and earnings because this group is most likely to be responsive to economic incentives. The coefficients obtained by correlating the plant quit rate with the level of gross earnings are negative in all save one quarter for Glasgow males and Birmingham females, while there are only two positive signs for Birmingham males. If the quit rate is related to absolute and percentage changes in earnings, no such systematic relationship emerges. With Glasgow males and Birmingham males, the coefficients derived are positive in every third quarter when the absolute or percentage change in earnings is correlated with the plant quit rate. Positive signs are even more frequent in the case of Birmingham females.

For each group considered, therefore, quits (and separations) are a diminishing function of the level of gross earnings but are not systematically related to changes in gross earnings over a previous period. Given our previous discussion, this implies that observed wage differences are in some sense "real"; they do not simply reflect the existence of non-pecuniary factors outweighing the additional earnings offered by high wage plants. At any point in time, a labour market is in a greater or lesser degree of disequilibrium. Earnings (and net advantages) are not equalised in all plants so that the relevant earnings variable influencing labour turnover is the level of earnings rather than changes in that level. This conclusion may appear somewhat peculiar if one considers that a plant which experiences large increases in earnings over a

long period of time must eventually become a high
wage unit and vice versa. We might, then, expect
quits, which are negatively related to earnings' levels,
to be similarly related to changes in earnings.
However, changes in earnings are likely to be small
relative to the large wage differences in earnings'
levels ruling in the market. The effect of the former
factor is not, therefore, apparent over the short run.

Although high wage plants tend to have low quit
rates, the relationship between the level of gross
earnings and the quit rate is not very strong. The
extent to which we can "explain" differences in plant
quit rates in terms of differences in earnings levels
is given by squaring the correlation coefficients (r)
in Table 3.5 to give the coefficient of determination
(r^2). At best, r^2 is only 0.56 (Birmingham females,
quarter 22) indicating that we have "explained" just
over half the differences in plant quit rates. Generally
the association is much weaker, particularly for
Birmingham males. Approximately the variation in
plant quit rates accounted for by differences in gross
earnings is 10 - 33 per cent for Glasgow males, 10 -
50 per cent for Birmingham females and seldom more
than 10 per cent for Birmingham males. Differences
in plant quit rates do not, then, wholly or even mainly
derive from differences in earnings. We should,
however, consider briefly whether a stronger relationship would emerge between earnings and labour
turnover if less aggregative data was utilised.

The weak relationship between quits and earnings'
levels arises perhaps because our discussion does not
distinguish earnings and quits by occupational groups.
For females, this is hardly important for the great
bulk are semi-skilled. But the male labour possesses
a much wider range of manual skills. The occupational
"mix" of the labour force will vary from unit to unit
and, as occupation influences earnings and quits,
possibly analysis by the occupational group would

reveal a stronger relationship between these variables with no differentiation. This possibility was tested via the occupational earnings' returns of the EEF and the DEP. Repeating the analysis for skilled and unskilled males in Glasgow and for skilled, semi-skilled and unskilled males in Birmingham, the results by occupational groups differ little from those for all males and all females. In other words, the rate of recruitment and the percentage change in employment by occupational groups are not systematically related to any of the earnings variables - percentage or absolute changes in earnings or the level of occupational earnings. The relationship between labour turnover and earnings by occupational groups was tested for standard weekly earnings and gross weekly earnings. Which of these definitions is adopted has little effect on the results obtained. The quit rate and the separation rate by occupational groups are a diminishing function of the level of occupational earnings but are little affected by changes in occupational earnings. The coefficients obtained from correlating quits and separations with the level of earnings by occupational groups are not, however, larger than those shown in Table 3.5. Hence, we cannot dismiss the weak relationship between earnings and quits on the grounds of aggregation.

3.5 CONCLUSIONS

Recruitment rates and changes in employment are not positively associated with the level of plant earnings, or with changes in plant earnings. Differences in plant wage levels do not, then, arise simply because high wage units wish to recruit a relatively high proportion of the available labour supply. Nor do high earnings arise because some plants are trying to increase their labour forces particularly rapidly. Of course, high wage units are able to recruit labour more easily than low wage units and could more readily build up their labour forces if desired. Nonetheless, high wage units do not have these purposes solely in mind.

High earnings, however, confer certain other benefits. Most obvious is their ability to retain labour more easily. As we have seen, the quit rate, and therefore the separation rate, is inversely related to the level of earnings. Therefore, wage units probably incur lower costs in the recruitment, selection and training of new employees. A "high wage policy" may, then be perfectly sensible economically even where the plant is not attempting to expand employment. Nonetheless, the relationship between plant earnings and quits is a weak one. The advantage enjoyed in lower quit rates is therefore scarcely the only reason for the existence of high wage units.

The competitive theory of labour markets predicts that within a local labour market labour of the same type will tend to obtain the same earnings. Yet we have found large wage differentials between plants employing the same type of labour and they are not eroded with the passage of time. There are three possible explanations. First, that our occupational groups, even if defined as "turners," "fitters," "unskilled" and so on are not, in fact, homogenous. Second, that differences in earnings are offset by non-pecuniary factors so that net advantages are equalised and, third, that various imperfections in the labour market prevent, or seriously retard, any adjustment towards equilibrium.

Possibly, indeed, probably, work requirements and hiring standard vary between plants even where the labour falls within the same occupational group. For example, a turner may be called on to undertake a wide range of tasks which vary considerably in the degree of experience and skill required. "Turners" employed by high wage units may therefore possess

94

greater skills than "turners" in low wage units and hiring standards may vary accordingly. It is extremely difficult to assess the effect of differences in hiring standards. Discussions with the case study plants indicated that hiring standards are likely to differ from one unit to the next, but few plants made any attempt to carry through a systematic analysis of job content which could be related to the attributes of potential recruits. Hiring standards for manual workers are in many plants highly subjective depending on the whim of the personnel officer. Experienced personnel officers may, in most cases, be able to judge correctly on what appears to be a perfunctory appraisal but selection procedures are often extremely casual. Most plants hire the first recruit who meets their minimum requirements. Although this minimum varies from plant to plant, there is no need to question the results of previous studies, (Lester 1948 and 1954, Myers and Maclaurin 1943, Reynolds 1951) which found that differences in hiring standards are only a partial explanation of differences in plant earnings.

The evidence in this study is hardly conclusive, but it is consistent with Lester's finding that:

Notable differences in quality of the work force were evident only for two or three companies at the top of the wage hierarchy and for two or three at the very bottom, whose work forces were obviously poor in quality.

In between these extremes there appeared to be little evident correlation between quality and relative wage position. (Lester 1954, pp 74-5)

Variations in plant earnings can also arise because of differences in non-pecuniary factors. We return, then, to our initial problem, for the non-pecuniary elements which may enter into job choice are, potentially, very numerous and extremely difficult to quantify. What can be said is that if non-pecuniary factors are the chief cause of variations in plant earnings they must be extremely important for they have to offset very large differences in earnings. This is not impossible, for most studies of labour market behaviour indicate that job choices are not made simply in response to monetary considerations, (see Parnes 1954). No systematic examination of non-pecuniary factors was attempted in this study. "Fringe benefits" such as pension, life assurance and sickness schemes were the only element not entering directly into the wage packet which proved susceptible to measurement. In the event, fringe benefits were greatest in those units where wage earnings were high so that one cannot explain differences in earnings on these grounds. Visits to the case study plants did not provide any indication that low wage plants enjoyed any advantage over high wage units with respect to non-pecuniary factors. Indeed, as far as physical conditions of work are important, these are generally more favourable in high wage units. This is hardly conclusive, for the relevant assessment is not that of the observer, but of the employee. However, while more detailed research on job aspirations and motivation is urgently required, the present evidence yields no hint that differences in earnings are largely due to differences in non-pecuniary factors.

Non-pecuniary factors, differences in hiring standards and differences in quit rates may explain some variations in plant earnings in a labour market. Such explanations can be accommodated without doing violence to the competitive theory, but it would do violence to the facts to suppose that there is no need to modify our view of labour market behaviour. Labour market theory must recognise that large differences in earnings may arise because of what Lester (1952) has called "anticompetitive" and "impeditive" forces. Numerous imperfections exist preventing the market from attaining equilibrium, and while the concept of equilibrium has always been regarded as a pedagogical device rather than as a position which is ever realised in practice, departures from equilibrium may be much more substantial than commonly realised. Competitive pressures are restrained by anti-pirating agreements, by institutional bargaining arrangements, by the exercise of bargaining power, by custom, habit and practice, by the emphasis placed on promotion internal to the plant, by the application of the seniority principle in determining the incidence of promotion and redundancy, by the importance of kinship and friendship networks in hiring new labour and by imperfect know-ledge on the part of employers and employees. This by no means exhausts the possibilities. Differences between establishments in managerial efficiency, in product market conditions and in profitability are likely to be reflected in plant wage levels. Competitive pressures may still make themselves felt but the limits set to management action are fairly wide. Thus, the simple mechanistic model based on the "economic man" provides only a partial explanation of labour market behaviour.

REFERENCES
   Bowen, W G (1960) "Wage Behavior in the Postwar Period" Princeton University Industrial Relations Section
   Dunlop, J T (1957) "The task of contemporary wage theory," in "The Theory of Wage Determination" edited by J T Dunlop, Macmillan
   Hicks, J R (1963) "The Theory of Wages" second edition, Macmillan
   Lester, R A (1946) "Wage diversity and its theor-etical implications" Review of Economics and Statistics, volume 28, pp 152-9
   Lester, R A (1948) "Company Wage Policies," Princeton University Industrial Relations Section
   Lester, R A (1952) "A range theory of wage

97

G

differentials," Industrial and Labor Relations Review, volume 5, pp 483-500

Lester, R A (1954) "Hiring Practices and Labor Competition," Princeton University Industrial Relations Section

Long, J R (1951) "Labour Turnover under Full Employment" (University of Birmingham Studies in Economics and Society Monograph A2), University of Birmingham

Long, J and Bowyer, I. (1953) "The influence of earnings on the mobility of labour," Yorkshire Bulletin of Economic and Social Research, volumes 5-6, pp 81-7

Myers, C A (1954) "Labor Mobility in two Communities," in "Labor Mobility and Economic Opportunity" edited by E. W. Bakke, MIT Press

Myers, C A and Maclaurin, W. P. (1943) "The Movement of Factory Labor," Wiley

OECD (1965) "Wages and Labour Mobility"

Parnes, H S (1954) "Research on Labor Mobility," Social Science Research Council

Reddaway, W B (1959) "Wage flexibility and the distribution of labour," Lloyds Bank Review, October 1959, pp 32-48

Rees, A (1966) "Information networks in labor markets," American Economic Review, volume 56, number 2, pp 183-99

Reynolds, L G (1951) "The Structure of Labor Markets," Harper & Row

Robinson, D (1967) "Myths of the local labour market," Personnel, volume 1, number 1, pp 36-9

Robinson, D (1968) "Wage Drift, Fringe Benefits and Manpower Distribution," OECD

Rottenberg, S (1955) "On choice in labor markets," Industrial and Labor Relation Review, volume 9, pp 183-99

UK Social Survey (1966) "Labour Mobility in Great Britain, 1955-63," HMSO

Wedderburn, D (1965) "Redundancy and the Railwaymen" (University of Cambridge Department of Applied Economics Occasional Paper, number 4), Cambridge University Press

Wilcock, R C (1957) "Employment effects of a plant shutdown in a depressed area," Monthly Labor Review, volume 80, pp 1047-52

Wilkinson, R (1961) "Differences in earnings and changes in the distribution of manpower in the UK, 1948-57," Yorkshire Bulletin of Economic and Social Research, volume 13-14, pp 46-57

4 Socio-cultural influences on the operation of a wage payment system: an explanatory case study

by Dan Gowler

This study examines wage systems in the light of the employees perceptions of the effort bargain, that is their ideas about the relationship between effort and reward. It analyses and described how the values and beliefs of women workers in a specific cultural environment combine with economic, social and organisational factors to influence the relation between a day wage system and the level of productivity.

It must be noted, however, that though dealing particularly with one form of day wage system, the processes and problems described here are also to be found operating with varying effects and expression in all types of payment system.

4.1 THE PROBLEM

Salary and wage payment systems are of perennial interest to sociologists, psychologists, managers, trade unionists, business consultants and, more recently, the National Board for Prices and Incomes. Yet we know little about the values and beliefs which underpin and validate various methods of salary and wage payment.

There are, for instance, Hilde Behrend's paper (1959) which discusses managerial convictions about the efficiency of incentive payment schemes. For instance, she comments that:

> ... the use of incentive schemes rests on faith
> in - rather than proof of - the effectiveness of
> financial incentives; the results expected from
> payment by results have acquired the status of
> achieved results in spite of the lack of factual
> proof of the achievement.

This topic is also discussed by Shimmin (1959) and
Lupton (1961).

Baldamus (1957) notes that effort and wage control
theory is saturated with normative conceptions about
what is morally "right" or "wrong." Jaques argues
that there exists:

> .... an unrecognised system of norms of fair
> payment for any given level of work, unconscious
> knowledge of these norms being shared among
> the population engaged in employment work.
> (Jaques 1967, p 146).

These comments are confirmed by William Skinner,
who, discussing the problems of American managements operating production facilities in developing
economies, observes that:

> American managers are "born and bred" on certain
> principles - the recognition of individual effort,
> treating each individual differently, monetary
> incentives, and so on. It is natural that Americans
> view these principles as prerequisites to
> productivity. Silently and implicitly they have
> crept into the wage system of American inter-
> national subsidiaries; but analysis of local values
> is necessary. What seems fair and acceptable to
> the worker varies from culture to culture.
> (Skinner 1968, p 55).

This paper is an attempt to determine and analyse some
of these values, and examine the relation between the
attitudes and beliefs of a group of workers and supervisors and the operation of a measured day work wage

101

system. For a discussion of this and related types of wage payment systems, see Lupton (1964). This method of wage payment is particularly well suited to this analysis for two reasons:

1   The successful operation of a measured day work system is claimed to rely not only on efficient supervisory and administrative controls but also on "... the moral obligation to keep contracts willingly entered into, and to meet undertakings freely accepted" (Lupton and Gowler 1969).

2   Measured day work systems pose the problem of maintaining a high level of productivity in the absence of a direct financial incentive.

4. 2 STRUCTURAL IMPERATIVES
It should first be explained that structural imperatives are those forces in the situation, for instance market competition, plant layout, and costs, which cannot be avoided and therefore exercise a considerable influence on behaviour through the restriction of choice.

The fieldwork for this study was conducted during the first six months of 1967 in a light engineering company mainly assembling small components for the electronics industry, employing about 350 workers, chiefly women.

The factory is in a small town in the North West, which has a fairly stable population of about 20000. The locality has a relatively narrow economic base, with only one important traditional industry, fishing.

The recent expansion of the chemical industry in this area affected the occupational structure. For example, at the time of the research, over 50 per cent of all workers in manufacturing industry were employed by one chemical company. This will have important long term effects on the local culture and, coupled with the decline in the fishing industry, will

102

alter the community's rhythms of life. The town and its environs might well be described as a community in cultural transition. The factory was also interesting in that it comprised two workshops at about half a mile from each other. The smaller of these two, employing about 130 women, was established first in existing buildings. The larger unit was custom built at a later date.

One reason given by this company's management for locating its plant here was that it believed that there would be an adequate supply of female labour. However, since the firm established its factory, others have arrived and now compete for labour. Further, when this company arrived, it was paying wages well above average for the area. This is no longer the case, and the firm, though still paying relatively high wages for the district, is now matched by several other employers. The company still has the advantage that, because of a progressive personnel policy and the type of technology, the physical working conditions for employees are rather better than elsewhere locally.

The work is highly labour intensive, though recently the firm has introduced some semi-automatic machines, and this mechanisation will doubtless continue. The work also demands a high degree of manual dexterity and, the product being small, particularly good eyesight. It also involves a training period of several months which is costly for the company.

Production is not, then, machine paced, the pacing being achieved by the payment system and the supervisors. The work is highly repetitive and assembly methods are laid down and controlled by the firm's industrial engineers.

The assemblers are organised into production units, each in the charge of a male supervisor. Each production unit, which makes a variation of the firm's product, is divided into three sections, each completing a stage of the component.

In recent years, changes in the firm's product
market has reduced batch sizes and resulted in a
greater variety of products, which lead to problems
of workflow administration (see Figure 4:1).

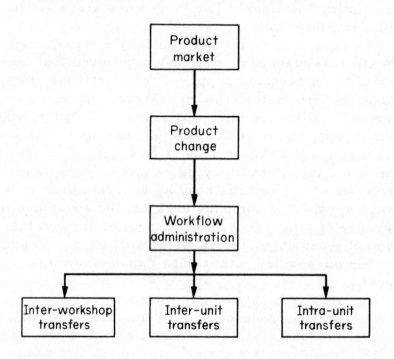

FIGURE 4:1   WORKFLOW PROBLEMS RESULTING
            FROM CHANGES IN A FIRM'S PRODUCT
            MARKET

These problems, resulting from adaptation of product
arrangements to product market requirements, had
two important consequences. Firstly, the firm must
now recruit a labour force flexible enough to meet
these changing requirements. Secondly, these changing
circumstances result in a considerable number of

104

inter-unit , intra-unit and inter-workshop transfers, which are so resented by the assemblers that they are one main cause of absenteeism and labour turnover. In fact, the assemblers dislike of inter-factory transfers is so strong that one manager said they were regarded by some workers "as worse than the sack." The reasons are discussed in detail later, but one stems from certain rules and procedures linking transfer arrangements to the wage payment system.

The wage payment system in use is a form of measured day work on the principle of a personal contract. The worker personally contracts to supply a given quantity of work of a given quality in return for a regular weekly wage. The crucial rule here is that a worker, once having contracted to attain a certain level of earnings/output, is not through her own fault allowed to fall back to a lower level. The management has since modified these rules, allowing workers a trial period on lower levels of performance. This regulation is enforced even if a worker is transferred to another unit, where she must master the assembly of a slightly different component. Thus, if after retraining, the transferred worker does not reach the original contract level she is likely to be dismissed. The supervisors did not help by occasionally using transfers as a disciplinary measure. Another difficulty is that this payment system puts pressure on certain workers, who appear to have internalised their obligations to management and are very distressed if they do not meet their earnings/output targets. This again appears responsible for some absenteeism and labour turnover.

This also puts pressure on the supervisors, who are responsible for maintaining and improving performance, while dealing with various other problems, such as quality, the deployment of labour, workflow difficulties and so on. For an example of the effects of similar structural pressures on supervisors see Gowler (1969). Some authorities argue that the maintenance of performance standards under measured day work systems is very difficult and that a restriction of output is built into such schemes. They suggest that workers treat the performance standards as the maximum performance which, when achieved, absolves from from further effort.

The analysis so far is summarised in Figure 4:2, which illustrates the structural imperatives in this situation. Workflow difficulties (box 1) were created by variations in product mix and batch size (arrow A) resulting from product market competition and technological change. This was exacerbated by the production arrangements, particularly the division of labour on the production units (arrow B). These

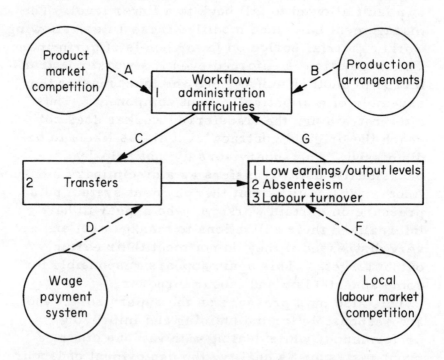

FIGURE 4:2   STRUCTURAL IMPERATIVES

workflow difficulties resulted in the redeployment of
labour (arrow C) and inter-unit, intra-unit and inter-
workshop transfers (box 2). These transfers, coupled
with rules and procedures regulating the wage payment
system (arrow D) had adverse effects on the workers
(arrow E) resulting in low earnings/output levels,
absenteeism and labour turnover (box 3). These
consequences worsened by the loss of labour through
competition in the local labour market (arrow F)
feedback (arrow G) to increase the workflow difficulties
(box 1) and so on.

This analysis reveals most strikingly the importance
of the supervisor in this situation, since he must deal
with all the structural pressures at point of impact,
on the shopfloor.

4.3 THE ROLE OF THE SUPERVISOR
The supervisors in this factory are responsible for
the output of components of a given quality, being also
required to maintain fixed production targets. These
responsibilities are linked with the workers' wage
payment system, in which management had set
standards of performance related to various levels
of pay. Each worker "contracts" for a certain
standard of performance for a guaranteed weekly wage.
It is generally accepted that this wage payment
system demands supervisors of high calibre, with
particular emphasis upon "human relations" skills.

Our research revealed, however, that the workers
did not regard the supervisors as competent in
either a technical or social sense, and certainly they
did not regard their power as legitimate. These
attitudes stemmed from the relative lack of technical
expertise on the part of these supervisors and also
from certain cultural values held by the workers.
What is means by a "relative lack of technical expertise" is not that the supervisors were deficient
in knowledge about the component being manufactured

107

but they were unlikely to be able to make one. At
least not at the speed and precision achieved by the
assemblers.

To take the cultural point first. In the fishing
community, where this factory stands, the masculine
virtues of physical strength, endurance and virility
were much admired. As one woman said of a
supervisor:

> What sort of man would do a job like that -
> standing watching a bunch of women all day.

This was confirmed when we recorded several factory
songs at the firm's annual dance, one clearly charging
the supervisors with transvestite behaviour. Obviously,
the role of the supervisor did not conform to the
workers' ideas about the proper division of labour
between the sexes in this sub-culture. The highly
charged subject of the division of labour between the
sexes is discussed in detail by Margaret Mead (1962)
and also by Bott (1957).

The role of the supervisor had undergone several
subtle changes over time, consequent of changes in
the wage payment system, the product market,
production arrangements and the local labour market.
They were responsible for highlighting the supervisors' lack of technical and social skills.

Firstly, the original wage payment system was
based on piecework, and the introduction of a
measured day work scheme, with its need for a
relatively high order of technical, administrative and
social skills, put a great deal of pressure on the
supervisors, who had little or no preparation for
this change. Some authorities suggest that less
direct supervision is required when an incentive
scheme operates, since the payment system itself
acts as a silent supervisor. Such systems are
believed to control the worker through the wage
packet - see for example International Labour Office

(1967). This situation, where a change in the wage payment system significantly influences the role of the supervisor, is illustrated by Figure 4:3.

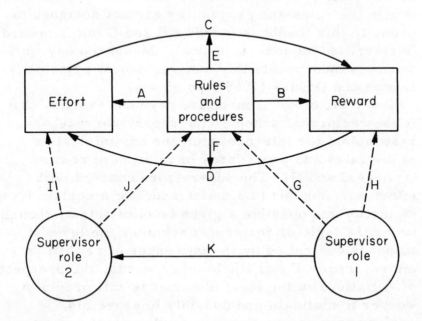

FIGURE 4:3 CHANGES IN THE SUPERVISOR'S ROLE

A wage payment system may be defined as a number of rules and procedures which relate effort to reward. Figure 4:3 is a diagrammatic representation of this definition. It shows that:

1   The rules and procedures circumscribe both effort (arrow A) and reward (arrow B)

2   They relate effort to reward (arrows E and C) in that a given amount of effort brings forth a given amount of reward

Figure 4:3 also shows that certain rules and procedures are specifically designed to encourage a feedback from reward to effort (arrows F and D). In this case, reward might be classified as reciprocal. Schemes incorporating this reciprocal principle are more generally known as "incentive" or "payment-by-results" schemes. Where the rules and procedures are not designed to promote this feedback (arrows E and C only) reward is classified as non-reciprocal. Measured day work schemes incorporate this non-reciprocal principle - Lupton and Gowler (1969), pp 45 - 53.

Under the original incentive payment system, that is the reciprocal scheme, the supervisor was responsible for interpretation and administration of the rules and procedures in relation to reward (arrows G and H). The supervisors concern with effort was reduced to a maintenance of a certain level of quality and possible a given level of output, though under the logic of reciprocal schemes the level of output is controlled by the influences of reward on effort (arrows F and D). In other words, the prospect of variations in the level of earnings will prompt a worker to maintain and possibly improve his performance, this operating as the silent supervisor.

The change in wage payment system from an incentive to a measured daywork scheme from a reciprocal to a non-reciprocal scheme (arrows E and C only). changes the supervisor's role (1) to role (2); see arrow K. Under the measured day work scheme, the supervisor became responsible for the interpretation and administration of the rules and procedures in relation to effort (dotted arrows I and J). His concern with reward is reduced, since the reward is now fixed. The supervisor must now replace the financial motivation and personally encourage workers to maintain and improve performance. This involves, of course, a quite different form of interaction with workers than under the incentive scheme.

The introduction of a new wage payment system was also accompanied by changes in the firm's product market with the emphasis now on smaller batches of higher quality components. The relation between batch size, management structure and industrial relations is discussed by Joan Woodward (1965). Quality became as important as quantity. Quality is, in the main, a technical matter, and the supervisors had no technical qualifications. Thus, the supervisors, because of the greater emphasis on quality and change in the type of wage payment system, had to involve themselves more with the assemblers on the units, exposing their lack of technical knowledge before workers not disposed to accept their authority in the first place. For a discussion of research and opinion on the relation between supervisory leadership and productivity see Dubin et al (1965).

Another very real problem for the supervisors was that, under this system, they were expected to encourage workers to opt for more pay by attempting higher levels of output, at the same time disciplining them when they did not maintain their contracted levels of output. The relations between workers and supervisors, the consequence of cultural and structural factors, were such that attempts to play this dual role seldom met with much success.

Another strain on the supervisors was that vacancies for clerical and administrative grades of labour locally were very limited, so they had very little chance of finding other acceptable jobs. During the period of our research the male unemployment figure in this area reached 8.3 per cent. Further, their chances of transfer or promotion were restricted because of their age, lack of technical qualifications and the fact that the firm was unlikely to expand its activities in this factory.

Finally, and perhaps not very surprisingly, the morale of these supervisors was very low. We often heard comments from them like "we are nothing but factory floormops" or "we are all misfits." Again

111

this did not help with the relations between them and their subordinates.

4.4 THE PRINCIPLE OF RECIPROCITY

There were other considerations which influenced whether workers decided to earn more money by improving their performance, apart from their relations with the supervisors. This involved, for example, the rights and obligations to one another as workmates, relatives, neighbours and friends. Fulfilling these led sometimes to a breach of management's regulations and conflict with the supervisors.

The regulation which appeared to be most important here was that a worker once having contracted to attain a certain level of performance was not allowed to fall back, even after transfer to another unit assembling a different component. Thus if, after retraining, a worker had not reached the originally contracted level of output, she might be dismissed. The whole matter was further complicated by the demands of the technology and workflow administration which resulted in a number of intra-unit, inter-unit and inter-workshop transfers (see Figure 4:1). One outcome was an unwillingness to contract for a higher level of performance and earnings. Management's justification was that, if workers adjusted their performance at will, the whole system would be undermined and revert to piecework, which they had already decided was unsuitable.

This unwillingness to attempt a higher level of performance was only prompted by the fear that it must be maintained after transfer. For, as far as the wage payment system was concerned, the workers we observed and interviewed stressed the personal nature of the contract made with the firm. This put many under some moral pressure, one result being a certain amount of labour turnover and absenteeism attributable to "nerves" and "nervous debility". This

112

is not surprising, since this type of wage system is
said to rely not only on efficient supervisory and
administrative controls, but also on the moral
obligation to keep contracts. In other words, the
workers took their reciprocal obligations to
management very seriously indeed.

Despite these problems, this payment system was
relatively well received in this factory, certainly
more so than in some others. When the management
was questioned on this, they either admitted being
mystified or attributed its success to the lack of a
militant industrial tradition in the area. This, it was
suggested, made the workers more amenable to a
relatively tight system of control and possibly more
likely to react to its pressures on an individual basis
by absenteeism, low levels of personal productivity,
or by seeking employment elsewhere, rather than the
collective action of strikes, go-slows and so on. There
is obviously something in this view, but it omits the
influence of a very special attitude to paid employment
in this community.

At the time of our research, less than 50 per cent
of the workers were members of a trade union. There
was also a considerable turnover in membership,
stemming in part from internal transfers and labour
turnover. Thus, the forces influencing the supply of
labour to the firm also affect the membership of the
trade union, which again "fedback" to the firm and so
on. Further, not only may labour turnover change
the social composition of the workforce as a whole,
see Legge (1970a), but it may also change the social
composition of trade union membership. This might
help explain the often sudden and apparently un-
accountable upsurge of aggressive action on the part
of a formerly passive or apathetic group. For a
discussion of factors that influence "grievance
activity" see the book by Sayles.

The fishermen in this community come under the

113

H

statutes regulating employment in the mercantile marine. Very briefly, these laws stress the contractual nature of the relation between the seaman and his employer, expressed and symbolised by the "signing of papers." If this contract is broken, say by "jumping ship" or not reporting for a voyage, he suffers relatively severe sanctions. Now many of the workers in the factory were socialised in this tradition. In fact, most of them had close male relatives employed in the fishing boats. Therefore, there was a situation where a payment system based on an individual contract was operating in a community where the bargain between employer and employee was already considered important and accompanied by strong sanctions, which was reinforced by experience at the workplace.

This situation does, however, create other difficulties resulting from conflicting values and obligations, which are discussed in detail later. But one quite striking conflict that arises here is, that while the workers are culturally disposed to accept the rationale of the wage payment system, they culturally rejected its administrators, the supervisors.

Another important influence on a worker's decision to earn more money by contracting for higher performance standards was the question of her obligations to her workmates. These workmates include, of course, friends, relatives and neighbours, each of whom could expect certain reciprocal rights.

One way a worker might meet her social obligations was the gift of completed assemblies, which enabled the recipients to honour their work contracts. This was, however, strictly forbidden, and any workers discovered were open to dismissal.

This gave rise to the conflict of values referred to earlier. For, on the one hand, the wage system. reinforced by management's sanctions and local values about the contract of employment, stressed the

114

principle of economic individualism, while on the other hand, the values of cooperation and friendly assistance were also highly regarded in this closely knit community. The influence of a "tradition of individualism" in relation to a wage payment system is discussed in Lupton (1963), p 92.

This conflict of values is worth exploring since its analysis holds several clues to why workers in this factory exhibited an unwillingness to attempt higher levels of output and earnings. As the management put it, there was "a great deal of slack in the system." This view was confirmed in that many workers appeared to have plenty of spare time towards the end of each day. This, naturally, considerably irritated the supervisors.

When questioned, the supervisors attributed this apparent restriction of output to irrationality, laziness, moral backsliding, a general decay of standards in society, and the evils of employing women, particularly married women. Very briefly, the argument here was that, because married women were mostly secondary wage earners, they were not interested in the extra money that a higher level of performance would give them. But the most popular explanation was the worker's fear of not being able to maintain performance standards after a transfer, a view also held by senior management. For they were experimenting in one part of the factory with the idea that workers might be encouraged to attempt the higher levels of earnings/performance if allowed to fall back to the lower level after an unsatisfactory trial period.

This analysis suggests that this restriction of output, the "slack in the system" results from workers balancing their obligations to the firm with their obligations to one another. In other words, in order to resolve two conflicting sets of reciprocities they maintained their output at a level which enables them

115

to exercise several choices. Thus, the workers contract for a level of output below that which they could theoretically attain. Workers were thus able to produce a "surplus." It is this surplus that enables the workers to exercise a choice, which goes some way to resolve the conflicts stemming from the complex interaction of values, beliefs, technology, job requirements, market forces and social structure. This analysis has been influenced by the work of Mauss on gift exchange - see Mauss (1954) - and to a recent development of these ideas by Firth (1968).

The first choice a worker might make would be to convert the surplus into spare time indulging in "conspicuous consumption." She might talk, go frequently and ostentatiously to the cloakroom, or just sit at her bench doing nothing. Certain workers flaunted this spare time before the supervisors, in what appeared to be a status-conferring activity, no doubt because it provided an open unassailable challenge to the dubious authority of the supervisors.

Another choice was to produce an actual surplus of components above her contracted level of output. This surplus did not have a cash value as it would under a conventional payment-by-results scheme, where each completed piece of work has a money equivalent. Workers were not paid for those components produced above the contracted level of output.

Workers admitted they gave completed components to one another, defending themselves on the grounds that one could never be sure of meeting the contracted level of output. They also claimed that their individual performance varied unaccountability and this was also reported by Shirley Wilson (1959) who conducted an earlier research project in this factory. Therefore, they argued, an exchange arrangement with another worker was useful as an insurance against variations.

116

This was not, however, a simple symmetrical exchange relationship, workers using each other as "banks." Some workers were in fact "carried" by others, the exchange relationships being asymmetrical. However, evidence suggested that some asymmetrical exchange were not tolerated indefinitely, the bonds of kinship and friendship not being strong enough to sustain a permanently unequal arrangement. But the withdrawal of support, the gift of completed components, could not be undertaken lightly, the possible consequence being that the worker would lose her job through not maintaining contracted levels of performance. In this area, with few alternative jobs, this was a very severe sanction.

The problem here was not that these women would be unable to find another job, since employment opportunities had been improving, though it must be repeated that pay and conditions in this firm were among the best in the area. The problem for many of these women was that their perceptions of the labour market were greatly influenced by the high levels of unemployment for males. Some had male relatives who were finding it difficult to obtain employment. Thus, there was a general impression that all job opportunities were scarce.

This also throws some light upon the worker's dislike of transfers which created two major difficulties. Firstly, it meant that a worker would find it more difficult to create the surplus which was so important in the delicate operation of balancing one's obligations to the firm and to workmates. Secondly, a worker transferred to another unit would need time to establish new exchange relationships, which were again important for feelings of individual job security and group membership.

Intra-unit transfers involved an entirely different class of work and great difficulty in maintaining performance, let alone creating a surplus. The management realised this and were more lenient on these cases. They had, in fact, created "transfer operators" trained to maintain a reasonable level of performance on the three types of work carried out within each unit. Special payment was made for this and workers were encouraged to become transfer operators. But the job was not popular. Obviously, one reason was that to create a surplus became more difficult, but also accepting the role was to:

1   Reject the principle of symmetrical reciprocity. A transfer operator, having no surplus could scarcely maintain a symmetrical reciprocal relationship. At least, she would find it difficult to establish a symmetrical exchange relationship on each of the three classes of work on a unit.

2   To enter into a relationship with the supervisors thought by others to be culturally unacceptable. For, in such cases, a transfer worker was admitting a supervisor's authority to move her from one class of work to another.

As a result, the job of transfer operator was not very highly rated, our experiments revealing that a transfer operator was held in much lower esteem than other types of worker, despite her wider span of technical competence. During our interviews we asked workers to rank the various jobs in order of personal preference. It does also suggest that job enlargement might, in certain circumstances, have hidden complications and disadvantages.

Another influence on a worker's decision to improve her earnings/output level has been discussed in Millward's article (1968) on the institution of "board" in this community. He describes how, when a girl first goes to work, she hands her wages to her parents, receiving in return an amount of pocket

118

money. Eventually, after going through a number of arrangements, a girl makes a contractual relationship with her parents paying them a fixed sum for her "board," (board and lodging) while keeping the balance of her wages for herself for personal use. This represents a marked change in status for the girl and, at the same time, makes to move up to a better paid level of performance more attractive. She can now keep the fruits of her extra efforts for herself. This institution has also been described by Legge (1970b).

The influence of this institution also goes the other way, since the status of being on board is so desirable that girls are prompted to opt for more pay to make this change a viable proposition. This decision is in turn influenced by what is believed to be a fair sum for a girl's board and lodging in this community. This is, in turn, related to the problem of the surplus since, after going on board, any attempt to move to a higher earnings/output level will inevitably reduce the size of the surplus. This suggests that the worker is not only faced with the problem of balancing reciprocal relations with both managers and fellow workers but also with balancing these reciprocities with members of her domestic group.

It also appears that the age at which girls in this factory have been going on board has been falling. This may have been influenced by such social factors as the school leaving age, which has increased since the last war, and the age at which firls marry, which has been falling during the past few decades - see Fletcher (1967), p 111. There has also been a general increase in wages in this area in recent years, making "going on board" a more attractive proposition. This will probably be the case as long as the customary sum for board lags behind general wage increases for young women in this locality. Both these factors, the customary sum for board and wage increases, are

119

influenced by more general economic conditions
affecting the cost of living.

4.5 CONCLUSIONS

Our analysis shows that a wage payment system is
subject to a number of structural pressures not
contained by the formal rules and procedures which
direct its operation. The importance of this proposition is discussed in Lupton and Gowler (1969).

In this situation, these pressures stem mainly from
changes in the labour and product markets. These
influences, combining with the rules and procedures
which determine the payment system, result in
difficulties with workflow and administration,
particularly with transfers of workers within and
between units (see Figure 4:2). These difficulties of
workflow administration, combined with the
expectations, values and beliefs of workers and
supervisors, give rise to yet another range of
problems.

Firstly it created difficulties for the supervisors,
since these various pressures resulted in problems
of role conflict, because it was difficult for supervisors to disentangle conflicting role expectations.
Furthermore, the workers did not accept the supervisor's definition of his role and, therefore, his
behaviour in certain situations. For the supervisor
was expected to encourage workers to higher levels
of earnings/output, at the same time disciplining them
when they did not maintain their contracted standards
(see Figure 4:3). This has been described as role-
activation conflict, that is "Where the conflict is over
which expectations should be activated, and in what
way, in relation to the particular problem situation"
Pugh (1966).

Secondly, the supervisors further difficulties, arising
from certain values held by the workers, concerned
their right to exercise any authority at all. This

120

challenge resulted from (a) their relative lack of technical competence, and (b) workers' ideas about the division of labour between the sexes in this community. This has been described as role-legitimation conflict, that is "What is the content of the particular role and what should in principle be included and what left out" - Pugh (1966).

In this situation the supervisors might perceive the situation in terms of role-activation conflict, while the workers might see it in terms of role-legitimation conflict. In any event, these difficulties must surely have depressed the level of individual and group effort.

Such difficulties might apply to any type of payment system, though exacerbated somewhat in these circumstances by the particular importance of the supervisor's role where, as here, a form of measured day work was operating.

Yet another range of problems is peculiar to this "personal contract" type of measured day work. The worker is expected to honour a contract and certainly was distressed if not able to do so. This distress was not wholly attributable to a fear of management sanctions if standards were not maintained, though conditions in the local labour market were such that, for such workers, acceptable job opportunities were limited. Therefore, management's ultimate sanction, dismissal, was not viewed lightly. Nevertheless, our observations confirmed that most workers really wished to uphold their obligation to return a given level of performance for a given level of pay.

This willingness to honour contracts did not work wholly to management's advantage since, given for example the problem of transfer, workers were wary of attempting higher earnings/output levels. Further, and more subtly, workers do not have a single moral obligation to management, but also multiple obligations to their workmates. Here is, of course, a classic conflict of interests. The main thesis put forward here is that workers contracted a level of performance which:

1 Would protect them against variations in their own performance

2 Would protect them when transferred to another unit, when they would, at least temporarily, be under pressure to maintain the contracted performance

3 Would enable them to meet their obligations to both management and fellow workers

This meant that there was a tendency to lower performance to a level at which they had a "surplus," enabling a worker to meet these three conditions. Yet this did create difficulties for the young worker domestically, where there might exist the expectation that the surplus would be reduced by the move to a higher level of earnings. The point is that the surplus, though fulfilling a social function with workmates, does not do so with, say, parents who view their daughter's occupational behaviour in the light of her status in the family. This then runs counter to the general tendency to lower the level of earnings/output since the effect of board encourages workers to create a smaller surplus. However, this influence is insufficient to lead workers to contract a level of earnings/output that would leave them without the social and psychological "space" provided by the surplus.

The form in which this surplus manifested itself, either in spare time or the completion of extra components for "banking" or "gift exchange," was influenced by culturally determined attitudes and values, which rested upon:

1 The social composition of the unit concerned, that is, the existence within the work group of reciprocal relationships

2   Relations with the supervisor in charge of the unit

3   The individual worker's status in her domestic group. This applied particularly to young unmarried girls and was, as described above, influenced by whether they are "on board" or not

This suggests that, despite the goodwill of all concerned, it was difficult to maintain effort without a direct financial incentive. These difficulties arose from the interaction of structural and socio-cultural factors. Further, these socio-cultural factors in the community subsequently introduced into the firm through the labour market warrant further interest and research.

ACKNOWLEDGEMENTS

The research findings discussed in this paper have been drawn from the early stages of a project which has been developing a theoretical model of the movement of earnings at plant level. A central concern of this project has been the investigation of the relation between the various forms of wage payment systems and the economic, technical and socio-cultural environment in which they operate. The influence of environmental factors on behaviour in organisations has been a constant theme in Professor Tom Lupton's work, and this paper owes a great deal to his guidance and encouragement. I must also thank my colleagues at the Manchester Business School for their interest and support, particularly Graham Barlow, Alan Brown, Karen Legge and my fellow fieldworker Neil Millward. I must also acknowledge a debt to Shirley Wilson whose earlier work (Wilson 1963) in the research location provided a firm and reliable base for this study. Finally, I would like to thank the managers and workers who cooperated so freely in this study and trust that this paper accurately reflects the very generous assistance I received from all concerned.

124

REFERENCES

Baldamus, W (1957) "The relationship between wage and effort," Journal of Industrial Economics, volume 5, pp 192-201

Behrend, H (1959) "Financial incentives as the expression of a system of beliefs," British Journal of Sociology, volume 10, part 2

Bott, E (1957) "Family and the Social Network," Tavistock

Dubin, R, Homans, G C, Mann, F C and Miller, D (1965) "Leadership and Productivity " Chandler Publishing Company

Firth, R (1968) "A general comment," in "Themes in Economic Anthropology," Tavistock

Fletcher, R (1967) "The Family and Marriage in Britain," Penguin

Gowler, D (1969) "Determinants of the supply of labour to the firm," Journal of Management Studies, volume 6, pp 73-95

International Labour Office (1967) "Payment by Results"

Jaques, E (1967) "Equitable Payment," Penguin

Legge, K (1970a) "The operation of the 'regressive spiral' in the labour market," Journal of Management Studies, volume 7, pp 1-22

Legge, K (1970b) "Paying mum and motivation," Personnel Management, volume 2, number 1, pp 30-2

Lupton, T (1961) "Money for Effort" (Problems of Progress in Industry, number 11), HMSO

Lupton, T (1963) "On the Shopfloor," Pergamon

Lupton, T (1964) "Methods of wage payment, organisational change and motivation," Work Study and Motivation, December 1964

Lupton, T and Gowler, D (1969) "Selecting a Wage Payment System," Federation Research Paper III, Engineering Employers' Federation

Mauss, M (1954) "Essai sur le Don" translated by Ian Cunnison as "The Gift," Cohen and West

125

Mead, M (1962) "Male and Female," Penguin

Millward, N (1968) "Family status and behaviour at work," The Sociological Review, volume 16, number 2, pp 149-164

Pugh, D (1966) "Role activation conflict: a study of industrial inspection," American Sociological Review, volume 31, number 6

Sayles, L R "Behaviour of Industrial Work Groups: Production and Control," Wiley

Shimmin, S (1959) "Payment by Results"

Skinner, W (1968) " American Industry in Developing Economies," Wiley

Wilson, S (1959) "A sociological case study of operator training: part 2," Occupational Psychology, volume 33, number 4, p 247

Wilson, S (1963) "Social Factors influencing Industrial Output," unpublished University of Manchester PhD thesis

Woodward, J (1965) "Industrial Organization: Theory and Practice," Oxford University Press

5   Internal wage structures

by D I Mackay

5.1   INTRODUCTION

Chapter 3 discussed the inter-plant wage structure, the
relationships between the earnings levels of different
plants located in the same labour market. Here we
draw on the results of the same study of engineering
establishments, but are concerned with the intra-plant
wage structure - the relationships between the
earnings of different occupational groups engaged by
the same unit. The intra-plant and the inter-plant
wage structure cannot be separated for economic theory
suggests that wage relativities in the plant will be
affected by the local labour market environment.
Changes in employment conditions, or in the wage
policies of rival units, may cause managements to
reconsider not only the level of earnings in their unit
but also the relationships between the earnings of
different groups of employees. However, while
ultimately relating our observations on the intra-plant
wage structure to external factors, the distinction
between the intra- and the inter-plant wage structure
provides a useful starting point.

There has been "an almost complete absence of
empirical investigation into plant-level wage structures
in the United Kingdom" (Lerner et al 1969, p 9). The
notable exceptions are Robertson (1960) and Robinson
(1968). Our first task is, then, descriptive, simply to
record certain features of wage payment methods and
of the structure of intra-plant earnings resulting, to
establish the nature of the problem. At present, we
cannot invoke economic theory because we do not yet
know the questions. Consider two apparently straight-

127

forward questions. Are the relationships between occupational earnings the same from one plant to the next or is the pattern of earnings' relativities unique to each unit? Is the internal wage structure rigid or flexible, that is, if one group of employees gains a wage increase for whatever reason, does this increase spread to all groups in the plant or is the wage structure flexible so that internal relativities change through time? Neither of these questions can be answered satisfactorily on a priori grounds. We must begin by establishing what happens in the labour market, then relating our findings back to labour market theory.

Let us take our last rhetorical question which has considerable relevance to economic theory and policy. The function of a plant wage structure is to reflect the balance, and changes in it, of the economic forces of demand and supply of labour. Wage differentials arise for many reasons. Certain occupations demand longer training or peculiar skills and aptitudes and, if the plant wants the correct "mix" of labour to operate efficiently, theory suggests that such occupational groups must be offered higher earnings than others. So we would expect skilled manual workers to have higher average earnings than the unskilled. But this is not all, for we also want to know how the wage structure alters over time in response to employment conditions in the market. If plants want to recruit more turners, for example, and are finding such labour particularly difficult to obtain, then in theory the earnings of turners will be bid up relatively. But does the wage structure behave in this manner? Do wage relativities within the plant change according to the ease or difficulty with which different types of workers can be recruited? Or is the wage structure inflexible so that wage increases for one group of employees become similar increases for other groups? Ross (1947) has suggested that wage determination

128

under collective bargaining cannot be understood
purely in terms of economic calculus. Notions of
equity and justice, of "equitable comparisons,"
provide the yardstick by which the success of union
officials and the "fairness" of wage increases are
judged. Such notions are derived from the existing
order.

> Change - always, everywhere, in everything -
> requires justification: the strength of conser-
> vatism is that it is held to justify itself. It is
> not, therefore, surprising that the maintenance
> of standards, absolute or comparative, should
> be woven as warp and woof into the texture of
> wage discussions ... (Wootton 1955, p 162)

Hence, wage settlements are interlinked. If one group
obtains an increase, then other groups will attempt to
re-establish the original relativities. If this is
accomplished the wage structure moves bodily upwards
through time.

Arguments for "justice" and "equity" largely based
on comparability have always been a feature of wage
claims and have considerably affected many wage
settlements. One consequence is the stability of
inter-industrial wage structure of developed countries
over fairly long periods- see Popola and Bharadwaj
(1970). Patterns of wage settlement also arise, a
few key bargains setting the pace for general wage
increases - see Knowles and Thorne (1961). The
force of comparability, nationally, is a major problem
which must be resolved before a successful national
incomes policy can obtain lasting success. (NBPI
1969, pp 22-4).

If social pressures can affect wage settlements
nationally, it is illogical to deny their existence at the
local, or plant, level. After all, employees are likely
to take as their point of reference the earnings and
status of other groups with whom they have regular

129

contact. Hence, the pressure to maintain "fair relativities" may be particularly intense within the plant. If this is so, the wage structure may be inflexible not being particularly sensitive to changes in the demand and supply for different types of labour.

5.2 WAGE NEGOTIATION MACHINERY
National agreements in the British engineering industry, negotiated between the Engineering Employers Federation and the Confederation of Shipbuilding and Engineering Unions, centre around two key wage rates for fitters and labourers. They establish national time rates, known as consolidated time rates, for these two groups which set minimum standards. The minimum rates also act as the basis on which overtime and shift premia are usually calculated. Actual earnings in the engineering industry, even for these two groups, bear little relationship to these minimum standards which merely provide a low floor, below which earnings for a standard working week cannot fall. The minimum time rates for other groups are related to those of fitters and labourers either through national agreements between the EEF and individual unions or, more frequently, through the application of "customary" or "recognised" differentials at district or plant level. The national agreements are described in Marsh (1965), pp 147-8 and NBPI (1967), pp 51-2.

The national minimum consolidated time rate is a "fallback" wage for pieceworkers and for timeworkers. In addition, the national agreement fixes the piecework supplement for fitters and labourers, providing that piecework times and bonuses should be so fixed that the worker "of average ability" can earn at least 45 per cent more than the basic rate. (The piecework supplement is therefore the payment through which national wage increases are incorporated in pieceworkers' earnings. In January 1968, a new piecework standard and an altered rate were introduced to the

130

national agreement. These changes have been ignored in the above discussion as they do not relate to the period 1959 - 66 and do not involve any fundamental point of principle.) Hence, the minimum standard for pieceworkers consists of a basic rate plus 45 per cent to which is added the piecework supplement.

The minima established in national negotiations bear little relation to actual earnings. For example, in 1966 the national minimum consolidated time rate for fitters would have yielded a wage for a standard working week of £10. 83$\frac{1}{2}$ whereas weekly earnings for fitters on timework averaged £22. 37$\frac{1}{2}$ (NBPI 1967, p 51, DEP 1966, p 30). The EEF estimated that in 1962 only 0. 4 per cent of fitters and 6 per cent of labourers were earning no more than their appropriate consolidated time rates - see Marsh (1965), p 182. It follows that negotiations below the national level are extremely important in determining actual earnings.

There are two further levels of negotiation, at district and at plant level. District negotiations are an historical anomaly of diminishing importance while plant or domestic bargaining has become more influential. The term "plant bargaining" is a misnomer, for it does not reveal the very fragmented nature of the bargaining process. For pieceworkers, bargaining seldom takes place on a plant or even a group basis. Piecework times and prices emerge from haggling between individual employees and ratefixers, with the shop steward and foreman acting as the first court of appeal. Bargaining on a group or factory basis is common only in the case of timeworkers.

The existing pattern of settlements in engineering results, therefore, from negotiations at two levels, national and domestic. The two are not unconnected, the chief link being that "a national agreement lifts the floor above which plant negotiations take place" (NBPI 1967, p 9). The links between national and plant bargaining are more tenuous than in many other

131

industries and the result is a system of wage settlements of virtually unrivalled complexity - see Knowles and Hill (1954). The timeworker may obtain, as the result of plant negotiations, a consolidated time rate above the district minimum and his earnings can be further supplemented by merit money, lieu bonuses, special allowances or fringe benefits not negotiated by any national agreement. The scope for variation in the levels of plant earnings is, therefore, considerable, particularly for semi-skilled workers whose earnings are largely unregulated at national or district level.

With pieceworkers, the scope for variations in plant earnings is, if anything, even more substantial. The national agreement provides a minimum piecework standard for the worker "of average ability," a monumental ambiguity providing unlimited scope for interpretation. Actual earnings depend on the piecework system and according to whether piecework times or prices are "realistic" or "slack." Further difficulty arises in policing the piecework system as time passes and as changes in material, means or methods of production require renegotiation of the initial bargains.

The institutional framework within which bargaining over piecework times and prices takes place has been identified as a major source of "wage drift" in engineering by Lerner (1965) and Lerner and Marquand (1962 and 1963). The extent of the difference between real earnings and nationally negotiated wage rates gives the earnings gap. Strictly speaking, the earnings gap is given by the difference between earnings and district rates but in the interests of simplification we shall ignore this complication. Wage drift is the rate of increase of the earnings gap over time, with overtime payments excluded. This is the definition adopted by Lerner and Marquand (1962). A number of alternative definitions of wage drift can be adopted - see Sloane (1967) - but the simplest concept to grasp, the rate of increase of the earnings gap (overtime excluded), will serve our purposes. Following Phelps Brown (1962), wage drift is held to occur when "The effective rate of pay per unit of labour input is raised by arrangements that lie outside the control of the recognised procedures for scheduling (wage) rates." As any system of piecework payments attempts, however unsystematically, to relate reward to effort we should, ideally, distinguish increased earnings due to increased effort from increases arising otherwise. In other words, we must differentiate statistical wage drift and "wage drift proper." Statistical wage drift is the rate of increase of the earnings gap (excluding overtime) and wage drift proper (see Rehn 1959) is the rate of increase in earnings which is not accompanied by extra effort. It is also necessary to allow for changes in occupational and industrial "mix" when measuring wage drift proper - see Turner (1956). In practice, the distinction is insubstantial and causes much of the controversy surrounding the subject. Statistical wage drift can only be measured at the macro-economic level, and so arises the difficulty of measuring that part of statistical wage drift due to increased effort and that part which is not.

It is useful to consider two types of wage drift. Primary wage drift arises when pieceworkers' earnings increase due to higher productivity or when any group of employees is able, due to labour shortages or bargaining power, to obtain a rise. Such drift disturbs "customary" and "recognised" differentials within the plant or between plants, and secondary wage drift follows attempts to restore customary relativities. Most authorities particularly stress the pieceworking system as promoting drift.

Typically, within the plant, the earnings of workers paid by results went up while those of workers on

time-rates, including some whose relative pay is
customarily high, did not, and then the sense of
what was fair, and the need to avoid trouble,
alike prompted a lieu bonus or other rise in
effective rates for the timeworkers. (Phelps
Brown 1962, p 348)

However, while it is widely accepted that wage
increases originate with pieceworkers and spread to
timeworkers there is no unanimity on the causes of
the primary drift.

The relationship between wage drift and the demand
for labour has been stressed by Phelps Brown (1962),
Rehn (1959) and the OEEC (1961) but several
investigations have failed to find a strong relationship
between them particularly within the British engineering
industry. Lerner and Marquand's initial position was
that "a high level demand for labour is a prerequisite
for most forms of wage drift to exist at all" (Lerner
and Marquand 1962, p 48) but a successfully smaller
role is assigned to labour demand in their subsequent
work. "Demand pull" is seen as explaining increases
in engineering earnings in the fully employed regions
of Britain, the increases being transmitted to less
fully employed regions by institutional factors
(Lerner and Marquand 1963). Later, Mrs. Marquand
concludes:

That drift is largely determined by institutional
factors which are not reflected systematically
in any of the aggregate series used as independent
variables. Even the level of demand for labour,
to which a central role in determining drift is
frequently ascribed, has no systematic influence
at all upon the behavious of drift at the aggregate
level, although there is a weak relationship
between drift and changes in the level of demand
for labour. (Marquand 1967, pp 17-18, Emphasis
in original)

These conclusions are supported by an investigation of the Coventry engineering industry by Knowles and Robinson (1969) which found wage drift was not related to the level of unemployment although it was influenced by the rate of change of unemployment. Nonetheless, the latter factor was not particularly influential so that factors apart from those reflected in employment conditions must apply.

Productivity increases have been seen by Turner (1956, 1960 and 1964) as the main influence promoting wage drift. Turner, like Lerner and Marquand, appears to have modified his initial position. In his case, increasing emphasis has been placed on the relationship between earnings changes and productivity increases. The position is further confused because Turner's analysis relates to manufacturing industry or to industry as a whole while Lerner and Marquand are exclusively concerned with engineering. Piece-workers again occupy a central position in the model. Short term drift is generated by technological progress which causes pieceworkers' earnings to rise. To maintain customary relativities, larger national increases are negotiated for timeworkers. Long term drift is also due to technological change which demands higher skills and, consequently, improved training, upgrading and payments "to make innovation acceptable in the workplace" (Turner 1960, p 120). Turner's thesis is, therefore, different from that of Lerner and Marquand who stress that improved methods of production may not require increased effort from the employee but do provide the pieceworker with a favourable bargaining position which he can exploit to increase his earnings. Hence:

> It is not the production of a greater output by male pieceworkers for the same output of effort that gives rise to wage drift; rather it is that opportunities for the negotiation of new piece-

rates arise whenever there are discontinuities in the production process (Lerner and Marquand 1962, p 52).

It is difficult to choose between these alternative explanations of wage drift. Both explanations allow for the existence of primary drift, through increases in pieceworkers' earnings, and for the subsequent appearance of secondary drift as timeworkers restore relativities. Lacking more detailed studies, it is impossible to separate out primary and secondary drfit making it difficult to single out the causal factors at work. Neither explanation appears completely satisfactory. For example, Turner's argument that increased earnings for pieceworkers results in more favourable national settlements for timeworkers is not applicable to the British engineering industry. Again, while earnings and productivity increases are related for the whole engineering industry, the relationship becomes weaker or disappears on analysis of individual sectors of engineering - see Lerner (1969) pp 32-5 and Nicholson and Gupta (1960). Further, some ie part, and possibly most, increased productivity arises without an increase in effort, due to additional capital investment, changes in workflow and in production scheduling, improvements in raw materials and the like. Even if we assigned all improvements in productivity to increased effort, much is left un-explained. This is illustrated by a rare case study of wage drift in engineering which found in a "well controlled piecework system operating in near ideal circumstances ... a wholly unproductive wage 'drift' of about 1 per cent per year. It is a strong argument that such wholly inflationary 'drift' is unavoidable in any piecework system" (NBPI 1968, p 50).

This does not imply that there is no connection between earnings and changes in productivity. But there is no evidence of increases in productivity being primarily due to increased effort by the piece-worker or of a strong association between productivity changes, increased effort and changes in earnings for the individual employee where piecework bargaining occurs. Hence, "for male pieceworkers in the engineering industry ... piecemeal negotiations have given rise to wage drift even when there has been no increase in productivity" (Lerner and Marquand 1962, p 52, Emphasis in the original). This is not to say that increasing productivity will not provide a general environment within which employees can strike favourable bargains. Reasonably, employers are less concerned about increased earnings when productivity is rising rapidly for then the effect on labour costs is small. Similarly, while some studies have found little relationship between levels of unemployment and wage drift this does not dispose of the "demand pull" argument. While small changes in unemployment around the full employment level have little effect on wage drift, doubtless drift would not continue equally given a major departure from a full employment position.

Great demand for labour, like increases in product-ivity, therefore provides an environment in which wage drift occurs. However, institutional factors, particularly the fragmented method of piecework bargaining, combined with discontinuities in the production process, allow individual workers or groups to obtain increases almost irrespective of demand conditions and changes in productivity. Bargaining arrangements are also likely to be an independent source of wage drift. Primary drift arising with pieceworkers disturbs customary relativities, in turn creating secondary drift as timeworkers try to restore the initial position.

The above review of the literature does little justice to the complexity of the argument. Still less does it resolve the fundamental questions as to how wage drift is generated. Nonetheless, we have illustrated one theme common to all authorities. This is that primary drift, for whatever cause, usually arises with pieceworkers. This created pressures on the wage structure and generates secondary drift. Yet comparatively little work has been undertaken within the individual plant, there being still much to learn about the wage payment methods adopted in engineering and about the behaviour of the intra-plant earnings structure which results from these payments systems.

5.3 WAGE PAYMENT METHODS
The discussion of section 5.2 suggests the most important distinction in wage payment methods is that between pieceworkers and timeworkers. Using occupational earnings returns for 1966, we show for male manual employees in Glasgow and Birmingham, and for those case study engineering plants for which the information is available, the number of plants employing timework, piecework or some combination of both these methods. The following text is exclusively based on earnings data for male manual employees for no occupational details are available for female employees. The bulk of female employees are, however, semi-skilled and are paid by piecework. Data for Glasgow plants derives mainly from EEF occupational earnings returns although, when not available, the DEP occupational earnings returns were utilised. The nature of these returns has been described in greater detail in Chapter 3. In Table 5.1 we have departed from the practice of Chapter 3 and combined results from EEF and DEP occupational earnings returns although the returns relate to different dates in 1966. This procedure is justified by the assumption that major short term shifts in methods of wage payment are unlikely to occur frequently. This procedure yields information

138

TABLE 5.1 METHODS OF PAYMENT, GLASGOW PLANTS, 1966

Occupational group	Number of plants					Percentage paid by	
	Timework only	Piecework only	Timework and piecework	Not applicable	Total	Timework	Piecework
Fitters	6	8	5	4	23	24.0	76.0
Turners	5	12	2	4	23	8.3	91.7
Unskilled	18	3	2	0	23	80.0	20.0
All workers	4	3	16	0	23	36.8	63.2

Source: EEF and DEP Occupational Earnings' Returns

139

for twenty three of the twenty seven case study plants
in Glasgow. In Birmingham, EEF occupational
earnings returns were not available. The coverage
of Table 5.2 is, therefore, restricted to fourteen of
the twenty five case study plants covered by the DEP
occupational earnings returns.

Table 5.1 shows the methods of wage payment
adopted by Glasgow plants for fitters, turners, unskilled and "all workers." The latter group comprises
all manual employees covered by the EEF occupational
earnings returns, including fitters, turners and
unskilled, but excludes the bulk of semi-skilled
employees for whom little earnings data is provided
by this source. The skill composition of the "all
workers" group in Birmingham is substantially
different, for DEP occupational earnings returns to
disclose details on semi-skilled workers. As Table
5.2 shows, many semi-skilled workers are paid
through piecework so comparison of the "all workers"
group in Tables 5.1 and 5.2 understates the true
extent of pieceworking in Glasgow relative to
Birmingham.

Most plants in both areas employed males on both
timework and piecework, and often these different
payment methods applied to employees in the same
occupational group. Of the twenty-three Glasgow plants
in Table 5.1 only four paid all manual workers via
timework and in only three units were all males on
piecework. Even this probably overstates the position
as semi-skilled employees who are largely on
piecework are poorly represented in Table 5.1. In
Birmingham, no plant was exclusively pieceworking
and only two employed all males on timework.
Pieceworking is more extensive in Glasgow than
Birmingham for all three groups where direct comparison is possible: fitters, turners and unskilled.
This is even true of "all workers" although, for
reasons stated, the comparison understates the extent

140

TABLE 5.2 METHODS OF PAYMENT, BIRMINGHAM PLANTS, 1966

Occupational group	Number of plants				Percentage paid by		
	Timework only	Piecework only	Timework and piecework	Total	Not applicable	Timework	Piecework
Fitters	1	1	4	14	8	42.4	57.6
Turners	2	2	3	14	8	25.2	74.8
Semi-skilled	2	0	11	14	1	40.5	59.5
Unskilled	13	0	1	14	0	99.2	0.8
All workers	2	0	12	14	0	51.8	48.2

Source: DEP Occupational Earnings' Returns

of pieceworking in Glasgow relative to Birmingham.

There are three reasons for the greater use made of male pieceworkers in Glasgow plants. First, female employees account for a greater proportion of the labour force in Birmingham and women, who undertake much routine work being paid largely by piecework, are excluded from the tables. Second, skilled males form a smaller proportion of the male labour force in Birmingham, and are more often engaged in toolroon, or in development or prototype work, than in Glasgow. In such "service" departments, where speed of working is not set by the production line, timeworking is the rule. Third come technological factors. In Birmingham, the engineering industry is largely concentrated on large batch or mass production of standardised goods. On the other hand, Glasgow engineering plants tend to specialise in "one-off" or small-batch, custom-built production of producer durable goods. The pace of work is therefore more easily controlled by management in Birmingham by regulating the workflow through the shop. In Glasgow, changes in product mix provide an acute problem of supervising employee effort. A common solution is to use the incentive element in a piecework system as a "silent supervisor."

Although pieceworkers are a smaller proportion of male manual employees in Birmingham, most plants in Birmingham, as in Glasgow, employ some pieceworkers. Therefore, should pieceworkers' earnings increase through time because of demand pull, productivity changes or institutional mechanisms, then such primary wage drift is likely to create friction within most units and may lead to secondary drift as timeworkers try to catch up. The difficulty of maintaining relativities between pieceworkers and timeworkers was stressed by almost all the case study plants employing both types of worker in Glasgow and Birmingham. Managers thought increases in piece-

142

workers' earnings the major source of primary drift and stressed the difficulty of controlling secondary drift. The problem of controlling pieceworkers' earnings, and hence labour costs, arises in rather different forms in Glasgow and Birmingham though the end-result is the same - an upward pressure on earnings levels due to a tendency of pieceworkers' earnings to increase over time.

In Birmingham, the traditional method of piecework payment is still commonly a price "per piece" (or unit of output). Though unsophisticated, this proves practical because of the more standardised nature of production, but even there changes in product mix or in method are sufficiently frequent to provide scope for haggling over new piecework prices. Many plants have no proper system of work measurement so that ratefixers rely largely on past practice, experience or guesswork. The inevitable errors are extremely difficult to locate and eradicate.

The Glasgow plants made much greater use of work measurement. Almost always, a standard time was set for each job as the result of work measurement, piecework earnings depending on the difference between the standard time and the actual time taken. This difference in practice reflects technological factors. A system of pieceworking on a price per piece basis would be extremely difficult to control within a small-batch technology. Hence, work measurement is more extensively employed to find a more "scientific" basis for matching effort to reward. Nonetheless, plant managers stressed the difficulty of preventing wage drift for much the same reasons as those described by Lerner and Marquand (1962). Nor was there any indication that wage drift was primarily due to "demand pull" factors. Earnings appear to increase at much the same rate in both markets despite substantial differences in employment conditions, and controlling wage drift within a pieceworking system was of as much concern to Glasgow as to Birmingham plant managers.

The increase of pieceworkers' earnings over time forced plant management to adjust timeworkers' earnings to maintain relativities or, at least, to prevent too great a difference in the rate of increase of earnings for these separate groups. This was not through national agreements, which provided for similar increases in the minimum standards for time-workers and pieceworkers. National bargaining takes place yearly, and, indeed, the period between such negotiations has lengthened recently (NBPI 1967). Meanwhile, timeworkers whose relative position has worsened, press for adjustments at the plant level. In any event, national agreements providing for larger increases for timeworkers would be inappropriate to compensate for wage drift in pieceworkers' earnings occurring in the plant. Increases for pieceworkers over a period vary substantially from one unit to the next creating different pressures which cannot be dealt with via a uniform increase. It is with piece - workers in their own plants that timeworkers make comparisons. It is therefore logical that plant managements should adjust timeworkers' earnings through domestic bargaining. Such adjustments can be achieved by a variety of methods: through establishing consolidated time rates above the agreed or recognised district minimum; through lieu bonuses or merit rates; through various special payments sometimes loosely related to output; or through systematic overtime working.

The payment of a consolidated time rate above the district minimum is widely used to preserve or adjust differentials between timeworkers and pieceworkers. The consolidated time rate is most important in the timeworkers' wage packet, but with pieceworkers only provides a floor below which his earnings cannot fall. All but three of the plants in Birmingham and two thirds of the plants in Glasgow had established a

144

consolidated time rate above the district minimum. In
fact, none of the timeworkers employed by the case
study plants failed to earn above the minimum levels
set through national and district negotiations. Thus,
all the plants in Glasgow and Birmingham which
incorporated the district minimum consolidated time
rate in the wage structure paid timeworkers a lieu
bonus in addition.

Hence, we have two methods of raising hourly rates
of pay for timeworkers. The first establishes a
consolidated time rate above the district minimum,
and the second adds a lieu bonus to the consolidated
time rate established as a district minimum. Quite
often plants add lieu bonuses to a consolidated time
rate already above the district minimum. Lieu bonus,
as its name implies, is a compensatory payment to
timeworkers. Method of determination varies considerably from plant to plant. More than half the
Glasgow case study plants made lieu bonus payments
to some group of timeworkers, or to all, and of these
every second unit paid a lieu bonus at a fixed rate per
hour. In Birmingham, lieu bonuses are more
regularly related to pieceworkers' earnings. The
rationale is to provide timeworkers with an incentive
to greater output. In practice, however, this aim is
often unrealised. In some cases, lieu bonuses are
paid to all timeworkers and then the bonus has much
the same effect as a consolidated time rate fixed above
the district minimum. Even where lieu bonuses are
restricted to certain groups of timeworkers, and
pressure to generalise such payments to other groups
is successively resisted, seldom is the size of the
bonus related to those pieceworkers with whom the
timeworkers on bonus are associated. In most plants
the size of the lieu bonus is determined by reference
to piecework earnings in the whole plant and, granted
exceptions, the incentive element must be relatively
weak.

145

Merit payments are also used frequently to adjust timeworkers' earnings. They were made by some one half of the case study plants in Glasgow and in Birmingham. In one Birmingham unit, merit payments were made to all timeworkers, although at varying rates, but more commonly are restricted to skilled timeworkers. Merit payments should show substantial variations between individuals with the same occupation for in theory they should be a reward for additional responsibility, special skills or other attributes not adequately reflected in alternative methods of wage payment. But usually most workers in the same occupational group receive the same merit rate or the spread of rates is comparatively narrow. A similar finding has been reported for engineering plants in Coventry by Knowles and Robinson (1969). Plant managements stress the difficulty of resisting pressure to narrow merit rates for workers of the same occupation or to extend merit payments to other groups. Sometimes the original purpose is lost and such payments are used, in the words of one Glasgow manager, as "a method of adjusting the wage structure in favour of skilled timeworkers." One reason is that managers find the existing system of merit payments difficult to justify. Only one Birmingham plant had made a serious attempt to evolve a more objective method of assessing merit rates. Otherwise where discretion exists, assessment is usually the responsibility of foremen or works superintendents who are seldom given any technical guidance. The subjective element is, therefore, strong and the system difficult to defend against charges of "favouritism." Because of the arbitrary nature and the difficulty of preventing them spreading to other groups, five of the twelve Glasgow plants had abandoned such payments by 1966, amalgamating them with consolidated time rate. This was not the trend in Birmingham where only one of thirteen plants abandoned merit awards over 1959 - 66.

146

Systematic overtime working is another method of adjusting the relationship between timeworkers' and pieceworkers' earnings. Average weekly overtime hours worked by timeworkers and pieceworkers were calculated for Glasgow plants from the EEF occupational earnings returns and for Birmingham plants from the DEP returns. The results are shown in Tables 5.3 and 5.4.

Overtime working is more important for timeworkers than pieceworkers in all periods shown, save one. It is clear, therefore, that the systematic use of additional overtime is widely used to adjust the earnings structure in favour of timeworkers. This conclusion is supported by Lerner et al (1969) and Robertson (1960). This is especially marked in Birmingham where in every period timeworkers averaged at least twice as many overtime hours as pieceworkers. In the former case, overtime usually averaged six hours per week, while for pieceworkers the average only once exceeded three hours.

This suggests the following conclusions. Two broad systems of payment for timeworkers are in general use. First, timeworkers are paid a consolidated time rate substantially above the district minimum. In a few cases, this has been consolidated into a guaranteed weekly wage for a standard working week. This is the simplest method although lieu bonuses, merit awards or other forms may be added to the consolidated time rate. Second, the consolidated time rate is equal to or close to the district minimum. Here there is always, among the case study plants, some supplementation to the consolidated time rate through lieu bonuses and, often, through merit awards. In principle, the latter system provides timeworkers with an incentive to greater output or a reward for special responsibilities, skill, etc. In practice, the incentive is seldom strong for rates seldom vary substantially within an occupational group and lieu

147

	June 1959	June 1960	June 1961	June 1962	1963	June 1964	Oct. 1965	Oct. 1966
Timeworkers	3.8	4.5	6.3	4.8	*	6.8	9.1	6.8
Pieceworkers	2.5	4.5	4.4	3.0	*	3.0	4.9	5.1

TABLE 5.3 AVERAGE OVERTIME HOURS WORKED, TIMEWORKERS AND PIECEWORKERS, GLASGOW PLANTS, 1959-66

Note: * No earnings returns were available for 1963.

Source: EEF Occupational Earnings' Returns

	June 1963	Jan. 1964	June 1964	Jan. 1965	June 1965	Jan. 1966	June 1966
Timeworkers	6.4	6.7	6.7	6.0	6.8	5.8	6.6
Pieceworkers	2.6	2.9	2.9	2.7	3.1	1.8	2.7

TABLE 5.4 AVERAGE OVERTIME HOURS WORKED, TIMEWORKERS AND PIECEWORKERS, BIRMINGHAM PLANTS, 1963-66

Source: DEP Occupational Earnings' Returns

bonuses are often fixed in amount or are tied to the earnings of pieceworkers, whose output is not closely linked with the effort of timeworkers. Timeworkers also work longer overtime hours than pieceworkers and there is a wide range of additional emoluments to specific groups such as "incentive bonuses" (some being in no way linked to output or effort), bonus payments on tonnage produced, bonuses linked to profitability, length of service awards, "dirty money," quality allowances and so forth. Length of service awards are relatively rare and usually account for only a small proportion of total earnings.

Few plants pay all timeworkers on the same general principles. The overriding impression is that the wage structure develops through a series of ad hoc decisions in which one expedient is piled on top of another to raise the earnings of timeworkers. The major factor is the need to maintain, or to prevent too great a fall in, timeworkers' earnings relative to those of pieceworkers. Such decisions are often made for particular groups with little thought of long term consequences. Once made, they are seldom reversible even if the original reasons no longer apply. In time, the wage structure becomes more complex and develops anomalies. It is not possible to explain the wage structure existing at a given time unless the historical process by which one form of wage payment was added to another to retain workers, to maintain relativities or tt satisfy other requirements is remembered. This does not indicate that economic forces are unimportant but the result of the system of wage determination is a wage structure which does not always reflect what would arise by the purely economic forces of supply and demand.

It is interesting to contrast the wage payment methods of Glasgow and Birmingham plants with those of the twelve case study plants located in North Lanarkshire, "New Town" and "Small Town." (See

149

Chapter 3.) No less than nine of these employed timeworkers exclusively and much wider use was made of job evaluation and measured day work than in Glasgow and Birmingham. Four Glasgow plants adopted systems of wage payment based on measured day work over 1959 - 66. No such trend was apparent in Birmingham. Thus, the methods of wage payment are much more easily understood. In part, this probably reflects the fact that all save one of the plants in these other areas had been established in the post 1945 period, most in the last 1950s and the 1960s. The methods of wage payment had not, then, been exposed for a long period to the pressures and strains operating on a wage structure. This was not, however, the only influence for there was a clear cleavage in the methods adopted by plants under British and American management. The six plants under American control employed timeworkers only and in three cases the wage structure consisted simply of an hourly rate based on job evaluation. In contrast, three of the six plants under British management employed mainly pieceworkers and the payment systems adopted for timeworkers invariably contained some form of payment in addition to a consolidated time rate above the district minimum. This supports the conclusion of one previous writer who has remarked, "As a broad generalisation it is suggested that American employers are more concerned to maintain control over internal wage structures than are British and Swedish employers" and that "In Britain ... some firms have made their wage structure so flexible as to abdicate all effective control" (Robinson 1968, p 69).

5.4   THE INTRA-PLANT EARNINGS STRUCTURE

The importance of domestic bargaining and the variety of payment methods result in a complex intra-plant earnings structure. The relationship between the earnings of different groups within the plant are, of

150

course, extremely important. The structure of earnings should encourage and recognise effort and skill and should be flexible enough to reflect changes in the demand and supply for different types of labour. Unfortunately, labour market theory does not provide any clear indication of what pattern of relativities might arise at any given moment. The relationships between the earnings of different groups might be the same for all plants or may show substantial differences from one unit to the next. Either observation can be reconciled with the economic model of the labour market behaviour. Nonetheless, an examination of intra-plant earnings structures at least establishes which if the two extremes is most realistic. Subsequently, by examining changes in plant earnings over time we can obtain some idea of how relativities change in response to employment conditions in the market.

We begin our examination of intra-plant earnings structures with Tables 5.5 and 5.6. Six plants in Glasgow and Birmingham were selected to illustrate the argument. The remaining case study plants for whom earnings data was available have been excluded to avoid unnecessary detail and because they contained a narrower range of occupations than the selected plants. Standard weekly earnings have been used as the basic unit of measurement because, for reasons outlined previously (Chapter 3), they provide the best indicator of the long run position. In each plant, standard weekly earnings for the occupational groups shown have been expressed as a percentage of the standard weekly earnings of unskilled timeworkers. In this case, DEP occupational earnings returns have been used for Glasgow plants as well as for Birmingham plants. These are preferred to EEF occupational earnings returns for the latter virtually exclude semi-skilled workers.

The relationships between the earnings of different

| Occupational | Plant number | | | | | |
group	G6	G9	G13	G14	G15	G16
Timeworkers:						
Fitters	NA	138	173	153	NA	121
Turners	NA	NA	149	140	NA	141
Semi-skilled	118	116	123	126	123	110
Pieceworkers:						
Fitters	143	158	NA	NA	NA	NA
Turners	152	147	NA	171	153	NA
Semi-skilled	129	NA	171	142	152	136
Unskilled	111	NA	129	121	NA	144

TABLE 5.5   STANDARD WEEKLY EARNINGS OF
OCCUPATIONAL GROUPS AS A
PERCENTAGE OF THE STANDARD
WEEKLY EARNINGS OF UNSKILLED
TIMEWORKERS, SELECTED GLASGOW
PLANTS, JUNE 1966

Source: DEP Occupational Earnings' Returns

Occupational group	Plant number					
	B2	B3	B5	B7	B9	B14
Timeworkers:						
Fitters	177	171	191	157	NA	135
Turners	NA	NA	206	157	130	130
Semi-skilled	125	122	121	124	112	128
Pieceworkers:						
Fitters	157	183	183	NA	NA	151
Turners	181	NA	187	189	NA	149
Semi-skilled	163	162	165	179	122	130
Unskilled	NA	173	NA	NA	NA	NA

TABLE 5.6 STANDARD WEEKLY EARNINGS OF OCCUPATIONAL GROUPS AS A PERCENTAGE OF THE STANDARD WEEKLY EARNINGS OF UNSKILLED TIMEWORKERS, SELECTED BIRMINGHAM PLANTS, JUNE 1966

Source: DEP Occupational Earnings' Returns

occupational groups correspond generally to those expected given the employment conditions in the labour markets. Skilled workers were particularly difficult to recruit in Glasgow and Birmingham while recruitment difficulties were least for the unskilled. In each quarter throughout 1959 - 66, the ratio of unemployment to vacancies in both areas was always lowest for skilled workers and always highest for the unskilled, semi-skilled workers occupying an intermediate position. Therefore, the earnings for fitters and turners should exceed those for semi-skilled and unskilled employees. Other factors will also be important, fo course, particularly the need to provide higher earnings for skilled workers to offset the costs of a long period of training. This expectation is borne out for timeworkers in both cities. In all plants, the standard earnings for skilled fitters and turners on timework exceeded the standard earnings of semi-skilled and unskilled timeworkers. Similarly, for pieceworkers alone, a fairly stable ranking emerges. Within each unit, fitters and turners on piecework tend to receive higher standard earnings than semi-skilled and unskilled pieceworkers. However, in plant B2 in Birmingham, fitters in piecework have lower standard earnings than semi-skilled pieceworkers and in two plants (G16 in Glasgow and B3 in Birmingham) standard earnings for unskilled pieceworkers exceeded those for semi-skilled pieceworkers.

The comparison becomes more confused with the inclusion of both timeworkers and pieceworkers. In each plant, semi-skilled and unskilled pieceworkers had higher standard earnings than timeworkers of the same skill. This may reflect greater effort by pieceworkers but, among skilled groups, timeworkers can earn more than pieceworkers with the same skill. Few comparisons can be made for these groups in Glasgow but in Birmingham skilled fitters on timework have higher earnings than skilled fitters on piecework

154

in plants B2 and B5, and in the latter unit turners on timework earned more that turners on piecework. The payment method has, on occasion, sufficient influence to submerge the effect of skill. In Glasgow, semi-skilled pieceworkers in G13, G14 and G 16 and unskilled workers in G16 had higher standard earnings than one or both groups of skilled timeworkers. In Birmingham, the same feature emerged for semi-skilled pieceworkers in B7 and for unskilled pieceworkers in B3. As the table provides only a few comparisons, it appears quite common for pieceworkers to have higher standard earnings than timeworkers with a higher level of skill. When gross earnings are considered, this tendency is comewhat less apparent although it is still quite strong. The difference between results based on standard and gross earnings arises because timeworkers tend to work longer overtime than pieceworkers. See Tables 5.3 and 5.4. Possibly we have, therefore, from what we have already learnt about wage payment systems, support for the conclusion that "all too often . . . reversed differentials are not the result of considered and agreed policy but of a haphazard development arising from ad hoc decisions" (NBPI 1967, p11).

Clearly the intra-plant earnings structure varies considerably from one unit to the next so that it is extremely difficult to establish any general rules. Taking fitters on timework as an example, then in Birmingham, their standard earnings varied between 135 per cent and 191 per cent of those of unskilled timeworkers. The spread for other groups is also large. Thus, despite substantial differences in the level of plant earnings, there is indication that all groups in a plant always have relatively high or relatively low earnings. See Chapter 3, Tables 3.1 and 3.2. The differences observed in intra-plant earnings structure makes it quite possible, although not usual, for a plant which is a high wage unit for one group of employees to be a low wage unit for another group.

As noted, it is difficult to evaluate the results in the light of theory for wage theory does not suggest that earnings relativities within plants must be the same for all units. Hence, differences in the structure of intra-plant earnings could arise from differences in the effort and "quality" of those employed. Again, plants may not experience the same difficulties in recruiting a given type of labour and the non-wage conditions attached to particular tasks are likely to vary between establishments. For these and other reasons, conceivably differences in intra-plant earnings structures could result from rational responses to economic and other pressures. We shall discuss this in section 5.5. Here we observe that the structure of intra-plant earnings is not the same in all units. Indeed, the outstanding characteristics of the earnings relativities in any plant is its uniqueness; there are as many intra-plant earnings structures as plants. Whatever the force of equitable comparisons, therefore, clearly they do not give rise to similar occupational differentials in each establishment. There is no "accepted" relationship between the earnings of different groups which the employee carries with him as he moves from plant to plant.

5.5 CHANGES IN OCCUPATIONAL EARNINGS

The cross-sectional analysis of section 5.4 revealed a very complex system of occupational differentials in which each plant is unique. Nonetheless, the form of analysis, at a given moment of time, cannot unambiguously answer whether we can reconcile intra-plant differentials with wage theory. The problem has, then, to be approached more indirectly. Wage theory predicts that where a particular type of employee is difficult to recruit, competition between employers for such labour will drive up the earnings relative to

156

those of other groups. Should such a tendency be observable, we could conclude that, to some extent at least, the wage structure was sensitive to economic pressures.

Table 5.7 shows for Glasgow case study plants the percentage increase, over 1959 - 66, in standard weekly earnings by occupational groups. Percentage changes in plant standard weekly earnings over 1963 - 66 for occupational groups in Birmingham are shown in Table 5.8, based on the same case study plants and occupational groups as those in Tables 3.3 and 3.4.

Before examining the changes in occupational earnings shown by the tables, we must set out the trends expected in the light of employment conditions in the markets at the time. In Glasgow, the ratios of unemployment to vacancies for fitters and turners were always substantially lower than those for unskilled workers in all quarters through 1959 - 66. The impressions conveyed by unemployment and vacancy data are confirmed by conversations with plant managers. While a number of case study plants reported occasional difficulties in obtaining skilled labour none found any difficulty in securing an adequate supply of unskilled workers. So, on the basis of labour market theory, a markedly favourable shift in the earnings of fitters and turners relative to those of labourers is predictable. One might also expect that of the two skilled groups, turners' earnings would show the more rapid increase in most plants. This is because the ratio of unemployment to vacancies was generally lower for turners than for fitters, and many case study plants reported difficulties in recruiting and retaining turners.

Toolroom workers were the category of engineering labour in shortest supply in Birmingham whether on the evidence of unemployment and vacancy data or the views of managers. In contrast, it was easiest to recruit unskilled males although with the very low levels of unemployment prevailing, some plants found

157

Plant number	Percentage increase in average earnings (excluding overtime)			
	Fitters	Turners	Unskilled	All workers
G1	25.0	23.3	11.6	20.3
G2	26.0	27.0	19.0	25.2
G3	61.7	46.1	45.7	52.8
G4	29.9	31.1	29.1	27.7
G5	37.7	43.8	14.6	41.7
G6	42.3	39.7	34.9	41.0
G7	52.0	72.7	58.8	55.6
G8	79.7	59.0	35.6	72.3
G9	30.5	36.5	19.6	34.2
G10	39.8	36.7	33.7	42.6
G11	42.7	35.3	33.7	43.0
G12	22.1	56.9	25.0	32.7
G13	59.2	72.3	66.7	61.3
G14	82.8	37.7	43.0	53.8
Average increase (unweighted)	45.1	44.2	33.6	43.2

TABLE 5.7 PERCENTAGE INCREASE IN OCCUPATIONAL EARNINGS BY PLANTS (STANDARD WEEKLY EARNINGS), GLASGOW PLANTS, OCTOBER 1966 TO JUNE 1959

Source: EEF Occupational Earnings' Returns

Plant number	Percentage increase in average earnings (excluding overtime)			
	Toolroom	Semi-skilled	Unskilled	All workers
B1	15.0	16.9	55.7	21.2
B2	7.9	9.6	70.2	27.8
B3	1.7	26.6	2.9	13.6
B4	23.0	-3.7	-13.7	7.3
B5	24.6	19.5	19.5	20.1
B6	36.0	-	32.8	27.4
B7	20.5	26.0	19.4	22.4
B8	26.0	30.5	1.4	29.1
B9	21.4	26.8	26.0	27.6
B10	26.7	21.3	38.1	22.1
B11	31.3	22.5	27.5	23.4
B12	20.1	34.8	27.9	31.1
B13	18.3	20.3	28.3	19.0
Average increase (unweighted)	21.0	20.9	25.8	22.5

TABLE 5.8 PERCENTATE INCREASE IN OCCUPATIONAL EARNINGS BY PLANTS (STANDARD WEEKLY EARNINGS), BIRMINGHAM PLANTS, JUNE 1966 to JUNE 1963

Source: DEP Occupational Earnings' Returns

even this difficult. In Birmingham, therefore, one
would expect that as plants attempted to obtain
sufficient labour the earnings of toolroom workers
would increase relative to those of semi-skilled and
unskilled employees while the rise in earnings would
be least for the latter group.

Inspection of Tables 5.7 and 5.8 indicates how far
these expectations are borne out in practice. In
Glasgow, standard weekly earnings for skilled turners
increased more rapidly than standard earnings for
unskilled workers in no less than thirteen of fourteen
plants. The earnings of the latter group lagged behind
those of skilled fitters in eleven of fourteen cases. If
gross weekly earnings are used as the unit of measurement, unskilled workers fare rather better but their
relative position still worsens in most establishments.
Clearly, then, greater competition for skilled workers
has changed intra-plant earnings' differentials in their
favour.

In other respects, there is less support for the view
that adjustments in the intra-plant earnings structure
will reflect the employment conditions in the labour
market. In every second plant in Glasgow, standard
earnings rose more quickly for fitters than turners.
There was, therefore, no clear trend in favour of the
latter group although this might have been expected in
view of the greater difficulty experienced in recruiting
turners. Increases in gross weekly earnings were
greater for fitters in eight of the fourteen plants
included in Table 5.7.   It is even more difficult to
reconcile the results for Birmingham plants with local
labour market conditions. Standard earnings for
unskilled employees increased more rapidly than those
for toolroom workers in seven of thirteen cases and
more rapidly than standard earnings for semi-skilled
workers in five of twelve cases. Increases in the
standard earnings of semi-skilled employees outstripped
those for toolroom workers in eight of twelve

160

establishments. Investigation of changes on gross earnings yields similar results except that even the slight trend in favour of semi-skilled workers compared to toolroom employees, in standard earnings, disappears for gross earnings. Therefore, no pattern at all results in Birmingham. None of the three groups improved its position relative to the others despite contrasts in the degree of difficulty in recruiting these different types of employees.

Therefore changes in intra-plant differentials are not wholly, or even mainly, explicable in terms of local labour market conditions. At the very least, changes in intra-plant differentials are not acutely sensitive to ruling employment conditions. It may be that the internal wage structure responds only slowly to economic pressures but, if this is so, the time lag, on the evidence of the above tables, must be considerable. Yet there is some indication in Glasgow of the influence of economic pressures, and possibly the failure of the intra-plant structure to adapt in the expected direction in Birmingham is due to secondary drift. Competition for labour which is particularly difficult to recruit might drive up earnings for such labour in each plant. Such primary wage drift will disturb customary relativities and create demands for compensatory wage increases for other groups. If conceded, the wage structure of each plant moves bodily upwards over time without the earnings of any group growing more quickly over an extended period.

A plant can adjust the earnings of different groups by a number of methods but the two extreme types are a general wage adjustment for all employees leaving intra-plant differentials unchanged and an adjustment of the earnings for a particular group which alters intra-plant differentials. Which effect predominates depends whether external labour market conditions or equitable comparisons within the plant is the major factor dictating changes. If external labour market

161

L

conditions dictate changes in the intra-plant wage structure, then the increase in earnings for different occupational groups depends on the balance, and changes in the balance, between the demand and supply for different types of labour. In short, persons in those occupational groups most acutely in demand have relatively large increases in earnings. If such primary drift did not give rise to secondary drift then reading down the columns of Tables 5.7 and 5.8 we would expect fairly similar increases in earnings while more substantial differences, related to supply and demand factors, would emerge across the rows.

Now, suppose that increases in earnings for one group, for whatever reason, cause secondary wage drift. In the extreme case, earnings for all groups in the plant would rise by the same amount in percentage terms. It is, of course, possible that secondary wage drift takes the form of similar absolute increases rather than similar percentage increases in earnings. We shall, however, ignore this complication. Such inflexibility is seldom realised in practice but, where equitable comparisons were important, differences across the rows would be less substantial than differences down the columns of Tables 5.7 and 5.8. In fact, in a number of plants the different occupational groups did obtain fairly similar increases in earnings over the periods covered - plants G2, G4, G6, G10 and G11 in Glasgow and B5, B7, B9, B11 in Birmingham. It seems that, if in any plant a group of workers receives an increase which is low relative to that obtained in other establishments, then all other workers in that plant also obtain a relatively low increase, and vice versa.

This should not be interpreted too literally. While most plant managements stress the importance of "established" or "recognised" relativities and while there is some evidence for secondary drift, Tables 5.7 and 5.8 do also show that substantial shifts in the intra-plant earnings' structure can and do occur (for example,

162

G8 and G14 in Glasgow and B1 and B2 in Birmingham). Nor is it possible to explain such drifts purely in terms of the difficulties experienced by plants in recruiting different types of labour. For example, in B1 and B2 there was a substantial shift in favour of labourers, for whom the labour supply position was always easiest.

Wage theory has, therefore, to be reconciled with very complex intra-plant earnings' structures. Such a reconciliation may be possible for, as we have seen, earnings relativities are not the same in all establishments. Yet it is not clear that employment conditions have a major impact on the evolution of intra-plant earnings' structure. The competitive model suggests that the rate of change of occupational earnings is a function of the relative ease or difficulty in labour recruitment. This is a good explanation of changes in occupational differentials between skilled and unskilled labour in Glasgow but no relationahip emerges between changes in occupational earnings and external labour market conditions when one considers skilled fitters and turners in Glasgow or toolroom, semi-skilled and unskilled employees in Birmingham; and this despite marked differences in the demand/supply position for these types of labour.

The failure of the internal wage structure to respond to external labour market conditions may, in part, reflect the strength of equitable comparisons within the plant. In both cities, the increase in earnings in several units was very similar across occupational groups. Even where this is not so there is a tendency for wage increases within the plant to be associated. Where one occupational group in a plant obtains an increase large relative to that won by the same occupational group elsewhere, then other groups within that plant also tend to obtain relatively large increases, and vice versa.

Despite this, equitable comparisons are not strong

163

enough to prevent any change in earnings relativities which can occasionally be very substantial as Tables 5.7 and 5.8 show. It is not clear why these shifts in the internal wage structure occur particularly in those cases where they do not seem to be related to labour demand and supply. Economic forces are not necessarily irrelevant in the process of wage settlement but nor are they necessarily of primary importance. Certainly the wage structures which exist in practice are extremely complex and do not at all points reflect the balance expected from purely economic forces. Primary drift stems largely from pieceworkers where the system of bargaining is extremely fragmented and where the management representative is subject to pressures which often make it difficult to evolve a consistent policy. Such primary drift causes wage demands from timeworkers and these are often settled ad hoc yielding many different types of payment for timeworkers in the same unit.

Probably the systems of wage payment in many engineering plants may make it difficult to establish effective control over increases in earnings or over the internal earnings structure which emerges at any point of time. Simplicity is not necessarily a virtue and any method must meet different objectives which are often difficult to reconcile. Nonetheless, the complex patterns of intra-plant earnings are scarcely primarily due to rational responses to differing needs and pressures. In many plants, particularly those under British management, little attention is paid to fundamental principles or long term considerations. Thus, it is hardly surprising that managements find it difficult to resist inflationary pressures on wage costs; nor is it to be expected that the internal wage structure will adapt readily to reflect the demand and supply positions for different types of labour. The economist's model is, therefore, not adequate by itself to explain the processes of wage determination within the plant.

164

REFERENCES

Department of Employment and Productivity (1966) "Statistics on Incomes, Prices, Employment and Production, number 19," HMSO

Knowles, K G J C and Hill, T P (1954) "The structure of engineering earnings," Bulletin of the Oxford University Institute of Statistics, volume 16, pp 272-319

Knowles, K G J C and Thorne, E M F (1961) "Wage rounds, 1948-1959," Bulletin of the Oxford University Institute of Statistics, volume 23, pp 1-26

Knowles, K G J C and Robinson, D (1969) "Wage movements in Coventry," Bulletin of the Oxford University Institute of Economics and Statistics, volume 31, pp 1-21

Lerner, S W (1965) "Wage drift, wage fixing and drift statistics," Manchester School of Economic and Social Studies, volume 33, pp 157-77

Lerner, S W, Cable, J R and Gupta, S (1969) "Workshops Wage Determination," Pergamon

Lerner, S W and Marquand, J (1962) "Workshop bargaining, wage drift and productivity in the British engineering industry," Manchester School of Economic and Social Studies, volume 30, pp 15-60

Lerner, S W and Marquand, J (1963) "Regional variations in earnings, demand for labour and shop stewards' combine committees in the British engineering industry," Manchester School of Economic and Social Studies, volume 31, pp 261-296

Marquand, J (1967) "Wage Drift: Origins, Measurement and Behaviour" (Woolwich Economic Papers, number 14), Polytechnic Department of Economics and Business Studies, London

Marsh, A (1965) "Industrial Relations in Engineering," Pergamon

National Board for Prices and Incomes (1967) "Pay and Conditions of Service of Engineering Workers" (Report number 49, Cmnd 3495), HMSO

National Board for Prices and Incomes (1968) "Payment by Results Systems" (Report number 65 supplement, Cmnd 3627-I), HMSO

National Board for Prices and Incomes (1969) "Fourth General Report" (Report number 122, Cmnd 4130), HMSO

Nicholson, R J and Gupta, S (1960) "Output and productivity changes in British manufacturing industry 1948-1954," Journal of the Royal Statistical Society, Series A (General), volume 123, pp 427-59

OEEC (1961) "The Problem of Rising Prices"

Phelps Brown, E H (1962) "Wage Drift," Economica, new series, volume 29, pp 339-56

Popola, T S and Bharadwaj, V P (1970) "Dynamics of industrial wage structure: an inter-country analysis," Economic Journal, volume 80, pp 72-90

Rehn, G (1959) "Wage Drift in Sweden," Trade Union Research Departments of the European Productivity Agency

Robertson, D J (1960) "Factory Wage Structures and National Agreements," Cambridge University Press

Robinson, D (1968) "Wage Drift, Fringe Benefits and Manpower Distribution," OECD

Ross, A M (1947) "The dynamics of wage determination under collective bargaining," American Economic Review, volume 37, pp 793-822

Sloane, P J (1967) "Wage drift: with reference to case studies in the engineering industry of central Scotland - part I," Journal of Economic Studies, volume 2, pp 23-49

Statistics on Incomes, Prices, Employment and Production, number 19, December 1966, HMSO

Turner, H A (1956) "Wages: industry rates, workplace rates, and the wage drift," Manchester School of Economic and Social Studies, volume 24, pp 95-123

Turner, H A (1960) "Wages, productivity and the level of employment: more on the 'wage drift'," Manchester School of Economic and Social Studies, volume 28, pp 89-123

Turner, H A (1964) "The disappearing drift (or, in defence of Turner)," Manchester School of Economic and Social Studies, volume 32, pp 155-96

Wootton, B (1955) "The Social Foundations of Wage Policy," George Allen & Unwin

6 The wage payment system: a primary infrastructure

by Dan Gowler and Karen Legge

Recent research work by members of the Wage
Payment Systems Project at the Manchester Business
School has revealed a phenomenon they have named
the "regressive spiral." The authors are
particularly indebted to Professor Tom Lupton, who
is directing this project, and who has generously
given his time and ideas, to contribute to this chapter.
Very briefly, the situation referred to as the regressive
spiral obtains:

> When organizations become increasingly less
> able to adapt to environmental pressures and
> finally enter a state of disequilibrium which
> becomes progressively aggravated. (Gowler
> and Legge 1970.)

We think this regressive spiral can apply to any factor
of production, that is, the supply of capital, land,
labour and managerial skill can be eroded when
dysfunctional forces become self-perpetuating.
However, discussion here is confined to the cross
pressures generated in the labour and product markets,
which strain the structure and processes comprising
a firm's social framework. Research also suggests
that certain rules and procedures, for example those
relating effort to reward, are important in containing
these pressures - see Gowler (1969a) and Legge (1970b).

We are thus, particularly concerned with the
consequences of an increasing and/or varied demand

168

for labour, coupled with a limited supply of labour, on the morale and productivity of a firm's workforce. Emphasis is also placed upon certain rules and procedures, particularly the wage payment system, which either attenuate or accentuate the problems stemming from an excess local demand for labour. Research shows that these problems sometimes become self-perpetuating and may result in the complete destruction of the social fabric of the organisation to the situation we call the regressive spiral.

This chapter has three main sections. The first is our "model" of the inter-relationships between the factors our research has revealed as important. This model follows what we have determined as the most likely chain of causation, though it must be noted that we are also concerned with the pattern of interaction between these variables. We feel it is necessary to make this distinction since, while the pattern of interaction between variables is sufficient at the level of analysis, causation and the weighting of variables becomes crucial at the level of action. In other words, those concerned with the implementation of decisions need to have some idea of the consequences of their actions. This naturally involves some notions about the likely sequence of events and the importance of the various factors deemed relevant in the situation.

The second section develops the importance of certain organisational infrastructures, particularly the wage payment system, for harmonious and effective interaction between the organisation and its environment. It lays stress on the structure of the wage packet and also discusses the tendency for certain elements of pay, e. g. overtime, bonus and basic rates, to expand at different rates. The influence of the differential rate of expansion of various elements of the wage packet on worker behaviour and attitudes is also considered.

The third and final section uses illustrations from

our fieldwork to demonstrate the operation of the regressive spiral and how in the very worst cases the social framework of the organisation collapses and then confronts management with a situation that requires radical and often unacceptable measures.

6. 1 THE MODEL

The most probable chain of cause and effect in that situation we call the regressive spiral is represented by the model in Figure 6: 1. This shows that, given a state of equilibrium as an arbitrary starting point, pressures in the product market (box 1) - the system involving the requirements of customers and the strategies of competitors - are transferred through management's marketing and sales/pricing decisions (arrow A) to the organisation via the technology (box 2). Our operational definition of technology is the fixed capital, for example plant, equipment and buildings, which with labour and managerial direction comprise the system of production. The technology either attenuates or accentuates these pressures (arrow B), that is, increases in demand for, or variation of, products and services might be dealt with by the plant with a minimum reorganisation of workflow administration or transformed into requirements for more flexible working arrangements, which then influence those rules and procedures comprising the formal organisation (box 3). This impact immediately confronts (arrow C) employees' job expectations (box 4). In the course of primary and adult socialisation people acquire and internalise values and beliefs, that is, expectations, which enable them to evaluate situations, make decisions and direct action. These expectations therefore help define the rights and obligations attached to any role. However, the contract of employment is never specific enough to encompass all these expectations and thus there arises ambiguity, mis-

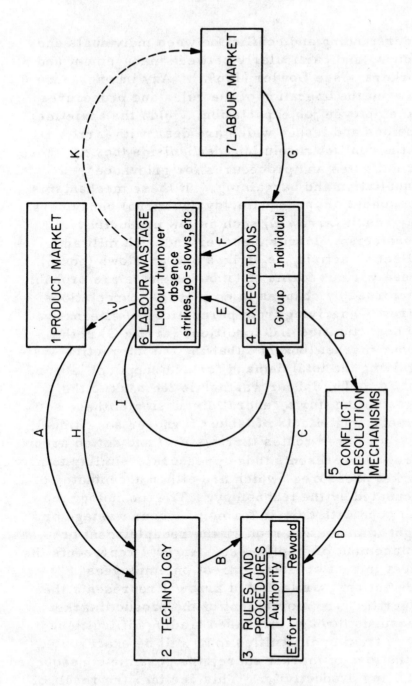

FIGURE 6:1 THE REGRESSIVE SPIRAL

understanding and conflict between individuals and groups, and particularly between management and workers - see Gowler (1969a). Any incongruence between the operation of the rules and procedures and employee job expectation, yields the anxieties, tensions and issues which are dealt with (arrow D) by the conflict resolution mechanisms (box 5), those formal rules and procedures for grievances, consultation and bargaining. If these mechanisms are absent or inadequate, dysfunctional behaviours may result (arrow E) such as low productivity, absenteeism, labour turnover and such militant collective activity as strikes and go-slows (box 6). These various forms of labour wastage are probably reinforced by changes in employees' expectations (arrow F) deriving from perceptions of alternative job opportunities and conditions (arrow G) in the labour market (box 7), that is, the interactive system involving the total demand for and supply of labour locally. The labour wastage is fed back to the organisation (for a general discussion of these self-perpetuating effects of labour turnover see Samuel, 1969) via three routes (arrows H I and dotted arrow J). Arrow H represents those pressures, similar to product market pressures, which are either accentuated or attenuated by the technology. The technology may also cope with certain forms of labour wastage or might immediately require the redeployment or replacement of employees. Arrow I represents the direct impact of labour unrest on employees' expectations, while dotted arrow J represents the longer term reinforcement of the product market pressures through increased trading difficulties. These trading difficulties may well be exacerbated by the loss of market share, the possible consequence of falling productivity. This decline, the result of labour wastage, may involve lower quality goods and services, long delivery dates, poor after-sales support.

higher prices and lower profit margins.

Clearly because every organisation is an "open system," (for a discussion of this concept see Emery 1969) the forces activating these vicious circles may be independently introduced through any of the "boxes." For example, as a result of generalised pressures in the environment, managements might introduce more efficient plant and machinery (see technology, box 2) which might promote such internal pressures as pay disputes, manning and job specifications, that might activate the regressive spiral through labour wastage (box 6). Also trade unions or managements might attempt to modify the wage payment system (see rules and procedures, box 3) or press for new forms of negotiation (see conflict resolution mechanisms, box 5) resulting in the build-up of pressures that culminate in the regressive spiral. A final example of these independently introduced pressures would be the situation where employees' perceptions of their individual or collective power (see expectations, box 4) are influenced by external factors, for instance when labour is scarce and jobs are plentiful, so as to promote use of collective employee power in overtime bans, strikes and go-slows (see labour wastage, box 6). Again, the possible consequence might be the organisation's entry into the regressive spiral.

Here, we are most concerned with those pressures introduced to the organisation via the influence (arrow G) of the labour market (box 7) on employee expectations (box 4). For example, competition in the local labour market might influence employees to leave the firm, increasing labour turnover (box 6), which then is fed back to the organisation (arrows H and I) and also in the long term to the product market (dotted arrow J). The labour wastage from this interaction of internal and external forces is also fed back to the labour market (dotted arrow K) quantitatively in labour turnover, and qualitatively, in the influence of these activities on possible employees' image of the firm and the influence on other managements' and trade unions' perceptions of the situation and the effect of these views on movements in local wage rates and earnings. This is, in fact, the birth of local wage spirals which interact with other localities and regions inevitably leading to national wage inflation.

Two further aspects of our analysis now arise. Firstly, it implies the primacy of the product market and secondly, the importance of the structure of the organisation and the market environments in which it functions.

Figure 6:1 illustrates the primacy of the product market, in that, given a state of equilibrium as an arbitrary starting point, it is management's decisions about the product market and their subsequent effects upon the organisation which are most likely to promote the regressive spiral. The forces generated in the labour market are a compounding factor. The reasons for this hypothesis of product market primacy are:

1   It is consistent with our observations of management's decisions, that there often appears to be a preference to face risk in the labour market rather than in the product market, thus precipitating (2)

2   Those changes in products, technology and related variations in the demand for labour, both qualitative and quantitative, which constantly threaten to generate the regressive spiral

3   Further, it links our analysis with conventional economic theory, where the demand for labour is seen as a derived demand, since it stems from a demand for goods or services. In other words, the decisions taken about the quantity and mix of

products influence the demand for quantities
and qualities of labour, given the nature of the
technology concerned

This does not deny the importance of the labour market.
As noted, a mismatch between the supply of labour and
the organisation's demand for it might independently
introduce the regressive spiral. However, the
regressive spiral is likely to be a combination of both
product and labour market forces, though we give the
product market influence the heaviest weighting. The
increasing market orientation of modern management
makes this realistic.

So far our analysis has been processual, i.e., it has
been concerned with activities, but it is necessary to
abstract from this diachronic process some structural
representations to produce a classification of
organisational forms useful for comparison. Thus,
we introduce the second aspect, the concept of
structure. We define structure as "...an ordered
arrangement of parts, which can be treated as
transposable, being relatively invariant, while the
parts themselves are treated as variables." The
growth of the dysfunctional, self-perpetuating forces
described here may be said to be processes operating
according to the following definitions.

1   Such processes operate through the structures of
     both the product and labour markets. We define
     markets as the total demand for, and supply of,
     any commodity within the boundaries customarily
     drawn for those transactions

2   Such processes are mediated by the infrastructures
     comprising the organisation. We define
     infrastructure as a construct which acts as a
     moderator between resources and economic
     achievement

175

These market structures and organisational
infrastructures, like the technology, either
attenuate or accentuate the forces of supply and
demand for goods and services and the labour which
contributes towards their production.

6.2 MARKET STRUCTURES AND ORGANISATIONAL INFRASTRUCTURES

Product and labour markets are variously structured
but here we only distinguish attenuative and
accentuative structures. A market is attenuative
when there exists interorganisational agreements
and/or customary arrangements impeding the forces
of supply and demand. Including, for example, trade
unions, professional organisations and government
agencies. For example, agreements about prices,
market share, conditions of employment and wages;
in economists' terms, the form of competition in the
market. Conversely, a market is accentuative when
its structure allows the forces of supply and demand
to operate without the intervention of social institutions.

Infrastructures may be subdivided into primary and
secondary. Primary are those regular, patterned
activities and relationships determined by the formal
rules and procedures of the organisation, for instance,
wage payment systems, job specifications, and
official information systems (reports, manuals,
budgets and so on). The latter rules and procedures
are those regulating institutions, which are designed
to direct employees towards the attainment of
organisational goals. Primary infrastructures are
thus those non-discretionary elements of occupational
roles, that is, those employment activities either
prescribed by managements or formally agreed
between managements and employees or their
representatives. They are, therefore, all the formal
mechanisms of organisational control which, with

176

plant and equipment, convert resources into goods and services, and correspond to box 3 in the model in Figure 6:1.

Secondary infrastructures are those activities and relationships consequent on the informal or discretionary elements of occupational roles. They are all the social activities which develop around the performance of any task. They are not specified by the primary infrastructures but are yet interwoven with them to such an extent that it is only possible to distinguish them analytically. This is not quite true since the work of Elliot Jaques (1961) on the "time-span of discretion" has resolved some of these difficulties, see also Fox (1966). These secondary infrastructures are not consciously designed and therefore may not necessarily direct employees towards organisation goals. These activities are, however, institutionalised and subject to the controls regulating social behaviour in the sub-cultures concerned. For example, customary and traditional rules which workers use to regulate levels of output and degree of cooperation with the management. Primary and secondary infrastructures may therefore perhaps conflict. Finally, secondary infrastructures correspond with box 4 in the model.

Primary and secondary infrastructures may also be classified as attenuative or accentuative. Thus, when either infrastructure restricts employees' choices, it is said to be attenuative. Conversely, when they do not, they are accentuative. This assumes, of course, that the restriction of employees' choices is the consequence of appropriate and matched control systems, since the constraint of employees' choices might, if inappropriate, accentuate an organisation's difficulties. The appropriateness of primary and secondary infrastructures is discussed later, but we assume that, together, they constrain behaviour within and

177

without the organisation.   Where there are many
constraints and choice is very limited, the
structure is attenuative; where there are few
constraints with relatively free choice, the structure
is accentuative.

Secondary infrastructures, like primary infrastructures, are forms of social control, but more
diffuse and variable than the formal control systems.
Whereas managements' sanctions are relatively limited
and defined, the sanctions wielded by workgroups
have a wide and varied range.

All this is now represented in a simple matrix.
For all the structures represented in Figure 6: 2
have one thing in common, they represent the various
forms of social institution which exercise a constraint
on behaviour and which combine to give
organisations and societies their stability and
continuity.

The cells in Figure 6: 2 may be variously
combined, but we assume that some combinations
are inherently unstable.

The stability of the various combinations of market
structures, technologies and infrastructures, that is,
their propensity to enter the regressive spiral,
depends largely upon the organisation's conflict
resolution mechanisms (box 5, Figure 6: 1).

We now illustrate how we use the concept of
infrastructure, with particular reference to how
conflict resolution mechanisms moderate between
grievances and the reformulation of the rules and
procedures and/or change in worker expectations.
This process is represented by the interaction
(arrows C and D) between boxes 3, 4 and 5 in
Figure 6: 1.

Conflict resolution mechanisms are located in both
infrastructures.   Formal rules and procedures about
the settlement of grievances, joint consultation and

178

bargaining come within our definition of primary infrastructures. However, most day-to-day conflicts are resolved by people acting out their occupational roles which include expectations about behaviour in conflict situations. Insofar as this conflict resolving behaviour is the acting out of the non-discretionary elements of occupational roles, for instance a supervisor exercising his formal job rights to deal with a shopfloor dispute, they are within our definition of primary infrastructures.

The conflict resolving behaviour which acts out the discretionary elements of occupational roles, that is, when conflicts are resolved by individuals acting outside the formal requirements of their jobs, come within our definition of secondary infrastructures. Unfortunately, while one can distinguish formal and informal mechanisms in theory, it is very hard to in reality, since the boundaries of discretionary and non-discretionary elements in occupational roles are inevitably blurred. Moreover, conflict resolving behaviour that was originally discretionary and formally unrecognised, for instance, informal shop steward activity, it likely to become recognised and incorporated into the formal procedures for settling grievances and dealing with disputes, as when shop stewards join the joint consultation and negotiating machinery. This recognition enables this previously informal conflict resolving behaviour to be overtly and legitimately used to lubricate and compensate for the prior inadequacies in the original formal procedures.

We can, however, reasonably generalise that conflict resolution mechanisms reside mainly in the primary infrastructures and therefore are attenuative, since they are designed to restrict certain forms of behaviour. The question of inadequate and inappropriate conflict resolution mechanisms, that is those defined as accentuative, are discussed later when the whole question of "match" or "fit" between market structures, technologies and organisational infrastructures is dealt with. We would finally state, however, that the self-perpetuating nature of the regressive spiral tends to persist as the conflict resolution mechanisms, inadequate to marshal and contain the associated accentuative pressures, are less able to provide adequate feedback for the necessary restructuring of the primary infrastructures to accommodate these pressures.

6.3 THE WAGE PAYMENT SYSTEM: A PRIMARY INFRASTRUCTURE

A wage payment system is a set of rules and procedures which relate some kind of effort to some kind of reward (Lupton and Gowler 1969) and so comes within our definition of a primary infrastructure.

A wage payment system is, however, a special type of infrastructure, since it fulfils three moderating functions:

1   It moderates between employee job expectations (secondary infrastructures) and job requirements (for instance those primary infrastructures concerned with workflow administration)

2   It helps determine the level of earnings and thus moderates between the organisation's internal labour demand and the external labour supply

3   It functions in certain circumstances as a conflict resolution mechanism, that is, wage increases stemming from changes in the wage payment system may resolve issues and difficulties which are the result of other organisational problems

	Market structures		Technology	Organisational infrastructures	
	Product	Labour		Primary	Secondary
Attenuative	A	B	E	G	H
Accentuative	C	D	F	I	J

FIGURE 6:2 THE WAGE PAYMENT SYSTEM AS A
PRIMARY INFRASTRUCTURE

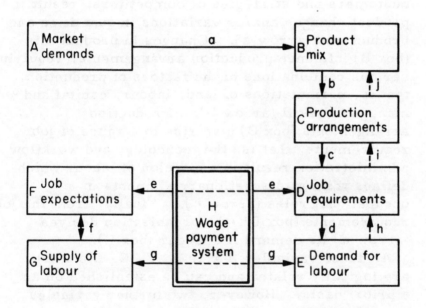

FIGURE 6:3 CLASSIFICATION OF MARKET
STRUCTURES AND ORGANISATIONAL
INFRASTRUCTURES

Figure 6:3 shows how the wage payment system functions in the three ways itemised above. It is really no more than a simplified version of our original model and shows the crucial nature of It is really no more than a simplified version of our original model and shows the crucial nature of this primary infrastructure. We feel this restatement of the model is necessary since it compresses and simplifies a rather long and involved analysis while highlighting the wage payment system as a special type of primary infrastructure. The authors have become only too aware that "the systems approach," though promising in its power to enlighten, is sometimes tedious in its apparently necessary repetitions.

Very briefly, Figure 6: 3 shows how market demands (box A), as determined by the requirements of customers and strategies of competitors, result in product changes and/or variations in quantities and product mix (arrow a). Changes in product mix (box B) influence production arrangements, requiring various combinations of the factors of production, that is, permutations of land, labour, capital and managerial skill (arrow b). Production arrangements (box C) give rise to a range of job requirements, that is, the technology and workflow administration result in a division of labour which defines the non-discretionary elements in occupational roles (arrow c). Finally, from the job requirements (box D), the organisation derives (arrow d) its demand for labour (box E).

All these variables (boxes A, B, C, D and E) are logically related and can be established on an a priori basis. However, two further variables complicate the situation making the conversion of market demands into a production programme more than a mere technical exercise.

Firstly, there is a relation (double-headed arrow

e) between job requirements and job expectations
(box F). That is, if job expectations, in terms of
pay, working conditions, social satisfaction and
so on, are not congruent with job requirements, the
job is likely to become and/or remain a vacancy.
These two variables are not, however, in a
straightforward one-way cause-and-effect relationship.
A job incumbent has expectations that are modified
in the light of working experience, his coming into
contact with certain occupational requirements, but
often job requirements are informally and formally
manipulated in the light of job expectations. An
example is when the hours of work are extended, not
for increased production, but to augment the wage
packet through overtime. Thus, job requirements
are "bent" to meet earnings expectations, and this
is often done in collusion with the lower levels of
management.

Job expectations also influence and are
influenced by the supply of labour (doubleheaded
arrow f). Employees' expectations react to
conditions in the labour market while, at the same
time, the labour market (double-headed arrow g)
is influenced by the expectations. Employers only
advertise vacancies which they believe to be
realistic in terms of pay, conditions and so on.
Finally, if the demand for labour is not satisfied,
for whatever reason, the firm may have to revise
its job requirements to meet shortages in its work
force (double-headed arrow h).

The shifting balance between the labour market,
job expectations and job requirements, represented
by the system D, E, F, G and H, may oblige the
firm to alter its production arrangements (dotted
arrow i). This "feedback" through the system to
the type and quantity of product manufactured
(dotted arrow j) may place the firm in
difficulties when meeting customers' demands, and

with subsequent adverse effects on the firm's costs, profits and competitive position (Gowler 1969a).

The wage payment system (box H) is important here since it functions as an equilibrating device. In other words, it contains the pressures developed by variations in job expectations, job requirements and the supply of and demand for labour. However, if the wage payment system is inappropriate, it will not contain these pressures and may even serve to exacerbate them. These functions of the wage payment system, that is, how it mediates between job requirements and job expectations, and its influence on the relation between the demand for and supply of labour is discussed in detail later.

The pressures developed by the shifting balance of the variables described above influence both (a) the level of earnings and (b) the size of certain elements in the wage packet. Since (a) and (b) are obviously related, our discussion emphasises (b), which we believe the most fundamental issue.

The expansion of various elements in the wage is a function of:

1   The wage payment system, which determines the number of elements in the wage packet, for instance a basic rate, shift and overtime premiums and a production bonus

2   Worker behaviour, for instance the number of hours he works and the intensity of his efforts

3   The variations in (1) and (2) above which stem from the changes in job requirements that arise from alterations in production arrangements and the demand for labour (Gowler 1969b)

An example of the expansion and contraction of one element in the wage packet is illustrated in Table 6:1. It shows in a large process plant a shortage of labour,

184

the consequence of increased local competition for workers, coupled with fluctuating production requirements to produce high and increasing levels of overtime working. The result was an increase in the overtime element in the wage packet.

Year	Overtime in average total pay (%)
1962	27. 5
1963	23. 3
1964	25. 2
1965	26. 9
1966	29. 0
1967	29. 3

TABLE 6. 1 EXPANSION OF THE OVERTIME
ELEMENT IN A WAGE PACKET

Here, the "weakest" element in the wage packet, overtime payments, reacts to the pressures in the system. However, given another wage payment system operating in the same circumstances, another element, for example, bonus payments, might react similarly.

The really crucial point is that each element in the wage packet is subject to varying rates of expansion and contraction. Further, the forces which impinge on one element may not on another. For example, the basic rate is likely to be influenced by collective bargaining at national level, while other elements are influenced by such conditions at the local level as overtime and bonus payments. This is not to deny that many elements in the wage packet are linked. Thus, when one element is influenced, other elements are likely to react. For example, general economic conditions may create, through the processes of national collective bargaining, an increase in basic rates, which might then influence the overtime payments related to them. So, each element in the wage packet is likely to be influenced by a range of forces, reducible to three distinct types:

1 Changes stemming from decisions made outside the plant; for instance across-the-board awards

2 Changes stemming from decisions made inside the plant; for instance increases negotiated by representatives of the parties concerned at local level and rates bargained by workers and rate fixers

3 Changes stemming from the "multiplier" effect of one wage element upon another

Recent research found that workers hold clearly distinguishable attitudes to each of the elements in their wage packets. Moreover, they tended to balance and evaluate each of these elements in relation to one another. These wage elements were seen as a system and a change in any one of them alters relative significance of each of the others.

In this situation, it was discovered that workers felt there was an imbalance in the effort-reward relation. In general, they attributed this to the small size of the basic rate. There were two main criticisms: (a) the basic rate was said to be too low in relation to what obtained elsewhere, and (b) it was claimed to represent too small a proportion of the total wage.

Another set of attitudes revealed that there was a strong sense of uncertainty brought about by workers' perceptions of insecure and unstable elements in the wage packet. These were reinforced by a perceived mismatch between the job requirements/opportunities provided by the production arrangements and the expectations raised by the job evaluation aspect of the wage payment system. For example, workers claimed that skill and responsbility were rewarded better than physical effort, and this was certainly in line with what management said about the logic of the job rate system, which was based on an earlier job evaluation exercise. The problem was that higher job rates did go to workers whose tasks required skill, intelligence and responsibility, but the technology and organisation of the work provided few opportunities to demonstrate these abilities. Consequently, many workers felt frustrated, for while they had accepted the problem of rewards determined by the original job evaluation system, they were unable to take advantage of it through the lack of the right job opportunities.

The outcome was increasing absenteeism and labour turnover, which then became self-perpetuating and led to the firm's entry into the regressive spiral.

This analysis suggests that certain forces influence the expansion and contraction of the separate elements in the wage packet. Also, given that workers' attitudes are clustered around these wage elements, expansion and contraction in them is likely to result in changes in worker behaviour. Thus, when variations in the size of certain wage elements promote negative attitudes towards them, as in the example, labour wastage is likely to result. In extreme cases, this may become powerful enough to produce the regressive spiral.

The wage payment system described above is a very good example of an accentuative primary infrastructure (cell I, Figure 6:2). In other words, not only has this wage payment system become undermined by the distortion of certain wage elements, but this very distortion has reinforced the pressures in the situation so as to promote the gradual wastage of the firm's labour force; it has helped generate the regressive spiral.

Here, the firm had either to attenuate some of the pressures, for example, by changing product market policies and/or stock holding policies, and/or redesign

187

the crucial infrastructure, that is, restructure the wage packet by changes in the wage payment system. The latter might also help reduce some of the labour market pressures in the situation. Thus, changes in the wage payment system might result not only in the revision of the number and size of wage elements, thereby influencing behaviour in the firm's internal labour market, but might also result in higher levels of total pay which then might help reduce external labour market difficulties by improving the supply of labour to the firm

6.4 THE REGRESSIVE SPIRAL
Changes in the product market, to varying extents, depending on the influence of technological constraints upon workflow arrangements, affect the deployment of labour. Changes in the product market are of two types, quantitative and qualitative, or some permutation on the possible combinations.

1   In quantitative terms, the volume of the products produced can:
    (a)   change overall, the volume of each product increasing/decreasing in proportion to its present size;
    (b)   change overall, while the individual products change proportionally in relation to each other;

2   The volume of each product produced can change proportionally in relation to each other, while the overall volume produced by the firm can remain static

3   In qualitative terms, new products can be introduced

4   Combinations of (1a), (1b), (2) and (3) can occur

Similarly, manpower requirements can change both quantitatively and qualitatively, in terms of both

numbers and skill mix required, while the resulting
redeployment of labour can occur in terms of space
(movement from one operation to another, from one
work term to another) or time (restructuring of shift
working, increased/decreased overtime hours).
Clearly, the redeployment of labour in these terms is
subject to the above categories of manpower requirements. If ability to recruit in the local labour market
is constrained for any reason (by wage levels offered,
limited supply of specific categories of skill labour),
certain types of product change, combining with
certain technologies to determine manpower requirements, predispose an organisation towards specific
if various combinations of redeployment. For example,
if type (1a) product change occurs (a quantitative
change) in constrained labour market conditions,
manpower requirements in terms of numbers (man
hours) required, will probably be met by increased
overtime. If, however, the changes that occur require
a reallocation of man hours upon specific products (2)
yet with no overall increases in output, transfers are
a more likely solution than overtime working (at
least initially), while the introduction of new products
(3) with the probable retraining and familiarisation
problems involved, is likely to require both forms of
accommodation. Moreover, because redeployment in
a physical sense (either in terms of time or space)
frequently is associated with changes in skill mix
required, especially in the case of product changes
(1b) and (3), again combinations of types of redeployment of varying degrees of severity can occur. With
the advent of a new product, for example, an operator
could conceivably be transferred on to a lower skilled
job, on a different work team, while concurrently
being asked to work overtime, depending on the range
of adequate alternatives perceived by management.

Thus, changed job requirements invariably alter
levels or type of effort demanded; if the structure of

189

the payment system does not allow for appropriately
adjusted levels of reward, adjustment will take place
elsewhere in the system.   The repercussions of such
redeployment in terms of labour wastage hinges on
the ability of the wage payment system, through its
accommodation in financial terms of the changes in
job requirements, to maintain equilibrium in the
effort-reward relationship.   For, as stated previously,
the wage payment system is the first infrastructure,
in the event of change, to moderate and, if necessary,
through its own restructuring contain the direct
confrontation of job requirements with expectations,
and thus ultimately to reconcile the demand with the
supply of labour (see Figure 6:3).   While the confrontation between conflicting job requirements and
expectations within the firm centres around the wage
structure (that is, via the implications for the labour
force, in the light of the stability of the effort-
reward relationship, of differential rates of expansion
and contraction of different elements in the pay packet),
the necessary accommodation of pressures of supply
and demand for labour centres around the wage levels
the system's operation allows.   The fact that the
structures of the wage payment system influenc the
level of earnings it allows, underlines the relationships postulated in Figure 6:3.   In other words, while
it is the relationship between the structure of the wage
packet and job requirements and expectations (arrow
e, Figure 6:3) that helps to regulate the allocation of
labour within the firm (the internal labour market)
the level of earnings, which derive directly from this
structure, influences the organisation transactions
with the environment (the external labour market)
(arrow g, Figure 6:3).

The adjustment of the system to changed job
requirements can be either voluntary or involuntary.
In the first category falls the conscious restructuring
of dysfunctional aspects of the primary infrastructure

190

(for instance the rules and procedures relating effort to reward) through the use of adequate and appropriate conflict resolution mechanisms; in the second category, uncontrolled adaptation through wage drift, grade drift, lowered effort levels, etc. Moreover, adaptation, taking place over time, can be characteristically continuous (involving a constant monitoring over time) or discontinuous (limited to periodic crisis management). Where permanent and appropriate mechanisms of conscious adjustment exist in the primary infrastructure (than is formal institutions for conflict resolution) adaptation is logically more likely to be continuous that where such institutions are either non-existent or inappropriate. The "regressive spiral" of labour wastage, illustrated by the case studies below, characteristically occurs when the adjustment of the system to market engendered pressures is both involuntary and discontinuous.

6.5 CASE STUDY A

In a garment factory, manufacturing by sectionalised flow techniques, with female direct labour deployed in stable work teams, product market changes dictated production changes (2) and (3); in other words, intensive production change of a chiefly qualitative nature. Job requirements, involving decreases in individual batch size and increases in style range, demanded that over a given period od time, the workforce learn to work with a greater range of machines and materials than hitherto, and in addition, to perform a wider range of sewing operations. The changed job requirements logically demanded redeployment of labour over space: if a new garment of very different styling to those previously assigned was assigned to a work team, first line supervision could arrange for its production via the external or internal transfer of operators. Redeployment could take the following forms. First line supervision could:

191

1   Have the members of the work team retrained
     on unfamiliar operations/machines/materials

2   Have moved on to the work team (if available)
     operators familiar with the operations required
     (with the corollary that some members of the
     work team would therefore be redeployed off
     the team)

The initially less likely possibility remained, if in the
process of retraining on the new garments high levels
of labour turnover and absenteeism ensued, of having
moved on to the work team operators unfamiliar with
the operations required.
     The implications of either of these decisions
involves repercussions for the status system and hence
social fabric of the factory. If first line supervision
chose (1), the decision remains of which operators
are to be trained on which operations. The problem
becomes acute if, while the previous garment
comprised many either low skill/high skill operations,
the new garment has an opposite skill mix of
operations. For this could mean that of the operators
who had previously worked a high skill/low skill job,
some would have to be retrained on either higher or
lower skilled jobs than those to which they were
accustomed. In either case, the wage payment system
is a crucial variable in the successful operation of the
redeployment. For those redeployed on a higher
skilled job, if the payment system is largely of a
reciprocal nature there exists the problem of maintaining earnings levels during retraining periods and
before a standard performance is reached. Reward
is classified as reciprocal when certain rules and
procedures are specifically designed to encourage
feedback from effort to reward and/or status. When
rules and procedures are not designed to promote
this feedback, reward is classified as non-reciprocal.

Thus, the level of the unstable element in the pay packet can contract markedly, and if allowance is not made for this via the expansion of timework elements (for instance training allowances) overall as well as in relation to the incentive element, severe distortion of the effort-reward bargain can occur. If the effort-reward bargain becomes seriously out of balance, it is likely to be either further undermined, or corrected via such conflict expressions as labour turnover, depending on the speed and quality of the feedback to management, itself dependent partly on the sanctions thus expressed. If, on the other hand, a largely non reciprocal payment system (defined in Lupton and Gowler, 1969) operates, but redeployment on a higher skilled job involves movement to a higher job grade, the problem of selection while maintaining group cohesion is intensified, especially as workers often hold conflicting views as to which qualities should be used as criteria for selection. Frequently criteria attached to social roles (for example length of service) are used in preference to sometimes related, but often divorced purely occupational criteria (for instance level of competence in the job). Thus, the worker with longer service but a lower level of competence than the selected man, feels that his length of service is being unfairly ignored, or vice versa. For those retrained on a lower skilled job, the insecurity attached to a loss of status can well be matched by financial insecurity, resulting from loss of skill allowances attached to the former job. Thus, given the utilitarian and symbolic role of money, the wage payment system, in the threatening environment of job restructuring, can either contain or aggravate the insecurity stemming from potential loss of earnings, in the face of a deteriorating effort-reward bargain, and that stemming from potential loss of status.

The feelings of job insecurity (in terms of both earnings and status) resulting from redeployment

N

outside the work group, are potentially even greater than those resulting from redeployment within the work group. The operator is likely to experience if not job change at least some slight job modification (with the potential for earnings loss outlined above), at the same time as experiencing the withdrawal of the social support of a familiar work team and supervision. Indeed, the redeployed's relationship towards his new work group and supervision is likely to be fraught with tension and possibly antagonism. Firstly, the operator is placed in a situation, even if already trained in the operation he is to perform, of some unfamiliarity vis-à-vis his job. In the factory under discussion, even if the basic work process and operations were familiar, the machines operated and materials handled were likely to have minor differences and their own idiosyncracies. In cases where operators to be retrained on new jobs were transferred on to different work teams, owing to specific labour shortages, the full burden of learning a new skill/machine/material, and possibly all three, combined with the removal of social supports. The operator's adaptation to the job change with which he is faced involves the danger of appearing inept and inexperienced before new team mates, for whom his acceptance in social terms may initially depend on the speed of his learning processes. The operator, therefore, has to adapt to changed job requirements with little or conditional social support, at a time when he is most in need of it. Moreover, as the redeployed operator has initially no length of service and ensuing informal status in the work group, his relationship with supervision vis-a-vis the latter's informal allocation of overtime, good/bad jobs and so on is disadvantageous. When transfer and retraining is, in addition, used as a disciplinary measure, the problems outlined above are compounded. A recent research project (Ni Bhroin, 1969) has yet again confirmed these findings.

194

In dealing with these, again, the wage payment system is a crucial variable. The problems inherent in the above situation would be greatly aggravated if a group bonus scheme comprised a major element in the wage packet, or if, as in this case, sectionalised flow production combined with a linear piecework scheme determined that a slow inexperienced operator occupying a strategic position in the chain could affect the earnings potential of other operators in the work team. Indeed, if any major element in the wage packet (as, for example overtime and/or bonus) is variable, and does not allow for an equal opportunity in its achievement by redeployed as well as established workteam members, the ability of the wage payment system to match job requirements with expectations is seriously jeopardised. Alternatively, a high day-rate with suitable training and transfer allowances could do much by way of absorbing the potential friction between changed job requirements and unaccommodating job expectations.

Unless the pressures associated with the redeployment of labour over space are contained by a primary infrastructure such as the wage payment system (or resolved by it via the renegotiation of the effort-reward bargain - and hence the restructuring of the payment system of job requirements or both - through conflict resolution mechanisms) the difficulties of redeployment will be compounded, and their self-perpetuation will lead to pressures on other parts of the total system.

In this case-study, the wage payment system was inadequate to cope with pressures engendered in the product market. High levels of redeployment in the terms discussed above were confronted by a wage payment system where the major element was incentive based, on standards that took no account of the new levels of job change and shortened production runs. Hence, incentive earnings contracted sharply but without compensating increases in flat rate training allowances.

> The hours spent learning unfamiliar machines
> and operations, in ironing out the snags on
> incoming garments were subjectively considered
> by machinists to involve more effort than working
> at full speed on an accustomed operation, machine
> and garment, yet the monetary return on the fall-
> back timework rate was seen to be lower than on
> piecework over standard performance. The
> effort-reward relationship had shifted unfavourably
> (Legge, 1970b).

As the firm operated in an area of high competition for female semi-skilled labour, the state of the labour market aggravated rather than alleviated the situation. The labour turnover that resulted from continued redeployment on the work team, in face of the inability of the wage payment system to maintain equilibrium in the effort-reward bargain, meant that the remaining workforce, owing partly to the firm's difficulties in recruiting in a tight labour market was faced with further redeployment both on and off the work team to cover the work of a learner or absentee in order to maintain the flow of production. Also, given the increasing shortness of production runs, it was frequent that, by the time a replacement had been trained to do the job of a leaver and assigned to a work team, the team could be about to start, or have started, a new production run, requiring a different skill mix, and hence a further period of training for the replacement, further aggravating the replacement's effort-reward relation, the consequent labour turnover and an intensification of the cycle.

Moreover, the pressures on the system exacerbated the latent conflict inherent in the organisational structure, between such departments as production make-up and production engineering, between make-up and cutting departments and so on as well as between different levels in the hierarchy. For example, the product changes (2) and (3) inevitably led to a higher percentage of badly cut constituents than on production runs prior to the product changes. If experience of the material and printing was relatively limited, there could be substantial stretching needle cutting, distortion of stripes and machine trouble. All these factors resulted in more work and responsibility for supervision, and in more irritation and loss of potential earnings for the operator. Added to this, the role of first line supervision, initiating labour re-deployment, while they themselves were pressurised by the greater workload involved in the increase in number of production runs, often led to strained relations on both sides which aggravated growing labour turnover problems.

But the difficulties resulting from inappropriate supervisory reactions to a dynamic stress situation can themselves be self-perpetuating. To cope with the lower productivity resulting from rising levels of labour turnover and absenteeism, supervisory style may become harsher and more authoritarian; retraining and transfers may increasingly be used as arbitrary disciplinary measures, further promoting lower productivity via further labour turnover and absenteeism. With the increasing aggravation of the vicious circle and ensuing complexity of problems, supervision may further retreat to the apparent security of rigidly defined rules and procedures, thereby further exacerbating the situation.

Moreover, high labour turnover and group frag-mentation are likely to lead to the breakdown of informal means of inducing conformity in work roles. If, on the one hand, a tightening up of work standards and on the other a clamping down on informal privileges associated with job rights, overtime, retraining allowances and so on lead to a substantial number of long service workers leaving, or more likely, withdrawing into apathy and uncooperativeness, their role of socialising new employees, via myths and rituals, into the norms and expectations attached to the performance of their work roles, and located in the secondary infrastructure, would be lost. This would further necessitate a reliance on the more bureaucratic and rigid socialisation procedures of the primary infrastructure, probably inadequate and inappropriate to the dynamic situation. In other words, if the primary infrastructures (that is, the wage payment system and conflict resolution mechanisms) that initially cope with environmental pressure fail, the aggravated stress situation could well foster the "vicious circle of bureaucracy" that Crozier (1965) has described.

The total situation represented here is characterised in Figure 6:2 as a combination of:

C   an accentuative product market

D   an accentuative labour market

F   an accentuative technology

I   an accentuative primary infrastructure (wage payment system)

J   an accentuative secondary infrastructure (frustrated expectations leading to a general deterioration of social relationships and a breakdown of informal control system

Further discussion of this case study will be found in Legge 1970b.

6.6 CASE STUDY B
In a factory of process technology, manufacturing consumer goods, product market changes dictated production changes (1b) and (3); changes, therefore, of both qualitative and quantitative nature. Here, however, the technology acted as a buffer in relation

to qualitative changes. Such changes as those involving product mix did not require the learning of new skills (hence the possibility, via redeployment, of a changed social composition in the work team), as a high degree of variation in detail was tolerated by the plant. In other words, a range of skills was built into the technology, rather than learnt by the individual operator. Thus, the infrastructure of the technology to come extent contained market pressures that in the case of a less sophisticated technology would have to be contained by the wage payment system or another primary infrastructure. The quantitative changes, however, given constraints in the labour market on the rapid recruitment of labour, involved redeployment over time, that is a high degree of overtime working.

The consequences of this form of redeployment was to increase the size of an unstable element in the wage packet, which in this situation in any case contained a large number of perceived insecure elements (for example, job rate, shift allowance, twice-yearly bonus, overtime payment), the operators often commenting that all payments additional to their basic rate "could be taken away at any time." The increasing amount of overtime worked was considered by the operators to upset their effort-reward relationship, as they claimed that, given the low basic rate, increasingly a smaller proportion of their total earnings, they were having to work too long for too little. Yet, on the other hand, the inflation of their earnings by high levels of overtime working, led operators to extend their financial commitments, giving the overtime a self-sustaining growth, inevitably resulting in pressure on management to maintain and extend it.

> In consequence, where expanding wage expectations were being met at the expense of increasing wage disparity, workers' attentions were focussed on the contribution each element made to the security and stability of their take home pay (Gowler, 1969a).

199

Thus, operators' attitudes towards redeployment through overtime working, and towards their monetary return for this was essentially ambiguous. On the one hand, they frequently desired it in order to make up their earnings to an acceptable level, but on the other, especially when production arrangements called for long periods of twelve hour shift working, they sometimes felt they were compelled to work more overtime than they needed to attain their earnings target. Moreover, young single men often complained that the compulsion to work overtime, for whatever reasons, interfered with their external social life. This redeployment, therefore (unlike the redeployment over space described in the previous case study, where operator reaction was almost completely negative) being at times welcome, complicated rather than simplified the role of first line supervision. For there were times when operators were demanding overtime from the foremen who were reluctant to give it, and times when the foremen were demanding overtime working from the operators who felt, at that point, they had worked enough. Their conflicting attitudes to overtime and to the ensuing increase in insecurity of their earnings levels, fostered a stressful situation between operators and supervision owing to its ambiguity.

Moreover, tension between supervision and workers was further exacerbated by their mutually ambiguous attitudes towards another element in the wage packet: job rates. Given the low basic rate, operators' attempts to increase their earnings resulted in claims for higher job rates, and pressure on first line supervision to concede them. Supervision, therefore, was placed in an ambiguous situation. On the one hand concession of job rates could be used to gain cooperation when production arrangements required the working of more overtime hours than operators would voluntarily wish to work; on the other, there was pressure from middle management to control an obvious wage drift mechanism. As far as operators were concerned, although increases in their job rates, increasing earnings, were welcome at one level, they also increased the size of perceived insecure and unstable elements in the wage packet, towards which operators had decidedly ambivalent attitudes. This then too contributed towards the absenteeism and labour turn-over which were among those forces that encouraged the upward drift. Thus, again, the demands and concessions by operators and supervision were, if at different levels, frequently at odds with each other, increasing the strain and potential antagonism between both parties.

The ambiguity of operators' perceptions of the effort-reward relationship resulting from this form of redeployment, led to the organisation being trapped in what has been described as a "double bind."

> The situation was that when overtime working diminished, male workers tended to leave because they found they were unable to manage on their now reduced incomes. When overtime working increased, there was a loss of male labour as a result of absenteeism, i.e. men taking time off after long, tiring periods of overtime working or deliberately substituting overtime hours for 'normal' hours. Thus, the men's dissatisfaction with their effort-reward relation was exacerbated by variations in the amount of overtime working. (Gowler, 1969a)

In other words, a vicious circle operated whereby labour wastage from either labour turnover or absenteeism, contributing to a general labour shortage, served to increase the amount of overtime necessarily worked and with it, therefore, further loss of hours via absenteeism, perpetuating the cycle. Moreover, the situation of the "double bind" tied the hands of management in tackling the labour shortages resulting from redeployment over space meant that if management had been able to eliminate it, labour turnover would have correspondingly been reduced, in this situation, given the positive attitudes of some operators towards it as a means of inflating their earnings (even if aggravating their effort-reward relation), diminished overtime in fact resulted in labour turnover. To prevent labour wastage through turnover in one section of workers (via maintaining overtime levels) was to increase it among another section (via absenteeism).

The total situation described here, may be represented in terms of Figure 6:2, as a combination of:

C   an accentuative product market

D   an accentuative labour market

E   an attenuative technology

I   an accentuative primary infrastructure (wage payment system)

J   accentuative secondary infrastructure (frustrated expectations leading to general deterioration of social relationships and breakdown of informal control system)

Further discussion of this case study will be found in Gowler, 1969a.

6.7 FURTHER IMPLICATIONS OF LABOUR WASTAGE

The most dangerous problems resulting from labour wastage are those unforseen consequences that are outside management's range of prediction and of which it has little experience in coping. Into this category must be placed one of the most insidious effects of the regressive spiral - whether initiated by redeployment over space of time - the "hidden selection" of labour, working through the mechanisms of labour turnover

202

and absenteeism, and resulting in a gradual change in the social composition of the workforce, in terms of age, sex, required skills, preferred working hours and, consequently, productivity potential. Detailed case study description of how this process operates can be found in two previous publications. We propose here to discuss rather the implications of the selection that occurred.

Following the labour turnover resulting from the redeployment described in case study A, management, refusing to restore equilibrium to the effort-reward relationship by adjusting either job requirements (effort levels) or restructuring the wage payment system (reward levels) in effect adjusted it by achieving lower levels of job expectations, through tolerating the previously avoided recruitment of increasing numbers of non-British and part time labour. Both these categories of labour accentuated training problems aggravated by the high levels of labour turnover, that resulted from and induced the increasing amount of redeployment, the consequence of product market change. The process of training non-English speaking operators was impeded by language problems while, for the part time operators, the problem associated with training the older worker were linked with motivational problems (see Clay, 1960) in that many of the women had returned to work for social rather than purely economic considerations.

Their response, therefore, to the challenge presented by the wage payment system, to rapidly complete training on a low flat rate in order to graduate on to higher incentive earnings, was inferior to those employees to whom the economic motive was uppermost. But this changing direction of recruitment had less immediate repercussions. The slow working pace of the part time and some sections of the non-British labour, owing to the interdependence of production roles in the workflow arrangements, at

203

times adversely affected the earnings potential of other groups of workers, such as full time workers whose social roles (for instance engaged or newly married) acted as powerful economic motivators. The effect of this process was to push out of the system its most productive workers. Moreover, the tendency to increasingly recruit coloured workers showed indications of having the often asserted effect of pushing out white workers and accentuating the difficulties of their recruitment. It is feasible that potential employees, of primarily economic motivation, could cease to be attracted to a firm owing to stereotyped images associated with workplaces with high levels of coloured workers ("they depress the wages"; "the employers can run the place like a sweat shop"), while female employees, working at least in part for social reasons, would consider the workplace unlikely to fulfil their need for suitable social intercourse. A firm in this situation could well experience a comparatively rapid change in the social composition of its labour force, necessitating, if tolerated, a reorganisation of training and personnel policies and the choice of the wage payment system based on appropriate motivators - see Millward (1968) and Legge (1970a).

Perhaps, even more dangerous in the long term, are the effects of the "hidden selection" of labour on the age structure of the organisation. In situations where its labour is coming under pressure in terms of job insecurity (through redeployment and changed supervision, with their frequent concomitants insecure and fluctuating earnings levels), it appears with both case study A and B that the age groups most prone to high labour turnover are those which in occupational terms are in the middle age range. The major reason for this is the social roles occupied by these employees at a crucial stage in their life cycle. For men it is the age band when high and steady earnings

204

levels are essential to finance new and permanent responsibilities; for women, too, the period involves the necessary saving in the years of courtship and early marriage, before the ensuing period of child rearing. In other words, the middle age range represents the period for employees when external financial commitment is at its highest. Thus, the members of this group, irrespective of sex, cannot afford to remain with a firm unable consistently to provide a relatively high and steady income, while for females in this group, high wastage will normally occur in any case, through changes in social role (that is pregnancy). For these female workers who are unmarried but self-supporting, the pressures normally associated with the primary rather than secondary wage earner will occur, and a certain level of income will have to be maintained that stands at risk in a situation of job insecurity.

Thus, if product market changes have repercussions that in employees' perceptions adversely affect work-flow arrangements and threaten the level and stability of earnings, it is likely that a bimodal age structure among hourly paid workers will develop (that is, the establishment maintained is of workers at both ends of the age structure, while the middle age range is denuded). The very young workers are less likely to leave as pressures to maintain regularly a high income level do not exist to the same extent as for workers in the middle age range. For older workers, different pressures operate to prevent high wastage through labour turnover. In practice, for these workers, labour turnover would involve the surrendering of both formal and informal privileges attached to long service (for instance greater security of job rights specifically and employment in general, greater opportunity to avoid undesired redeployment, greater opportunities of job choice and possible promotion, a favoured position in an "overtime club," choice of

holiday period, pension rights and possible condone-
ment by supervision of a gradual slackening of effort
levels, etc.), at the risk of being at a disadvantage
through age in the labour market. The problems
associated with re-training the older worker, are
again relevant here. The importance of the reciprocal
influence of labour turnover and age distribution have
been discussed here, but there is another variable to
be related to these, sex. For example, the age
distribution of women workers will be important,
particularly with regard to reasons for leaving. Thus,
independently of, say, problems generated by pressures
on workflow administration and the wage payment
system, women with a certain age band will be likely
to leave through marriage and/or pregnancy. Such
factors acting both as rewards and sanctions for
stability bind the older worker into the firm, often
irrespective of attachment or non-attachment to the
intrinsic factors in his job, and in spite of the
potentially threatening situation of the deterioration
of the effort-reward relationship of less privileged
workmates. The process whereby the worker is
bound into a firm and ultimately trapped in it has
been termed by the authors as that of "institution-
alisation."

The problems inherent in a bimodal age structure
accentuate these outlined above and in case studies A
and B. Firstly, if the age structure is heavily biased
towards the upper age group, it can become increasingly difficult, especially in the employment of
female labour to recruit younger employees, and
maintain an optimum size labour force. Further case
studies collected in the garment industry provide many
illustrations to this effect, as the following quotations
indicate: "The average age of the operatives was very
high, which meant that young girls would often leave
after a few weeks simply due to lack of young
company"; "There is a high turnover among new

206

recruits in their first month, mostly due to younger
girls preferring not to work with older women. "
This is perhaps the greater long term danger of a
bimodal age distribution. For if the latter bulge is
not balanced by the equal recruitment and retention
of younger workers, a self-selection process will
progressively accelerate the proportional increase of
this age group at the expense of the younger group. If,
within an organisation, there exists a disproportionate
number of older workers, with long service and hence
powerful claims on the preservation of their job and
income security (in the terms outlined above), when
environmental pressures attack this security through
increased redeployment over space and/or time
without adequate primary infrastructures to absorb
the dysfunctional repercussions upon earnings levels,
informal social relationships and so on, the younger
age group is likely to suffer disproportionately (for
instance the younger men will be more frequently
involved in redeployment over space, loss of over-
time/perceived excessive overtime, etc). Numbers
of them may then opt out of the firm, thereby
increasing the disadvantageous pressure on the
remaining younger workers, unless the dangers of the
process are recognised, and the firm maintains its
labour force by either restructuring primary infrastructures or, less constructively, and at the expense
of much internal conflict by trading on the institutionalised state of its older workers.

Secondly, general social changes are intensifying
the problems of firms with a bimodal age structure.
Firms experiencing difficulties in maintaining job and
income security for all categories of workers (and
especially for those without the formal and informal
privileges attached to length of service) will increasingly
find younger labour as intolerant of earnings insecurity
(and therefore of organisations where the primary
infrastructures do not shield labour from potentially

207

dysfunctional effects of redeployment over space/or time) as that of the middle age range. On the one hand, the younger age group increasingly takes on the characteristics of the middle age group (see, for example, the younger age at marriage in British society today, the higher birth rate among recent marriages (Kelsall, 1967), the frequent aspiration among the younger age group for home ownership, etc.). On the other, there is its development as an intensively exploited consumer market in its own right. The recent legislation on the age of majority enabling 18 year olds to take on full adult commitments in terms, for example, of marriage and responsibility for contracting debts seems relevant here. In more than one case study, the process had been observed over time whereby the denuded state of the middle age band has escalated, eroding the younger age band. Bimodal age structures, often a symptom of organisations under pressure, have a tendency to become mono-modal, with the implication, in terms of labour wastage, of gradually eroding the organisations' potentially most valuable labour, before that which remains itself melts away via illness induced absenteeism, retirement and death.

A bimodal age structure, a frequent result of the inadequately contained processes of redeployment discussed above, serves to accentuate such consequences of environmental pressures. For not only does it tend to diminish the supply of labour to the firm in quantitative terms, but, largely as a result of this, to sap the firm's resources, in terms of the quality and flexibility of its labour, at a time when it most needs these characteristics to compensate for numerical shortage. As a result, the compensating redeployment increasingly polarises the two age groups which aggravates the process of hidden selection of labour. If a firm's labour supply is largely composed of very young and older workers, problems arise in the deployment of labour, especially when, in a given work group or section, there are operations of differing skill levels, and where the number and proportion of high and low skill operations change in relation to each other. When the number of high skill jobs is increasing the problem arises, as mentioned previously, of finding enough operators of sufficient skill. The supervisor may well be forced to look beyond the hard core of older, skilled operators and train younger men. Yet, once the skill level of these younger men is increased, the problem arises as to whether, with further product change and possible alteration of production arrangements, there will be enough skilled operations to go round. If there are not, it is likely that the younger men will be deployed on the less skilled operations (with likely unfavourable repercussions on their earnings potential) while the older workers retain the high skilled operations that remain. If the supervisor, afraid of high labour turnover (with its repercussions on both past and present training costs, as well as general disruption) among the younger workers, allows a proportion to remain on high skilled operations, at the risk of transferring older institutionalised workers on to lower skilled jobs than those to which they are accustomed, labour turnover may be diminished, but at the cost of low levels of effort and high absenteeism, if not overt conflict, on the part of the older workers. Alternatively, the system may adjust temporarily through some form of straight wage inflation such as by grade drift, or training allowances to compensate for earnings loss consequent on redeployment, but having an eventual feedback to the product market via the effect on labour unit cost, this course of action may further result in problem resulting changes in production arrangements.

If, alternatively, production arrangements call for operations of differing skill levels, but proportionally static for long periods, a different situation may emerge. The older workers will retain control over the more skilled (and probably higher paying) operations, while there is a constant draining labour turnover of the younger men on the less skilled operations, seeing the likelihood of promotion, (and hence increase in the stable elements in the wage packet) at the best slow and at the worst non-existent. The younger labour that remains is likely to be unambitious and apathetic, with low levels of productivity, reinforcing the older workers' hold on the better jobs. Yet it is to this pool of labour that the firm would normally look for potential first line supervision, after passage through jobs of increasing seniority and skill content. If the firm attempts to cope with the loss of its high calibre young labour through wage inflation on the lower skilled jobs, disputes over the re-establishment of customary differentials may well occur. If it attempts to cope by redeployment of its institutionalised workers the conflict expressions mentioned above may emerge.

In both situations, the pressures that dictate a pattern of workflow arrangements influence the adequacy and appropriateness of other primary infrastructures which, in turn, influence the possibility of a bimodal age structure occurring. The bimodal age structure is then likely to aggravate the pressures and inadequacies which initially gave rise to its existence.

6.8   CONCLUSIONS
The foregoing discussions suggest two points:

1   When production changes stemming from changes in the product market are coped with by redeployment (there existing constraints in labour market against recruitment to increase the size of the establishment), unless the wage payment system is appropriate to match changed job requirements with expectations, in

such a way as to maintain a perceived favourable equilibrium in the effort-reward relationship, labour wastage is likely to occur, and is likely to be self-perpetuating.

2   While the forms of labour wastage (labour turnover and absenteeism) are similar in both case studies, the processes by which they occur depend upon the whole range of variables shown as interacting in Figure 6:1. For example, not only does the structure of the product market influence the type of product changes undertaken, but the type of technology will attenuate or accentuate the extent to which the logically predictable type of redeployment will result in actual redeployment. Moreover, as emphasised throughout, the relationship between redeployment and labour wastage will depend largely on the ability of the wage payment system to establish a new equilibrium between changed job requirements and the expectations.

It is necessary to concentrate on the processes by which similar forms of labour wastage occur, owing to their implications at the level of action, that is, for policy making. Of the two forms of redeployment discussed here, as far as the workers' occupational roles are concerned, it is considered that redeployment over space is more severe. If the payment system is inappropriate - in common with workers redeployed over time - his effort-reward relationship deteriorates, but to a far greater extent his status and general social relationships within his work group are threatened. In other words, while the occupational role of the worker redeployed over time is in qualitative terms largely unchanged, that of the worker redeployed over space can be radically altered in terms of operational content, status, supportive social relationships, etc. Thus, when the vicious circle of a regressive spiral operates unchecked, the speed and severity of labour wastage can far outstrip that

resulting when only redeployment over time exists.
But equally, as mentioned above, because the workers
have no ambivalent feelings towards this form of
redeployment, its cessation can lead to a relatively
rapid improvement in a firm's labour situation,
which, given the "double bind," has not been found to
be immediately the case with cessation of the latter
form of redeployment.

Decisions taken in the product market, therefore,
by patterning forms of redeployment, the pressures
from which, if aggravated rather than contained by
the wage payment system, can push the organisation
into a regressive spiral of labour wastage, also
influence the ability of the organisation to arrest the
spiral quickly. If the wage payment system cannot
contain environmental pressures, their dysfunctional
diffusion can be halted by the other crucial variable
of the primary infrastructure: conflict resoution
mechanisms.

Indeed, the quality of the existing conflict resolution
mechanisms are inevitably tested when the rules and
procedures relating effort to reward come under fire
in disputes seeking to adjust levels of reward (for
example, differentials, disputes, bargaining over
rates) or the pattern of job allocation with its
relationship with rewards (for example, disputes betwee
men and supervision over transfers to other work teams
allocation of jobs of higher/lower skill content than
those previously worked, allocation of overtime, etc.).
Invariably, when environmental changes upset a control
mechanism (for instance the rules and procedures
relating effort and reward) in which both sides in
industry have interests and reason to manipulate,
conflicting expectations (job requirements or job
expectations) confront each other as industrial
relations problems, to be resolved by specific
procedures. The latter, if appropriate, can function
to restructure the relationships postulated in Figure

212

6:3, so that the total system achieves a new equilibrium. However, the likelihood of adequate and appropriate conflict resolution mechanisms existing alongside an inadequately functioning wage payment system is slight almost by definition. The problems in arresting a regressive spiral largely centre around the fact that inadequate primary infrastructures tend to cluster and, through the process of interaction, mutually aggravate a system already under environmental pressure.

REFERENCES

Clay, H M (1960) "The Older Worker and his Job" (Problems of Progress in Industry, number 7), HMSO

Crozier, M (1965) "The Bureaucratic Phenomenon," Tavistock Publications

Emery, F (1969) "Systems Thinking," Penguin

Fox, A (1966) "The Time-span of Discretion Theory: an Appraisal," Institute of Personnel Management

Gowler, D (1969a) "Determinants of the supply of labour to the firm," Journal of Management Studies, volume 6, pp 73-95

Gowler, D (1969b) "Wage Drift: the Shadow and the Substance," Guardian Business Series

Gowler, D and Legge, K (1970, in press) "The Regressive Spiral: an Essay in Organizational Pathology," Institute of Personnel Management

Jaques, E (1961) "Equitable Payment," Heinemann Educational

Kelsall, R K (1967) "Population," Longman

Legge, K (1970a) "Paying mum and motivation," Personnel Management, volume 2, number 1, pp 30-2

Legge, K (1970b) "The operation of the 'regressive spiral' in the labour market," Journal of Management Studies, volume 7, pp 1-22

Lupton, T and Gowler, D (1969) "Selecting a Wage Payment System" (Federation Research Paper III), Engineering Employers' Federation

Millward, N (1968) "Family status and behaviour at work," Sociological Review, volume 19, number 2, pp 149-164

Ni Bhroin, N (1969) "The Motivation and Productivity of Young Women Workers" (Human Sciences in Industry Study, number 4), Irish National Productivity Committee

Samuel, P J (1969) "Labour Turnover: towards a Solution," Institute of Personnel Management

7 Wage structures and internal labour markets

by Derek Robinson and W M Conboy

A wage structure is a set of relative wage levels for
different occupations and is, therefore, a hierarchy
or league table of wages for a number of occupations
or jobs. Here, we shall concentrate on the relationship of wages of different occupations in the same
plant, and so will discuss internal plant wage structures.
The term wage structure implies something more than
just an observed set of relationships; it suggests that
there are reasons for them. Thus, when we speak of
a wage structure we often imply that some expected
relationship will or should hold. For example, it is
generally accepted that the wage structure should be
such as to pay skilled men more than semi-skilled,
who in turn should receive more than unskilled.
Traditionally, skill content of an occupation or job has
been vital in determining views about wage structures
and what they ought to reflect. Other factors can
influence the wage structure such as pace of work, its
pleasantness and the physical surroundings, danger,
effort, length of training, shortage of members of the
occupation and so on. There may be various views
held by different groups of workers about the "proper"
wage structure, and there may be differences between
the planned and actual wage structure. Many sectional
claims for wage increases assume not merely that the
workers should receive an absolute increase but also
relatively as against other groups in the plant. (We
are deliberately excluding external relativities, that
is comparisons with wages of groups of workers, in

215

either the same or different occupations, in other plants.) Thus, pressure to change differentials is regarded as synonymous with efforts to change the wage structure.

National collective bargaining in engineering does not seek to lay down a universal standard wage structure although it does produce consolidated time rates for some skilled occupations and for labourers. This might be thought to imply a wage structure because it produces guidelines that suggest the relationship that ought to hold between the wages of the various occupations. But as the engineering agreement sets minimum levels and not standard rates the implied wage structure is not very definitive. The industry accepts that plant-level additions are often made, although the reasons and the amounts often lead to considerable disagreement between the two sides of industry. Even if the national wage rates seem to provide a wage structure, at least for certain occupations, it is not necessarily maintained at plant level, for plant increases seldom produce the same effective wage structure as implied by the national rates. Thus, it is reasonable to expect two wage structures in engineering. Even so there is still an implication that the wage structure at plant level will reflect and be based upon certain pre-determined factors. The implication that a wage structure should reflect deliberately chosen factors is somehow bound up with the very use of the term no matter at what level the structure is determined and no matter what specific factors have caused it to be what it is. Thus, although we have defined wage structure as a set of relative wage levels for different occupations, there is also some philosophy or set of explanatory factors underlying the particular relationships which is not the result of random factors.

However, the wage structure is not necessarily based on factors carefully and rationally assessed with

216

different weightings agreed for its various features,
as sometimes suggested for job evaluation pay schemes.
Sometimes the structure reflects the bargaining
strength of specific groups of workers, being one
reason why the actual structure differs from the
agreed or formal structure. The reality of bargaining
power can lead to the forced acceptance of changed
differentials. Nor does the existence of a wage
structure mean that it is basically accepted by those
concerned. Some groups may wish to change it, and
more particularly their place within it, but being
currently unable. Nevertheless, they may hope that
soon circumstances will change, when they will
achieve "justice."

7.1 METHODS OF MEASURING WAGE LEVELS

There are different ways of measuring wages. The
relative position of different groups of workers within
a firm varies according to the measurement used.
Gross pay is the total amount of pay received for
work done in the given week. This means that from
the gross pay for the pay-week arrears or adjustment
from previous weeks are deducted, as are holiday
payments. There are three main items, pay
received for normal or standard hours worked, overtime
payment (including flat rate element and premium) and
shift payment. Excluding all overtime payment, the
actual standard week pay remains. A comparison of
gross pay and actual standard week pay shows the
importance of overtime to the worker or occupation
concerned. If shift premium is deducted and the total
divided by the number of normal or standard hours
worked, (that is, excluding the overtime hours) the
resulting figure is defined as standard hourly earnings
which were used in Chapter 2. This is a useful measure
of wages when making comparisons between different
firms or between different occupations in the same
firm as it excludes the additional payment received

for shiftworking which is a special payment for inconvenience and therefore excluded from the
comparisons. For some purposes, it is desirable
to put the standard hourly earnings on to a weekly
basis so that they can be compared with gross pay.
Merely to take actual standard week pay less shift
premium would be misleading as groups of workers do
not necessarily work a full forty hours of standard
time. They may lose time because of illness,
absenteeism or early leaving. Thus, for any sizeable
group of workers whose average total hours are greater
than forty we would expect their average normal hours
to be between 37.5 and 39.0. Also, there are some
elements of pay which do not vary with hours worked
but are a flat-rate element in weekly pay. This might
be a good timekeeping allowance or a flat-rate merit
or long-service addition. We have therefore devised
a measure of computed standard week pay which is the
amount received if the worker or group works a full
forty hours at normal, non-overtime rates, without
receiving a shift premium. It will generally be the
same as forty times the standard hourly earnings but
in a few cases will differ from this for the reasons
given.

From the viewpoint of a company's labour policy it
is not clear which measure of pay ought to be used.
Most comparisons by Employers' Associations in
engineering use standard hourly earnings, which
sometimes include shift premiums. In the DEP
average earnings and occupational earnings series it
is not possible to remove shift premiums.
Conversely, for many aspects of labour market policy
gross pay, including overtime, is a crucial factor.
Thus, to the extent that workers are influenced by pay
in different employments it seems they look at total
pay. This explains the advertisements referring to
"opportunities for overtime" and so on. We do not
really know the relative importance of these two

218

measurements to employers, groups of workers
making wage claims on the basis of comparability or
internal differentials and individual workers choosing
a place of employment. More research is needed.
However, the wage structure of a plant may change
considerably according to which measurement is used,
as is seen in Table 7.1, which shows various
measurements of pay for the six main skill groups.

For computed standard week pay the structure is
what is expected given the generally prevailing views
about the importance of skill differentials. If shift
premiums are excluded and standard week pay reduced
by men working less than forty hours of normal time
(column 4) the positions begin to change. The skilled
direct men still lead, but are now followed by the
semi-skilled indirect men, while the skilled indirect
men fall to third place some $72\frac{1}{2}$p behind the semi-
skilled men. Columns 2 and 4 are merely two
different measures of standard week pay. Column 2
is the ideal case of comparing "like with like" by
computing everyone up to forty hour week working and
excluding the effects of different shifts; Column 4
includes the effects of short week working (missed
shifts and lateness) and receipts from shift premiums.

Column 7 shows that the ranking order is again
changed when overtime pay in included. Semi-skilled
men now lead, followed by the skilled indirect with
the skilled direct group third. In all three measures,
the ranking order of the semi-skilled indirect men and
the two small unskilled groups remains the same.
Thus, even when workers are classified in the six
broad skill groupings used in Table 7.1 the wage
structure and ranking order can change, and the
amount of differentials between groups almost
certainly change when different measurements of pay
are used.

(1)	(2)	(3)	(4)	(5)	(6)	(7)
Skill group	Computed standard week pay £	Ranking order	Actual standard week pay £	Ranking order	Gross pay £	Ranking order
Skilled direct	16.32½	1	16.20	1	19.57½	3
Skilled indirect	15.80	2	15.41½	3	19.88½	2
Semi-skilled direct	15.48½	3	16.14	2	20.95	1
Semi-skilled indirect	13.09	4	13.14	4	17.70	4
Unskilled direct	12.39	5	12.39	5	16.19	5
Unskilled indirect	10.81	6	10.81	6	12.03½	6
All	15.17		15.17		19.41	

TABLE 7.1 RANKING OF DIFFERENT MEASURES OF PAY BY SKILL GROUPS - FIRM 101

Note: Direct workers are those in production departments, indirect are those in non-production. Thus, a skilled fitter in an assembly shop will be in skill group 1, while a skilled fitter in a maintenance shop will be in skill group 4.

220

7.2 METHOD OF PAY

The method of payment, or wage payment system in operation for the different groups, might also affect the relative earnings position. This is illustrated in Table 7.2

The three lowest ranking groups in Table 7.1 which did not change their ranking order - semi-skilled indirect, unskilled direct and unskilled indirect - are omitted for simplicity and because here only one method of payment was used. Thus, the six groups in this table come from the first three groups in Table 7.1. The orderly and expected skill differentials of computed week pay in column 3 of Table 7.1 now change as the semi-skilled direct pieceworkers earn more than the time rated skilled indirect workers. For actual standard week pay (including shift premium but still excluding overtime), the positions change considerably, and the ranking coefficient of the two measurements of pay is only +0.257. If the three excluded skill groups were included the ranking coefficients would be higher and more positive as these groups do not change their position at the bottom of the various league tables. The two pieceworking semi-skilled groups now head the league table. This reflects the impact of shift premium and to a lesser extent short week working. The ranking of gross pay is even more interesting. The semi-skilled piece-workers on a high flat-rate base lead while the skilled direct pieceworkers are last. The ranking coefficients between computed standard week pay and gross pay is -0.600 emphasising the inverse relationship between these two measures of pay, This brings out the importance of shift payments, but more importantly of overtime pay, in changing the internal wage structure and differentials.

The changing order of different skill groups according to the measurement of pay adopted does not occur in all firms surveyed but does frequently.

(1)	(2)	(3)	(4)	(5)	(6)	(7)
Skill group and method of payment	Computed standard week pay £	Ranking order	Actual standard week pay £	Ranking order	Gross pay £	Ranking order
Skilled direct (time) (a)	16.49	1	16.27½	3	20.26	3
Skilled direct (piece) (b)	16.12	2	16.11	4	18.60½	6
Semi-skilled direct (piece)	16.06	3	15.53	2	19.58½	5
Skilled indirect (time)	15.52½	4	15.09½	5	19.88½	4
Semi-skilled direct (high flat rate) (c)	15.37	5	17.17½	1	23.94	1
Semi-skilled direct (time)	14.94½	6	15.06	6	20.46	2

TABLE 7.2 GROSS AND STANDARD WEEK PAY OF SELECTED SKILL GROUPS BY METHOD OF PAYMENT

Notes:

(a) These men were timeworkers on the "national" consolidated time rate plus a lieu bonus. About a sixth of them also received supplementary payments of some kind but this accounted for less than 3 per cent of the gross pay of those receiving payments and just over $\frac{1}{2}$ per cent of the gross pay for all the time workers in the group.

(b) These men were "pieceworkers" on the National Supplement of (at that time) £7.38$\frac{1}{2}$ per week. Payment-by-results was paid on a time system with conversion factor.

(c) These men were pieceworkers on a high "fall back." The fall back rate was normally equivalent to national consolidated time rate. The payment-by-results was again paid on a time system with conversion factor. They differ from the timeworkers with lieu bonus in that their bonus earnings are dependent on their own (individual or group) efforts and not on the efforts of others.

223

Overtime earnings and the method of payment for
different groups of workers can reverse the wage
structure implied in the national agreement, or in
the internal labour market. The choice of the wage
measurement is, therefore, crucial for comparison
and possibly different groups of workers use different
wage measurements when pressing for wage increases
intended to change the existing structure. Little is
known of the impact of comparisons on internal wage
structures and which measurement is more likely
to lead to compensatory claims is debatable.

7.3 WAGE STRUCTURES OF SKILL GROUPS THROUGH TIME

Figures 7:3 - 7:5 show the relative importance of
pay of the six main skill groups in two firms for a
pay week in each month from October 1966 to
December 1967. The levels in October 1966 provide
the base of 100 and the subsequent months are shown
as movement in an index permitting quick assessment
of the percentage increase in the pay of the different
groups over the period. In firm 43 there was
considerable variation in the increases received by the
different groups from month to month. Group 1 had a
particularly large increase in July while group 4,
the indirect skilled workers, tried to compensate for
this in the following month. The internal differentials
altered considerably over the fifteen months as total
percentage increases varied from 10.8 per cent for
skilled direct workers to 4.3 per cent for unskilled
indirect workers. The variation in increases for the
six groups is even more marked for firm 17, where
skilled direct workers received a 20 per cent increase
and unskilled indirect workers 6.1 per cent. The
latter group are timeworkers who have periodic
adjustments in their basic rate, but evidently they fall
behind quite quickly when direct workers are increasing
their earnings. Both firms emphasise the dangers in

224

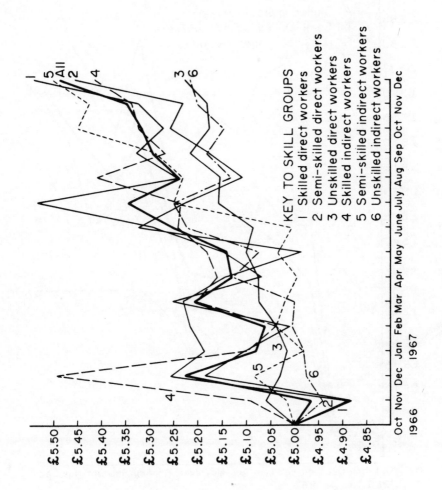

FIGURE 7:1 INDEX OF COMPUTED STANDARD PAY
           THROUGH TIME
           Six main skill groups and all workers
           (October 1966 to December 1967, Firm 43)

225

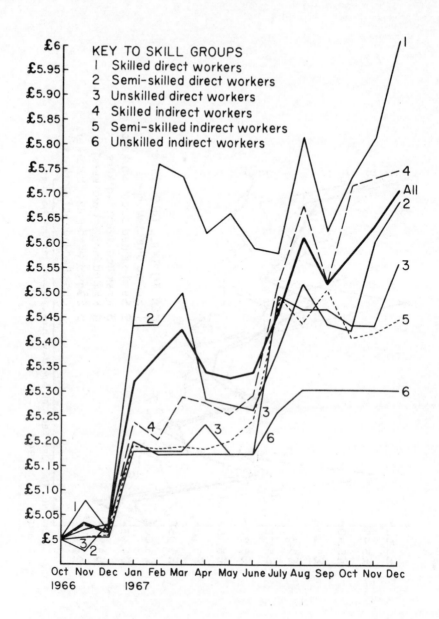

KEY TO SKILL GROUPS
1 Skilled direct workers
2 Semi-skilled direct workers
3 Unskilled direct workers
4 Skilled indirect workers
5 Semi-skilled indirect workers
6 Unskilled indirect workers

FIGURE 7:2 INDEX OF COMPUTED STANDARD
           THROUGH TIME
           Six main skill groups and all workers
           (October 1966 to December 1967, Firm 17)

forming too strong a conclusion on the wage structure based on figures for a single week.

Internal wage differentials are not rigid. In some firms there is consistent readjustments. Thus, examination of the movement in average standard week earnings within the plant can be misleading. During the period April to June, the plant average increase in firm 17 was in fact pulled up entirely by the relatively very large increases received by skill group 1. Standard week earnings can also fall. If there is a ratchet effect on pieceworkers' pay possibly it is more aimed at piecework prices, for earnings themselves which are the result of piecework prices and output move down as well as up. The fluidity of internal wage structures means that firms may well have more flexibility of action than is often thought, providing that they fully appreciate the nature and causes of the flexibility and can produce policies to use it constructively.

7.4 COMPONENTS OF PAY

As noted, there are several items in a gross pay packet. These commonly consist of time rate, or pieceworkers' supplement and payment by results, lieu bonuses, supplementary payments such as merit rates or long service allowance, waiting time allowance, shift premium and overtime premium. Their relative importance varies between skill groups and occupations and also for one occupation or skill group through time. Figures 7:3 - 7:5 show the relative importance of different components of pay for three pieceworking groups over a period of fifteen months, based on the earnings of individuals in one pay week each month. These men are "high flat rate" pieceworkers, the firm paying them the consolidated time rate instead of pieceworkers' supplement. The flat rate element and the payment by results components are separated into earnings in normal hours and earnings in overtime

227

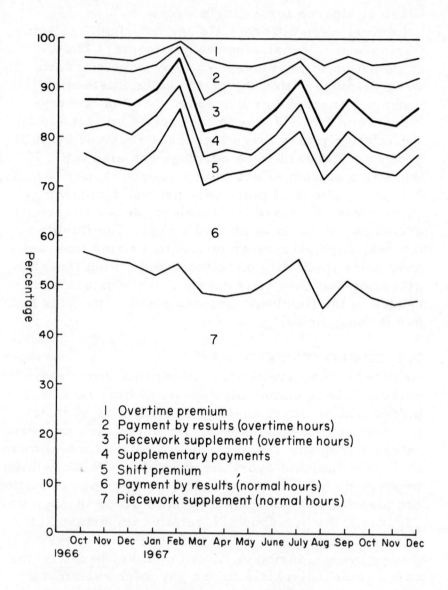

1 Overtime premium
2 Payment by results (overtime hours)
3 Piecework supplement (overtime hours)
4 Supplementary payments
5 Shift premium
6 Payment by results (normal hours)
7 Piecework supplement (normal hours)

FIGURE 7:3   COMPONENTS OF PAY OF SKILLED
DIRECT PIECEWORKERS
(October 1966 to December 1967, Firm 17)

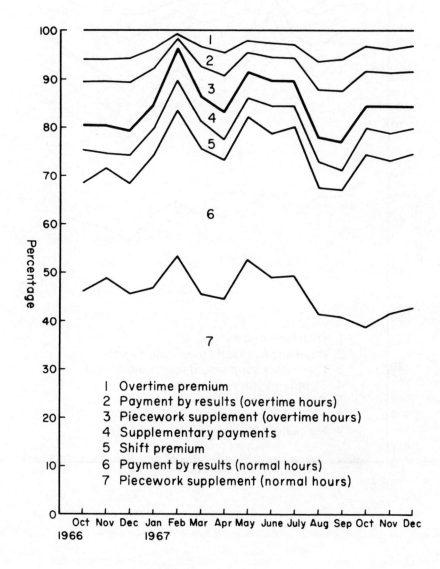

FIGURE 7:4   COMPONENTS OF PAY OF SKILLED
INDIRECT PIECEWORKERS
(October 1966 to December 1967, Firm 17)

229

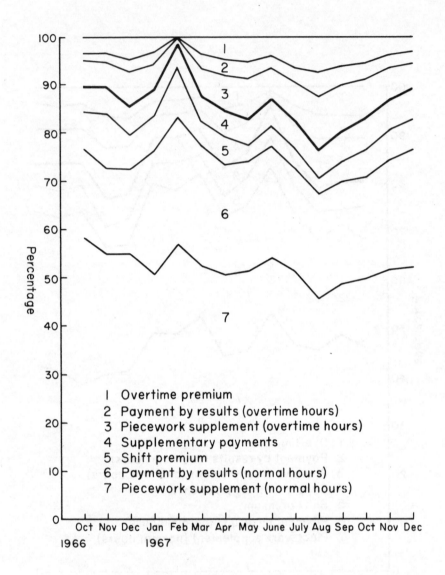

FIGURE 7:5 COMPONENTS OF PAY OF SEMI-
SKILLED PIECEWORKERS
(October 1966 to December 1967, Firm 17)

230

hours. This allows us to show together the total earnings in overtime, flat rate, payments by results and premium as a combined percentage of total pay. The thick black line separates earnings in normal hours from overtime pay thereby simplifying the changes in the importance of overtime earnings. The supplementary payments are not allocated between normal hours and overtime hours so that the total percentage of pay received in respect of overtime working is slightly understated. Shift premium is not paid for overtime hours and so comes within the total for normal hours.

Clearly, the relative importance of the various components changes through time. For example, in October 1966 56.8 per cent of the gross pay of skilled direct workers came from piecework supplement earned in normal hours, 19.9 per cent from payments by results in normal hours, 4.8 per cent from shift premium, 6.0 per cent from supplementary payments and a total of 12.5 per cent (6.2 per cent piecework supplement, 2.3 per cent payments by results and 4.0 per cent overtime premium) (strictly overtime should be a little higher as some of the 6.0 per cent supplementary payments were in respect of overtime working). The proportion from piecework supplement fell so that by December 1967 it represented only 47 per cent of gross pay. The same trend is observed for the other two skill groups. The proportion coming from payment by results rose, from 22.2 per cent to 33.5 per cent for skilled direct workers, from 26.9 per cent to 37.3 per cent for skilled indirect workers and from 20.4 per cent to 27.2 per cent for semi-skilled direct workers. This suggests that the hourly payments by results earnings rose over this period, a conclusion established by average hourly payments by results for the three groups.

Table 7.3 shows the average hourly piecework

Month	Skilled direct	Skilled indirect	Semi-skilled direct
	P	P	P
Oct. '66	10.95	16.70	8.90
Nov. '66	10.95	16.05	8.90
Dec. '66	10.75	17.60	8.85
Jan. '67	14.95	20.35	13.10
Feb. '67	18.00	19.85	13.00
March '67	16.55	22.75	13.25
April '67	16.20	22.00	12.25
May '67	16.15	19.45	12.10
June '67	15.70	21.20	11.80
July '67	15.40	22.10	11.65
Aug. '67	18.05	22.15	13.25
Sept. '67	16.10	21.20	12.30
Oct. '67	16.95	27.15	11.65
Nov. '67	18.00	26.90	12.95
Dec. '67	20.05	26.85	13.65

TABLE 7.3   AVERAGE HOURLY PIECEWORK
EARNINGS OF THREE SKILL GROUPS

October 1966 - December 1967.
Firm 17

earnings of the three skill groups from October 1966 to
December 1967. This steadily increased. This could
have been the result of increased productivity so that,
with constant piecework prices, hourly earnings rose
with higher output, or it could have been the result of
increases in the piecework prices themselves with
little increase in output per hour. Details of
productivity are not known so no conclusions can be
drawn. Our general impression from various pieces

232

of information is that the piecework system in this firm was under considerable pressure during this period so that we interpret these figures to indicate a general loosening of piecework prices and some degeneration of the control mechanisms. It is interesting to note months 4 and 5, January and February 1967, when all three groups show a rise in the hourly piecework earnings. There was short time working in February because of a dispute, and average hours worked fell from about 41 - 43 hours according to skill group to about 29 - 31 hours. The increase in piecework hourly earnings indicates that the groups concerned tried to maintain their total weekly pay, or at least offset some of the fall in gross pay, by increasing their piecework earnings either by extra output per hour, or by bringing forward piecework tickets "from the back of the book," that is submitting for payment in this week piecework jobs completed previously and kept back to provide some stability of pay in the event of unforseen factors as instanced here. Possibly also some groups anticipated the dispute and started unloading piecework tickets to provide a cash reserve during a strike. The unloading of accumulated piecework tickets is not uncommon among pieceworkers and must be borne in mind when making comparisons of pay of different groups of workers in single weeks.

The importance of looking at components to understand what is happening within the firm can be seen if Figures 7:3 - 7:5 are contrasted with Table 7.4. The Table shows that for two of the skill groups the percentage changes in gross pay and computed standard week were very similar indeed while for the other skill group, skilled indirect workers, computed standard week pay rose by 7 per cent more than gross pay. Yet the figures show there were some significant changes in the importance of the various components suggesting that changes are taking place which would have been missed on a simple comparison of the two general earnings figures.

| Skill group | Percentage increase in: | |
	Gross pay	Computed standard week pay
Skilled direct	24.3	23.9
Skilled indirect	13.8	20.8
Semi-skilled direct	15.8	15.9

TABLE 7.4   PERCENTAGE CHANGE IN TWO
MEASUREMENTS OF EARNINGS FOR
THREE SKILL GROUPS OCTOBER
1966 - DECEMBER 1967

While a common practice, in some firms a worker may be paid by more than one method of payment system in the same week. Table 7.5 gives the breakdown of the pay packets of three individuals in a pay week in December 1967. All three were paid by both time and piecework methods during the week. Interestingly, individuals A and B both worked overtime and received waiting time allowance, which accrues when for uncontrollable reasons such as shortage of materials or machine breakdown piecework earnings are impossible.

A study of individual worker's pay packets emphasises the number of elements in or components of gross pay. The greater the number of components the larger the number of points at which pressure for increased earnings can come. Moreover, the existence of a number of opportunities to the firm to increase earnings and thus ease any pressure provides a desirable degree of flexibility in a wage system allowing quick wage adjustment. There is considerable

234

Component	Amount			%	A Hours	%
	£	s	d			
Overtime premium	10	7		2.88	4.50	10.17
Consolidated time rate	1	1	2	5.75	4.50	10.17
Lieu bonus		5	0	1.36	4.50	10.17
Piecework supplements	9	5	2	50.33	39.75	89.83
Payment-by-results pay	5	16	2	31.57	39.75	89.83
Waiting time	1	9	10	8.11	3.75	8.47
Shift premium	–			–	–	–
Special allowance	–			–	–	–
Gross pay	18	7	11	100.00	44.25	100.00

TABLE 7.5   COMPONENTS OF GROSS PAY: INDIVIDUAL WORKERS
(15 DECEMBER 1967)

B*

Component	Amount £ s d	%	Hours	%
Overtime premium	4 3	0.99	2.50	6.25
Consolidated time rate	8 8	2.02	1.50	} 3.75
Lieu bonus	4 2	0.97	1.50	} 3.75
Piecework supplements	10 8 0	48.59	38.50	}96.25
Payment-by-results pay	6 6 0	29.43	38.50	}96.25
Waiting time	2 0 7	9.48	5.08	12.70
Shift premium	1 13 1	7.73	-	-
Special allowance	3 4	0.78	-	-
Gross pay	21 8 1	100.00	40.00	100.00

* Shift worker on a $37\frac{1}{2}$ hours normal week

TABLE 7.5 COMPONENTS OF GROSS PAY: INDIVIDUAL WORKERS (15 DECEMBER 1967)

Component	Amount £ s d		C* %	Hours	%
Overtime premium	4 2		1.21	2.50	6.25
Consolidated time rate	4 9 3		25.94	18.00	{45.00
Lieu bonus	2 3 3		12.57	18.00	45.00
Piecework supplements	6 12 7		38.54	22.00	{55.00
Payment-by-results pay	1 18 9		11.26	22.00	55.00
Waiting time	-		-	-	-
Shift premium	1 12 8		9.50	-	-
Special allowance	3 4		0.97	-	-
Gross pay	17 4 0		100.00	40.00	100.00

* Shift worker on a $37\frac{1}{2}$ hours normal week

TABLE 7.5 COMPONENTS OF GROSS PAY : INDIVIDUAL WORKERS
(15 DECEMBER 1967)

debate on the merits and demerits of a simple versus a complex wage system and structure, often hinging on the choice between flexibility and the lack of adequate control mechanisms often implied in a complex multi-factor wage system. We do not believe it is possible to generalise; the appropriate wage system depends on the factors and conditions present in any particular firm. The best account of the factors applicable in selecting a wage payment system is that of Lupton and Gowler (1969)

7.5 OCCUPATIONAL WAGE STRUCTURES

Previous discussion has referred to the wage structures of different skill groups and methods of payment. From details available from a different survey we can calculate internal wage structures relating to separate occupations although the various methods of payment were not known. The base of the structure is the standard hourly earnings of unskilled labourers in each plant, which are taken as 100. This includes all labourers in the plant, that is, machine shop, stores and washhouse attendants. Each internal wage structure was calculated separately so that although labourers represent 100 in each plant the actual amount of standard hourly earnings in the different plants are not the same. For example, in Table 7.6, in plant 2 the average labourer's hourly earnings were £0.5755 and the toolsetter's equivalent to 172.7% of this, a differential of 72.7 per cent. In plant 14 labourers received £0.4172 and toolsetters 203.5 per cent of this amount. Toolsetters in plant 2 received £0.9931 an hour while those in plant 14 had a higher differential over labourers in their plant than did toolsetters in plant 2, though in terms of actual money amounts they received less. The wage structures are therefore entirely internal, and external comparisons of relative amounts received by members of the same occupation cannot be made. But in plant 8 the wage

Firm	Labourers' standard hourly earnings	Skilled				Semi-skilled				
		Welders	Fitters	Tool-setters	Electricians	General machinists	Welders	Electricians' mates	Crane drivers	Internal truck drivers
2	0.5755	170.7	172.3	172.7	145.8	147.0	132.4	117.2	107.8	107.4
8	0.4458	n.a.	185.5	147.4	115.4*	127.8	n.a.	n.a.	n.a.	111.0
14	0.4172	n.a.	n.a.	203.5	174.4	n.a.	200.5	n.a.	152.6	152.6
15	0.5218	n.a.	163.7	165.7	157.8	155.4	n.a.	126.7	116.3	118.3
27	0.7458	105.7	114.9	119.9	118.3	108.4	108.7	101.9	n.a.	96.6
39	0.6172	136.5	135.3	n.a.	131.5	139.5	n.a.	n.a.	n.a.	106.6
37	0.4682	n.a.	233.9	214.2	175.4	145.0	151.2	150.3	n.a.	113.3

n.a. not applicable. No members in that occupation are employed

* Staff, not works

TABLE 7.6 EXAMPLES OF INTERNAL WAGE STRUCTURES IN LM1 –
FEBRUARY 1970

Per cent differential over labourers

	Minus 0.0–4.9	5.0–9.9	10.0–14.9	15.0–19.9	20.0–24.9	25.0–29.9	30.0–34.9	35.0–39.9	40.0–44.9	45.0–49.9	50.0–54.9
Skilled											
Fitters			1					1		1	1
Machine tool fitters (maintenance)				1				1			1
Welders		1						1		1	
Toolsetters				1						1	
Toolroom operators				1						1	1
Electricians				2			4		4	4	5
Semi-skilled											
General machinists	2	1		1		2		2	2		3
Transport drivers	2	8	5	4	3	1	2	2	2	4	
Internal truck drivers	1	6	5	3	6	4	1				1
Electricians' mates	1	3	1	3	4	2	1	1		1	3

Per cent differential over labourers

	55.0 - 59.9	60.0 - 64.9	65.0 - 69.9	70.0 - 74.9	75.0 - 79.9	80.0 - 84.9	85.0 - 89.9	90.0 - 94.9	95.0 - 99.9	100 and above	Total
Skilled											
Fitters	1	4	1	4	1		1	1		1	18
Machine tool fitters (maintenance)	3	1	5	1	2		2		1	3	21
Welders			1	1	1		1	1		3	11
Toolsetters		2	1	3	3	2		1	1	5	22
Toolroom operators		1	4		1	1	2	1	2	10	26
Electricians	3	3	3	2	2		2				33
Semi-skilled											
General machinists	3	2	1	1							22
Transport drivers				1							30
Internal truck drivers											28
Electricians' mates											20

TABLE 7.7 INTERNAL WAGE DIFFERENTIALS IN THIRTY SIX FIRMS ON A LOCAL LABOUR MARKET. FEBRUARY 1970

structure gave toolsetters almost three quarters as much again as labourers, while in plant 14 it gave them twice as much.

Table 7.7 shows the spread of internal differentials for a number of occupations in thirty-six engineering firms in the same local market. There is always a wide range of differentials so that for example in one firm fitters receive only 14.9 per cent more than labourers per standard hour while in another they receive 134 per cent more than the labourers. Figure 2:3 also illustrates this point in relation to local labour market 1. The vertical columns showing the levels of standard hourly earnings in the different firms also show the internal wage structures for those firms. If every firm had an identical internal wage structure the diagram would be a series of horizontal lines which did not cross. When two of the lines representing different occupations cross it means that the occupational differentials between the two firms are reversed. For example, in firm 2 welders are paid more than toolroom operatives and machine tool-fitters while in firm 3 they are paid less. The differentials are reversed in the two firms. While there are some general relationships in internal wage structures, for instance skilled men generally receive more per standard hour than semi-skilled men, and while some occupational differentials are fairly constant between firms in their relative ranking in a hierarchy, there is little similarity in the actual relative differential as opposed to general ranking. Quite often the general pattern of occupational differentials is broken or reversed.

Table 7.8 shows details of the internal wage structures in twenty-five firms in local labour market 2. Again, there is no clearly established uniform wage structure common to all. Differentials are sometimes reversed, for example in firm I fitters have an 8 per cent advantage over maintenance fitters whereas in P they

242

Unskilled labourers in each firm = 100

Firm	Skilled fitter	Skilled toolmaker	Skilled maintenance fitter	Skilled maintenance electrician	Skilled turner and machinist	Semi-skilled operatives
A	-	-	-	125.3	-	119.1
B	-	152.5	139.2	143.6	-	135.9
C	140.6	143.8	143.8	143.8	142.8	121.1
D	-	-	140.3	-	-	181.8
E	179.2	190.2	158.0	154.7	157.4	133.2
F	-	177.7	157.8	157.8	142.4	212.7
G	117.9	122.3	110.4	112.1	117.9	116.4
H	-	164.9	-	159.6	145.2	126.2
I	156.5	162.4	148.2	-	150.6	120.0
J	161.9	146.3	123.8	132.5	144.4	108.8
K	147.6	165.3	146.1	147.3	163.8	162.1
L	151.2	-	-	-	152.4	140.2
M	140.3	156.4	156.4	146.3	135.6	115.8
N	137.4	137.4	139.0	137.4	136.3	119.4
O	-	270.5	165.8	-	-	123.6
P	144.0	167.7	150.7	156.4	-	121.5
Q	172.9	176.4	158.4	164.6	172.9	151.4
R	120.8	-	120.8	-	120.8	111.8
S	132.4	158.2	135.2	135.2	132.4	128.6
T	133.3	128.6	111.1	114.0	-	127.0
U	132.8	154.6	-	127.3	148.0	130.4
V	129.0	-	-	-	139.8	-
W	148.1	-	148.1	148.1	194.8	128.6
X	-	-	-	-	-	112.6
Y	146.3	165.0	135.0	142.5	-	132.5
All	144.0	161.2	142.2	142.0	146.7	133.1

TABLE 7.8 INTERNAL WAGE STRUCTURES IN LM2.
AVERAGE STANDARD HOURLY EARNINGS
(NOVEMBER 1967)

are 6 per cent below maintenance fitters. Similarly, the differentials between fitters and toolmakers in firms J and K are practically identically reversed. Sometimes also the skilled/semi-skilled differential between certain occupations is reversed. In firm F, semi-skilled operatives earn more per standard hour than any of the skilled grades shown. In firm K, they earn more than fitters or the two skilled maintenance occupations. The overall (all twenty-five firms) average wage structure is shown in the bottom row. This illustrates two points. Firstly the "industry" average, of all twenty-five firms, only approximates the actual wage structure found in individual firms, and, secondly, although there may appear some general wage structure relationship overall it can be reversed in individual firms. For example, in the overall or "industry" average, fitters have a 44 per cent differential over labourers but of the eighteen firms employing fitters nine had a lower differential than this, eight a higher and one was the same.

Obviously wage structures in different firms in the same industry in the same town do not have to be the same; the internal labour markets can adapt to, or create, different wage structures. There seem few very powerful economic forces tending towards uniformity of wage structures and differentials within a local labour market. It is also clear that examination of wage structures in aggregate, for example consideration of the wage structure and differentials between different occupations throughout an industry, covers a very great diversity of actual differentials. Once again, averaging aggregate statistics mask the great variety found in practice when the detailed figures are studied.

Internal wage structures also change through time. The full data have not yet been fully analysed but it is clear that changes in differentials occur. For example, over the period April 1965 to October 1968 the fitters'

differential in some firms fell - 120 to 76, 95 to 77,
115 to 77 - while in others it rose - 50 to 68, 59 to
72. While a number of internal wage structures seem,
on cursory inspection, to remain reasonably constant
over three or even five years, there are changes
taking place and possibly previous differentials
become reversed for long periods of time. Moreover,
the changes in internal wage structures are not uniform
throughout the local labour market; changes in internal
differentials can be in opposite directions in different
firms. Once again, there are no powerful economic
forces within the local labour market which generalise
changes in internal wage structures.

7.6 DISTRIBUTION OF EARNINGS

We have concentrated on average pay - gross pay or
computed standard pay - as a measure of the
relative earnings of different occupations. Often this
is because the figures were averages reflecting the
widespread use of this statistical measurement in
industry. Often, however, the average is misleading
in hiding a considerable spread of pay between the
various individuals within the average. For example,
average computed standard week pay for the six main
skill groups in one firm in April 1967 were as set out
below.

	£	Ranking
Skilled direct	18.99	2
Skilled indirect	19.69½	1
Semi-skilled direct	15.21	3
Semi-skilled indirect	13.26½	4
Unskilled direct	10.81½	6
Unskilled indirect	11.21	5

This is the expected wage structure; the skilled men
earn more than the semi-skilled who earn more than
the unskilled. What is a little surprising is that the
skilled indirect workers earn more than the skilled

245

	£10	£11	£12	£13	£14	£15	£16	£17	£18	£19	£20	£21	£22	£23	£24	£25 and over	N
Skilled direct				1	3	6	5		7	8	6	4	3			3	53
Skilled indirect					1		2	9		6	6	1		2	4	4	36
Semi-skilled direct			2	6	12	13	13	3	10	1		2				1	61
Semi-skilled indirect		8	11	3	1	1	1	1								2	27
Unskilled direct	12	1															13
Unskilled indirect	8	7			1												16

TABLE 7.9 DISTRIBUTION OF COMPUTED STANDARD WEEK PAY IN ONE FIRM, APRIL 1967

direct. However, looking at the distribution of
computed standard week pay for each individual in
Table 7.9, the picture is less straightforward. Four
of the fifty-three skilled direct workers and one of
the thirty-six skilled indirect workers earned less
than £15 for a standard forty hours, while twenty eight
of the sixty-one semi-skilled direct workers and four
of the twenty-seven semi-skilled indirect workers
earned more than this £15. Taking a figure of £16,
then ten skilled direct workers earned less and fifteen
direct semi-skilled men more. Most skilled men
were pieceworkers although six were paid time rates
(one direct and five indirect workers). Five of the
semi-skilled indirect workers were on time rates as
were all the unskilled direct and fifteen of the
unskilled indirect workers. Even excluding the timeworkers means that at least three skilled direct
workers received less than semi-skilled workers.
The relatively orderly wage structure obtained by
using average earnings does not hold when the full
distribution is examined. Usually, distributions of
purely timeworking groups vary less than do pieceworkers but there is still some spread and overlap
between different groups, often the result of lieu
bonuses or other additions. Distributions of gross pay
generally show even wider dispersion and overlap
than do standard week earnings, as overtime is often
used by some less skilled groups to increase their
ranking in a league table of total pay,

   Figures 7:6 and 7:7 show the distribution of
computed standard week pay and gross pay for fitters
who worked at least thirty-eight hours in six firms.
The firms are in different parts of the country and so
do not represent a local labour market. The figures
are to illustrate the spread of pay for a specific
occupation and so emphasise the reservations to be
attached to the use of averages and conclusions drawn
therefrom. This reservation was mentioned in

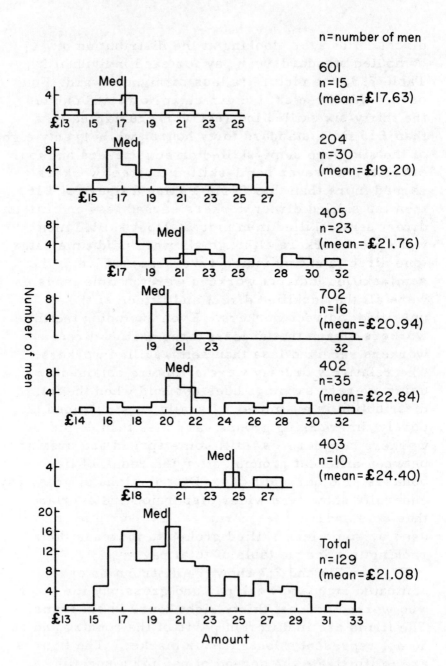

FIGURE 7:6 SKILLED FITTERS : DISTRIBUTION
OF COMPUTED STANDARD WEEK PAY

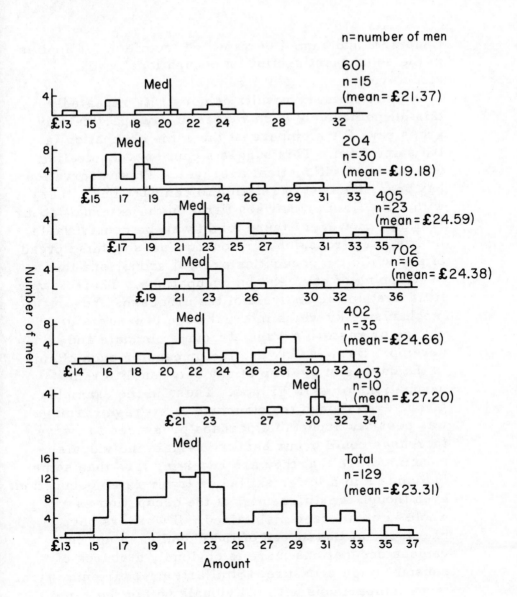

FIGURE 7:7 SKILLED FITTERS : DISTRIBUTION
OF GROSS PAY

Chapter 2 and cannot be repeated too often. It applies in the subsequent section on occupational wage structures.

Our preliminary results demonstrate repeatedly this phenomenon of wide ranges of pay, particularly gross pay, for members of the same occupation in the same firm. This suggests caution when dealing with simple arithmetical averages. This reservation has been stressed in relation to comparisons either within the firm or between firms in the external labour market. However, there might well be considerable internal repercussions or consequences of this spread of pay within an occupation or skill group, and the overlapping of pay between occupations. There is very little systematic analysis of the processes and mechanisms by which internal wage pressures to change or restore a wage structure emanate and develop. But possibly one factor causing such claims is the degree of overlap of pay between different occupations or skill groups. Thus, in the examples given, even though the structure of average earnings was possibly acceptable perhaps pressures for wage increases could occur because certain individuals become aware that they are receiving less than some individuals in a lower skilled or lower rated occupation, even though the differential of the occupation as a whole is on average maintained. If workers have knowledge of the spread of individual earnings in various occupations there is obviously a source of constant wage pressure. Similarly pressure may stem from comparisons with individuals within the same occupation.

From discussions with employers and workers, we have a strong impression that the comparison within an occupation or group is often based on gross pay with heavy emphasis given to overtime opportunities. In many factories overtime is not distributed equally between all workers. Some may not want to work overtime. Often, however, there seem to be groups of individuals who are able to work relatively large amounts of overtime causing discontent among other workers. There is then potential discontent for those feeling excluded from the "overtime club." This may express itself in pressure for higher earnings from some of the other components of pay, for overtime opportunities to be created for them or, and possibly more likely, in their leaving the firm. Precise and reliable information on why people leave firms is scarce but one reason often not brought out in interviews with personnel officers is the feeling that individuals have been excluded from their "fair share" of overtime. We have not completed our studies of the incidence and significance of overtime in the sample of engineering firms but this should be published by the Engineering Employers' Federation fairly soon.

Where there is a wide range of gross pay for members of an occupation the use of average earnings as an indicator of potential income when new recruits are hired almost necessarily involves the danger that some of the recruits will have their expectations unfulfilled. In practice, new recruits will probably not be able to move into the top quarter, or possibly even the top half, of the range of gross pay for their occupation, at least not immediately. They will, therefore, probably be disappointed with their earnings levels. This can be even more acute if they have been recruited or attracted to the firm by word-of-mouth recommendation of someone already employed there, often the most common source of recruits. Their informant is perhaps likely to be in the higher than average range of pay, this being a factor attracting the recruit. If the recruit is unable to obtain the expected earnings levels, the firm will probably have high turnover of recruits. Our experience suggests that a number of firms when complaining of difficulties in recruiting labour are really referring to high turnover among new recruits; the distinction between recruitment and retention is often blurred.

Even though recruits may be attracted by the level of earnings they think they can get at a particular firm this does not negate the arguments of Chapter 2 that economic forces leading to equality of pay in a local labour market are weak. Workers can move from low to higher paying employment without there necessarily being any tendency towards equality of earnings among firms. Possibly there can be a hierarchy of earnings and people progress up this by external mobility, but while firms obtain adequate supplies of labour they need not pay the same as other firms.

Although we have suggested that in some cases workers have some expectation of earnings levels in different firms or occupations within a firm there is very little evidence of just how much knowledge they in fact have. Sometimes trade union district committees or officials do have reasonably comprehensive knowledge of local average earnings in particular occupations. Sometimes they lack this, or their figures seem sketchy. Similarly, there is no clear picture of the state of knowledge of relative earnings within individual plants. In some cases, shop stewards collect wage slips from members and so are in a position to collect accurate information for some workers. In others, workers are not prepared to disclose their earnings even to their shop stewards. Whatever the state of knowledge within any particular group, there is much less knowledge between groups, even within one plant. This is even more marked the more that different groups are organised by different trade unions. This lack of accurate figures is often highlighted when there are disputes about relative wages within a plant, particularly when the subject is the relationship of skilled workers' pay and that of semi-skilled process or assembly workers. For example, skilled workers may receive a lieu bonus and wish to relate this to the piecework earnings of the semi-skilled grades. They may quote particularly high semi-skilled earnings which are correct for a specific week, but the semi-skilled grades may argue that their earnings fluctuate with output or because of short time working. Here. both may be using figures arithmetically correct but based on different periods. Or the semi-skilled pieceworkers may argue that only certain individuals earn the quoted levels the general picture being less favourable. These inter-group disputes are sometimes based on genuine ignorance of the real state of affairs, and are also sometimes the result not so much of lack of knowledge but of lack of agreement as to the wage relationship or structure that ought to exist. The different interests are partly expressing themselves in a statistical debate. In many firms, of course, this problem does not arise, or does not arise so often.

Much work must be done on the subject of knowledge within both external and internal labour markets. Perhaps if knowledge is improved labour markets will function more in accord with theory. On the other hand, perhaps the results will appear to be as though economic forces were working and yet result from institutional forces. Thus, if everyone knew what everyone else in the local labour market was earning, and there was some better definition of job content and work and skill requirements of different jobs called by the same name, then trade unions might well use the arguments of comparability to improve pay in the lower paying firms. They might succeed, not because labour was moving to the higher paying firms (who might not want additional labour) but because they used their bargaining within the internal labour market to obtain "justice or equality." Institutional pressures might then create the results we expect from theory and this can be one of the paradoxes of labour economics. The forces of comparability are often thought very powerful in union bargaining. At present, comparability arguments are often crude and based on average earnings or impressions of average earnings for certain groups with little attention paid to the question of whether or not the groups are in fact identical or even similar in anything but name. Moreover the claims may be based on what people believe to be true rather than what is or is not true. In some ways, this is the more important point. Collective bargaining pressures often result from what people believe to be the case, or believe to be "fair" and fairness and equity are subjective criteria not really precisely measureable. We believe, therefore, that the spread of knowledge about earnings of groups of workers in a local labour market, or within a firm, leads to institutional pressures towards uniformity. We are not sure whether this is good or bad but we believe that it will happen. Even so we do not expect rigid uniformity; there will probably still be differences within a local labour market. Sometimes, these reflect differences in ability and efficiency, sometimes the profitability and ability to pay of the company and sometimes bargaining strength. We also believe that the information companies require for their own purposes, for instance, of components of pay of different groups and their movement through time and of the distribution of earnings, will in time be obtained by both sides of industry and that, therefore, the tendencies we have forecast are more likely to occur. We believe that firms ought not to decide not to collect the detailed statistical information suggested here since they need it if they are to develop and control an effective wage payment system and structure. The dangers (and costs) of not obtaining such information exceed the possible upward pressure of wages resulting from an improvement of knowledge generally within the labour market.

254

7.7 CONCLUSIONS

The acceptability of a wage structure in practice is influenced by the type of wage payment system operating in the plant and the processes by which increases in pay take place. If the plant operates a time rated system with a single collective agreement covering the whole plant it might reasonably be assumed that the various trade unions or work groups are committed to the acceptance of the wage structure in the agreement, at least for the time being. This need not mean that each union or group believes that the structure is "right" and that their group are in a fair relationship to others. It might mean that they do not believe they are yet in a position to achieve their "proper" place. Nevertheless, in a sense such a formal plant-wide agreement represents some minimum of agreement between the various groups and parties as to the sort of wage structure that is currently acceptable.

On the other hand, a plant may have no formally agreed wage structure. There may be some process workers paid by payments by results and indirect workers receiving some combination of the the time rates and bonuses or allowances. The pieceworkers may increase their earnings by ad hoc rises in piece-work prices almost on a day-to-day basis. Timeworkers may then periodically press for some adjustment to their own wages to restore some previous differential. The fact that pieceworkers have been able to change the previous wage structure can, often, lead almost inevitably to pressure for compensatory changes by other groups to offset the resulting alterations in differentials. Moreover, as many of the increases in pieceworkers' pay results from fragmented bargaining by small groups there is no general agreement within the plant to change the wage structure. This means that it is, at the time, often very much easier to increase the pieceworkers' pay, but that subsequently there are pressures from other groups. If changes in the pay of any group or occupation have to be agreed by all the others, the process of changing the wage structure will probably be more difficult, but the changes once made have a better chance of remaining unaltered. If the changes were not agreed generally there is a much higher chance that the process of leap-frogging adjustments intended to restore some previous pressures which essentially reflect the fact that there has been no generally agreed wage structure in the internal labour market will continue.

We believe that the processes by which the realities of a wage structure are in practice determined exercise a crucial influence on the stability of that structure, and thus on the inflationary consequences of a leap-frogging series of adjustments and compensatory claims. It seems that in most engineering plants there is no generally agreed wage structure in terms of the reality of wage levels as opposed to some notional wage rate figures. Indeed, for straight pieceworkers, it is practically impossible to produce a pre-determined wage structure reflecting the realities of their earnings. This is not to imply that pieceworking is necessarily bad, but draws attention to one problem, often associated with it, but which might be offset by other advantages. In some cases, timeworkers' wages may be linked to pieceworkers' by a lieu bonus on a percentage basis so that their wages rise automatically as pieceworkers' earnings rise.

There is to some extent a choice between the flexibility provided by a system that permits immediate adjustments in wages in response to changes in output, bargaining pressures and so on, but which also carries the risk of constant involvement in dealing with counter-claims by other groups to restore the wage structure to some previous situation; and on the other hand a formally agreed plant-wide structure which

256

carries with it the implication that once agreed it will be in practice accepted by all the groups, occupations and unions, but because it involves obtaining the agreement of all parties every time any change at all is considered, has the possible disadvantage that it is slow to adjust to changing conditions and requirements.

In another area the internal and external labour markets impinge on each other. Securing an acceptable wage structure requires agreement within the internal market. The parties to collective bargaining have to agree about differentials. As suggested, the actual wage structure agreed upon will result from several factors and pressures which are determined primarily within the internal labour market. In some cases, the internal labour market pressures represent the transmission within the plant of forces determined externally as when craft unions press for certain wage levels or systems which are essentially determined by the craft union as a whole so that there is little if any scope for internal market changes and adjustments. The bargaining power of the various groups might exercise considerable influence on their place in the actual wage structure. However, sometimes management wishes to alter the wage structure determined by internal labour market forces to respond to perceived external labour market pressures.

Thus, if a firm is unable to recruit or retain members of a specific occupation it often seeks to increase their wages. This is often not a necessary condition of achieving a satisfactory labour supply but, in practice, if people believe it is necessary or helpful, they are likely to do it. The more formal the agreement setting out the wage structure the more difficult it might be to increase the wages of any one occupation. Here, firms may resort to various additions to wages which increase it without appearing openly to break the existing agreement. Thus, possibly every member of one occupation will receive an increase in merit money

R

which while supposedly granted on an individual merit basis can be used to give a unilaterally determined wage increase, as merit allowances are often not the subject of collective bargaining. Possibly other occupations will then press for increases to restore the initial wage structure. One company has dealt with this problem by having incorporated in its agreements a clause stating that "there are no fixed and inflexible differentials between day workers' rates, between day workers and pieceworkers and within or across market groups of jobs." A further clause permits wage increases where "the Company assesses that the rate has become uncompetetive."

Sometimes market forces require a wage increase if sufficient numbers are to be attracted and retained and then it might be necessary to seek to change the wage structure. In most developed countries, the shortage of computer programmers has led to their wages being higher than many believe warranted in relation to other workers. Economic forces have imposed a change in the internal wage structures in some companies, but interestingly others are now trying to devise ways of opening up further career prospects for programmers who, so far, have had high pay but poor promotion prospects outside their field. Possibly, with the creation of career prospects enabling programmers to move over into general management at a later date it may be less necessary to pay them such high salaries as programmers. This tries to alter the conditions in the internal labour market to overcome problems imposed by the external market.

Within certain limits, companies seem to have considerable freedom from economic forces when determining the internal wage structures. Some of these limits are set by external forces and some by currently accepted notions of what a wage structure ought to be like. The latter point, for instance, makes

258

it difficult sometimes to pay semi-skilled workers more than skilled, but not impossible (see Table 7.8 firms D, F and K). Internal labour market factors exert greater influence and are much more influenced by institutional forces such as trade union and work group bargaining strength and tactics, and it is clear from the great disparity in wage levels and wage structures that the internal bargaining strength of specific occupations is not merely a reflection of their external economic position as determined by general supply and demand conditions. There is considerable scope for each internal labour market to produce its own wage structure and indeed to adapt and change this through time.

Increased attention ought to be paid to the internal factors determining a wage structure. The method of payment as well as the degree of formality and comprehensiveness of bargaining over wage structures are no doubt significant in the process. The current emphasis on plant- and company-level bargaining implies that increasingly there will be pressures to formally establish plant-wide wage structures. If this occurs, probably the views of various unions and work groups about the proper wage structure and their place in it will come to the fore and lead to some difficulties. It will be necessary to secure some minimum agreement between the various groups as to the acceptable structure and, because this might require the ratification of some formal agreement, to reach such agreement might be difficult. When structures and differentials are informal there is no open commitment by the various groups to the resulting structure who are free to change it as they wish. Formal comprehensive agreements at plant or company level prevent this approach imposing a limit on unilateral action by specific groups. There might well be some conflict, therefore, between the desire to avoid the difficulties resulting from measures to establish a formal rational wage structure and the desire to end the current state of leap-frogging constant adjustment process. We believe that, on the whole, it is worthwhile to go through the difficulties involved in establishing an agreed structure.

REFERENCE
Lupton, T and Gowler, D (1969) "Selecting a Wage Payment System" (Federation Research Paper III), Engineering Employers' Federation

8 Practical conclusions

by Derek Robinson

This chapter draws together some of the conclusions
and points of relevance for policy-makers. It is based
on the previous chapters and also on the discussion
which followed the presentation of the original papers.
In some cases the following chapter will range wider
than the discussion chapters; for example, wage
systems were discussed at some length in the seminar
and, although only Gowler's chapters dealt with this in
any detail, the other contributors made a number of
comments which linked up with their quantitative work
on wage structures. Apart from references to
individual papers points made in discussion will not
be ascribed to individuals. The approach will be to
combine the arguments into a general discussion of
the issues.

8.1 ECONOMIC THEORY IN RELATION TO
PRACTICAL PROBLEMS

The starting point for discussion of wage structures and
local labour markets, and indeed for any topic which
tries to connect the behaviour of wages and their
appropriate level within the plant with effects,
activities and repercussions in the external labour
market, must be some interpretation of economic
theory. Implicit in managerial behaviour in wage
determination, particularly in conditions of high or
full employment, is some view of how the labour
market works. Whether this view is made explicit, or
whether it is even coherently formed, there is little
doubt that it underlies many actions in wage determination in practice. One of the problems is that

traditional economic theory of labour market behaviour is a sophisticated conceptual superstructure which is built on, and needs a number of assumptions about, rational behaviour and the free working of a market within which individuals are able to exercise a degree of choice. It also contains certain elements which are indeterminate and unquantifiable. Taken as a whole it may be regarded as a beautifully balanced and comprehensive set of interrelated concepts which provide a complete framework for the understanding of how individual workers choose their occupations and places of employment. The finely tuned and balanced parts of the theory fit together because it is assumed that the whole theory works, that is, it explains what will happen given the assumptions underlying it. However, from the viewpoint of someone actively involved in determining wage levels and wage structures in the context of a real labour market in which trade unions and informal workgroups exist and operate it may prove to be not so much a comprehensive explanation as a tautological trap which has little or no operative value.

The theory of the maximisation of net advantages can always be held to apply. No matter what differences in wages, fringe benefits, physical conditions of work and so on are seen to exist it is always possible to argue that there are (indeed must be) some other aspects of the employments which lead specific individuals to choose one employment rather than another. At the end of the day it may be that merely not having to go to the bother of changing one's job is in itself an advantage that helps explain why individuals do not move from a relatively low-paying firm (including all the quantifiable elements) to a higher-paying one. This would leave us with traditional theory intact but unable to make any statements stemming from a theoretical basis about the actual behaviour of groups of individuals in specific circumstances or the way in

262

which they will react to changes in circumstances.
This theoretical purity is of relatively little assistance
to those attempting to operate in a real labour market.

However, in practice, most commentators, and
certainly most practitioners, do not deal with the
full traditional theory. They tend to concentrate on
the wage aspect, on on wages plus fringe benefits.
They simplify the theory, and in doing so may well
distort it. Certainly they do it less than justice, but
this may be because they are looking for guidance to
action in the real world and are impatient with
theoretical explanations no matter how elegant these
might be, which cannot be applied to everyday
problems. The research work underlying the previous
chapters has stemmed from a desire to examine how
the facts of labour market activities so far discovered
relate to traditional economic theory.

8.2 THE WAGE/PRODUCTIVITY RELATIONSHIP

It is clear from the evidence produced that there is
very little uniformity between the standard hourly
earnings of members of the same occupation in
different engineering plants in the same locality.
Indeed there is a very wide range of average standard
hourly earnings between these plants. A comparison
of the spread of standard earnings in Birmingham and
Glasgow does not support the view that earnings levels
would tend to get closer together in tight labour
markets where the forces of competition would be felt
more acutely. This is a finding of some importance
as it suggests that what might otherwise be regarded as
"temporary distortions," which would be removed once
the full pressures of a tight labour market within
which employers really competed for labour were felt,
are more permanent and perhaps a regular feature of
local labour markets. It is possible, of course, that
there are significant differences between the other
conditions of employment in the various plants both as

regards rewards, fringe benefits, etc, and as regards
the effort bargain, pace of work, degree of skill
required and so on. If one wishes to argue that
workers of equal efficiency receive identical net
advantages, or that there is a tendency for them to do
so, then it is obvious that these other factors must be
exercising a very considerable influence, far more
indeed than most people would be prepared to concede
in practice. This point becomes even more marked
given the general condition that the addition of
quantifiable fringe benefits to wages tends to widen
rather than narrow the spread of wages alone.

It is often believed that wage differences are caused
by differences in the effort bargain, so that higher-
paying firms require a greater degree of skill, or
higher output of effort, from their employees than do
lower-paying firms in the same locality. Sometimes
this view is supported by reference to the generally
higher hourly earnings of pieceworkers who are widely
supposed to work faster or more intensively than
timeworkers. This sort of explanation is not
necessarily true in practice. There may be a number
of plants where pieceworkers do work harder or
faster than timeworkers in other plants; equally there
are plants where timeworkers are working harder or
faster than pieceworkers elsewhere. Moreover the
growth of measured daywork with higher rates of pay
and correspondingly higher daily norms is likely to
increase the number of situations where the accepted
view that piecework leads to higher output than in
other plants is invalid. For what we are comparing
is the rates of output of groups of workers in
different plants with different payment systems.
Arguments based on experiences within a single plant
which may have changed to piecework are not conclusive or even necessarily relevant. Discussion of
the various seminar papers confirmed the view that
there were many examples of pairs of plants in the

same locality engaged on very similar engineering work where the higher-paying firm, which also had the better fringe benefits and physical surroundings, had a lower rate of productivity. It has not been possible to test this relationship in any systematic and quantifiable way, but there are strong general impressions that the money and effort bargains of members of the same occupation in the same industry in the same town are by no means similar. Indeed, the relationship is often reversed, so that lower-paying firms may have a higher rate of productivity.

The method of payment operating in different plants cannot be taken as indicative of the level of the effort bargain, although it is of course relevant to the type and nature of the effort bargain made. The method of payment is also pertinent to the type of sanctions and pressures that may be open to the two sides of industry in their bargaining over money and conditions. The naive view that piecework contains a built-in regulator of the effort bargain - that is unless the effort is forthcoming, earnings will not increase - does not accord with the facts. Pieceworkers have various ways open to them of increasing earnings without necessarily increasing effort. Such methods include: increasing piecework prices following a change of materials, design or working methods; or, without any such changes, by receiving allowances of various kinds; by increasing the hourly rate for waiting time; or in some cases by double-booking so that waiting time is paid while piecework earnings are being earned. In a number of cases these increases will be granted with management agreement, or as a result of collusion between first line management and the work-group concerned. The important point is that it is no longer possible, if it ever was, to argue that all increases in pieceworkers' earnings come from increased output. The effort-money relationship is no longer regarded as a constant one.

265

Similarly, recent developments in collective bargaining which have increased the extent of measured daywork payment systems have changed the money-effort relationship for timeworkers. Traditionally the effort bargain for timeworkers has been but vaguely expressed; measured daywork requires a clearer and agreed statement of the effort bargain and in return offers higher time rates and a greater degree of stability of earnings.

It may be that the method of payment is more important from a local labour market viewpoint, not because of the implied effort relationship, but because different systems vary in flexibility and adaptability to changes in technology and production requirements, and because of the varying propensity of different payment systems to lead to higher wage increases. The control mechanisms available to different systems generate different internal rates of growth.

Payment systems ought not to be considered and established in isolation from the whole productive environment in which they operate. Conversely production or design decisions ought not to be taken in isolation from labour market factors, both external and internal. Gowler's work emphasises the inter-relationship of the different aspects of productivity processes, and produces a coherent analytical framework within which the various features and pressures can be examined. There are numerous examples of labour problems resulting from minor changes in product design. In some cases changes, initiated by sales or marketing divisions, which were considered as of relatively little importance, led to disagreement over the money-effort bargain because they required changes in methods, materials, or production workflow. Firms embrace many different activities and interests which all impinge to some degree on each other. A firm, like peace, is invisible. In many situations, it is thought that the labour aspects are ignored or left out of consideration when deciding on product changes. Gowler expressed this in discussion by saying that when considering product changes or new production plans there are three questions to be asked. Will it work? Will it pay? Will they work it? The third question is asked all to seldom and too late. If the full benefits of technological change are to be gained it is necessary to bring the third question, that relating to the acceptability of change on the shopfloor, into the preliminary discussion.

It is readily accepted that some aspects of production programmes create the opportunity for sustained and successful wage claims. When stocks are low and there are orders to be met there is a shift in the relative bargaining strengths within a firm, not only between workers and management but also between different groups of workers. Similarly at other periods in different circumstances power swings in the opposite direction. The statement that there is an active inter-relation between the different areas of activity within a firm - production, sales, investment and labour - is not therefore novel nor revolutionary. What is perhaps different in Gowler's work is the emphasis given to the degree of interrelationship between a wide range of different factors and the conclusion that many of the decisions often regarded as financial or pure production or marketing issues should be brought into a comprehensive programme of consideration and action from the earliest stages.

8.3 RELATIONSHIP OF INTERNAL AND EXTERNAL LABOUR MARKETS

One of the features brought out is the importance of the particular conditions existing in the internal labour market, an aspect which was also emphasised in the other papers dealing with wage structures. Internal labour markets vary from plant to plant within the same industry and may even vary considerably between different establishments of a multi-plant company. Generally internal labour markets in this country are governed by a series of informal rules, regulations and arrangements in contrast, for example, with the United States where there is a much greater degree of formal statement of the conditions and practices prevailing within the internal market. The British informality extends in many instances to substantive parts of the arrangements governing the internal market as well as to procedural matters.

The various research findings when considered together suggest that it is the interplay between the internal and external (particularly the local) labour market that provides a possible answer to many of the questions raised by the movements of earnings of different groups. Even granted the possible differences in labour between firms covered by the same occupational title there is still a very considerable diversity of internal wage structures within a locality. The external labour market pressures do not seem strong enough to impose a uniform wage structure in an industry, or at least in an industry where plant-level bargaining is practised. The pressures emanating from the internal labour market appear to be strong enough to create and maintain or change an internal wage structure to meet the particular requirements of the plant. It may be that some of the diversity would be explained if very detailed studies of particular internal labour markets over longish periods of time could be made. In this way, for example, light could be shed on the skill requirements of different plants, for it is already clear from evidence available from research work that the skill content of an occupation such as skilled toolroom worker, which is often regarded as reasonably consistent in job requirement, varies from firm to firm. In some firms semi-skilled process workers may be

268

given a few weeks on-the-job training and subsequently reclassified as skilled if they prove competent. However, even if these studies were possible, it does not follow that the corrections would necessarily be in the direction of greater uniformity. The institutional pressures within different internal labour markets are different as the bargaining strengths, opportunities and willingness to take advantage of the opportunities vary from plant to plant.

The "institutional" pressures may come from a number of sources. They may stem from different attitudes expressed through formal trade union machinery, or from the different personalities on either side of the bargaining table. They may come from informal workgroup pressures expressed either through some sort of collective bargaining arrangement or through informal or collusive action with first-line management. As has been discussed earlier, the different production processes and technologies require or permit different bargaining strategies which will lead to different results. The extent of centralisation in the company's wage and labour policies may exert an institutional pressure which is conducive to particular forms of wage movements; alternatively a more centralised wage policy in a company may result in a particular wage structure being "out of line" with others in the locality. Institutional factors in this sense, therefore, cover a wide range of factors, not all of which are customarily thought of as being institutional pressures resulting from formalised collective bargaining machinery.

While this study does not make a general claim that economic forces coming from the external labour market exert no pressure on an internal wage structure, it does seem to be the case that in certain situations external economic pressures are weaker than the internal institutional pressures coming from within the company. This suggests that the firm, rather than

being a helpless victim of economic forces beyond
its control, has a margin of opportunity within which
it can adjust its internal position and take independent
decisions regarding its wage structure and wage levels.
This margin of opportunity may be considerable in
scope and extent. For internal labour markets are by
definition as well as in observed fact to some extent
isolated from the external labour market. Labour
does not switch employment continually in order to
maximise net advantages. There is labour mobility
but there is much less than a comparison of different
rates of pay for the same occupation in the same
locality would suggest.

8.4 THE ARGUMENT OF COMPARABILITY

Where manual workers in engineering are concerned
it is much more likely that if terms and conditions of
employment in other firms are seen to be improving,
the first response of most workers, and of the trade
unions representing them, is to seek to obtain
equivalent improvements in their present place of
work. This is in part the explanation of the prevalence
of comparability arguments in wage claims.
Comparability is an attractive argument to use in that
it appeals to some previous state of affairs, which is
often implicitly assumed to have been a fair one, and
because appeals to traditional fairness are often
thought to be the most reasonable as well as the most
just. It may be that underlying the argument of
comparability is the view that, if similar improvements
are not offered, labour will leave or new recruits will
not be forthcoming, but this is an area about which
there is very little factual evidence. Given a state of
high employment and tight labour markets, it may
nevertheless be a widely held view, and certainly it
may be the case that an individual employer may be
unwilling to risk losing his labour force by testing the
extent to which labour is mobile in response to

270

changes in the relative eranings position. Certainly
many employers appear to believe that it is changes
in earnings that are important and must be matched,
and not necessarily earnings levels themselves,
although the continued use of such phrases as "the
going rate" or the "market rate for the job" are still
widely used. However, from Mackay's work it can
be seen that there is a relationship between earnings
levels and turnover. Whether this is a burden on the
individual firm will depend on the costs of hiring and
training new recruits. It should be noted that the
relationship is with earnings levels, and not with
increases, so that we do not know the effect on
labour turnover of granting or not granting compara-
bility-based wage claims.

From the evidence available there is little to
suggest even increases in earnings are uniform for
different firms. This may be because the time
periods covered in the surveys are too short. It may
be that there is greater uniformity of increases in
earnings over a longer time period or that the
recruitment and retention effects are felt in the longer
run which would lead to greater long-term uniformity
in wage increases, or even possibly in wage levels.
It is still possible to try and explain this in terms of
traditional economic theory. If wage increases given
elsewhere, or believed to have been given elsewhere,
are not matched by a particular firm, then the
workers in that firm may reassess their general
attitude to the firm as a place of employment in such
a way that they reduce the "value" of the intangible
returns received by them from that employment and
so reduce the net advantages of that particular
employment. This would lead them to change jobs.
In this way the comprehensive complexity of
traditional theory can be regarded as providing a
consistent explanation. But it does so in a way that
might not be acceptable to the practitioner, who would

prefer an explanation in terms of actual earnings levels. The problem with this is that it cannot satisfactorily explain the great diversity of earnings levels discovered in a local labour market.

Although there may not be any marked similarity in the increases received by members of the same occupation in different plants, at least over the period studied, there is evidence that the ranking of firms in a league table sense remains fairly stable over the medium term even though there may be more fluctuations in the short term. This suggests that firms may well have some view of the general relationship they want to have with other firms in their locality in terms of relative positions but this is not sufficiently strong to ensure that increases are uniform. It is possible to retain a general ranking position without giving exactly the same increases as other firms because there is such a wide spread of earnings levels for particular occupations. This means that there is often sufficient difference between the various firms for them to grant different increases without changing the overall ranking position. This is consistent with the evidence that ranking positions appear to be more stable at the top and bottom of the league table with more changes taking place in the middle where the difference between earnings levels is probably less.

From discussions with employers it does seem that increasing attention is being paid to the changes in earnings. Given the importance attached to institutional pressures in some of the papers this would appear to be right, but for institutional and not economic reasons. The forces in the internal labour market are likely to seize on increases given elsewhere as grounds for wage claims in their own plant. Moreover the tendency to focus attention only on the money bargain, and not also on the effort bargain, means that comparability claims resulting from these institutional pressures

272

will, if successful, appear to show the working of economic forces. There might be greater uniformity than hitherto; but because there may not be corresponding changes in the effort relationship, wages may not in fact be moving closer together. Thus, if comparability works only in respect of wage levels, or wage increases, and not also in terms of effort levels or changes, the apparent working of economic forces which will result from institutional pressures will, in fact, lead to a situation quite opposite to that postulated in economic theory. It does not follow that economic forces working in the product market will lead to any offsetting equalising pressures. For one of the features of local as well as internal labour market analysis is that firms who compete in the labour market may not be competitors in the product market and so they may be subject to quite different external economic forces in respect of ability to pay, profitability and so on.

8.5 ECONOMIC EFFECT OF PRODUCTIVITY AGREEMENTS

One of the criticisms made of the spread of productivity bargaining is that it leads to wage claims based on comparability of pay without there being any willing-ness to consider comparability of effort or working arrangements. The same argument can perhaps be applied to the more general comparability claims which seek to establish parity within the various plants of a multi-plant company or between different companies in an industry. Often these claims may refer to wage levels in quite different local labour markets. They do not in fact rely on economic arguments, based on the working of economic forces through a labour market, but on some general appeal to equity or fairness expressed in terms of money wages, with, perhaps, some notion of ability to pay lying underneath the claim. They are therefore essentially institutionally-based wage claims, not the result of economic factors. This is emphasised by the fact that relatively few productivity bargains lead to the firm increasing its demand for labour, indeed it may well reduce its labour force. In any case one outcome of most productivity bargains is that the firm reduces its claims on the labour supply in the external labour market, that is, its demand for labour from external sources, by reducing the number of people required to perform a given work load and/or by increasing the effective supply of labour to itself from its existing workforce.

Productivity bargains illustrate very well the distinction between internal and external labour markets. They can be seen as measures to change the wage and effort levels and relationships within the internal market in order to increase both pay and efficiency by reference to internal arrangements and practices. Even though changes in some of these practices and arrangements may require approval of some external agency, e.g. the executive committee of a trade union if the proposed changes appear to alter arrangements which are generally applied by the union throughout all firms, it is still essentially the case that the objective of the productivity agreement is to make specific changes inside individual plants or companies. An industry-wide productivity agreement may be seen as an attempt to make these changes for a number of internal labour markets simultaneously. The difficulty of doing this is seen in the relative absence of industry-wide productivity agreements which specify changes in much detail. From the labour market viewpoint, productivity agreements are attempts demonstrably to isolate the internal market from the external market by increasing the barriers round it. These barriers relate both to pay and effort conditions. Thus the fact that the firm is offering higher wages, or similar gross pay levels for less hours if overtime is

reduced or abolished, does not have the expected
"market" effect as the firm is not generally seeking to
recruit additional labour, although of course it may
still wish to replace natural wastage. The special
improvements in rewards are not linked with additional
claims on the external supply of labour.

From an external or local labour market position
there is therefore no necessary reason why other
firms should be required to follow the increase in pay
granted in the firms making productivity bargains. If
they do so it will be because of institutional pressures
from their own internal labour market based on a
simple comparability claim of wage levels.

Productivity bargaining also highlights one of the
major issues currently under discussion which is the
degree of formality and rigidity in the wage structure
and payment system. There is a fear that productivity
bargaining leads to an unwelcome degree of rigidity
so that it becomes more difficult and more expensive
to make relatively small changes in production
methods. In many parts of the engineering industry
it is necessary to make small changes in methods of
working almost daily. A payment system which
inhibits change might therefore have very undesirable
consequences for efficiency. Inhibitions can come
from the payment system and not just from the
existence of a written agreement which specifies the
areas of unilateral and joint control. If this is
recognised the question is no longer, "does productivity
bargaining reduce efficiency and inhibit managerial
flexibility, as well as lead to situations where workers
will store up restrictive practices to 'sell out' at a
later date?" The question should be, "does productivity bargaining make things worse?"

Usually productivity agreements do lead to a
greater degree of formality and the specific tasks,
demarcation areas and rules for the allocation,
mobility and flexibility of work of labour are set out

in more detail and agreed by both sides. Joint control
is substituted for unilateral control so that both sides
(or three, if we distinguish the official trade union
negotiators from the workgroup bargainers) gain control
over additional areas of activity and decision-taking by
sharing it with the others. Because specific changes
are being made, there is a strong tendency to set
them out in detail. The emphasis on areas of joint
control and the agreed terms that result from the
productivity bargain, by their very nature, focus
attention on the areas where such joint control has
not been agreed and published. In this sense there
may be more difficulties over these other areas in the
future. There may possibly be less flexibility and
more sticking to the letter of the agreement over those
aspects covered in the bargain. But whether this is
good or bad depends upon the terms of the individual
agreement and the conditions in and requirements of
the particular plant concerned. If there is need for
considerable flexibility within the plant then obviously
a productivity agreement which did not provide for
this would be bad; but so would any wage payment
system which similarly inhibited flexibility.

Given the increasing trade union concern over
managerial rights and prerogatives which is illustrated
by discussion of the status quo rule in disputes,
productivity bargaining can be seen as one method of
reaching some agreement over certain areas by
recognising joint control. The fact that management
might be regarded as having to share some control
should not be assessed in a vacuum. The next most
likely alternative to productivity bargaining ought to
be considered and the relative advantages and disadvantages of the alternatives assessed. If, as seems
likely, more and more areas of decision-taking are to
be subject to joint control in one form or another then
productivity bargaining becomes one possible method
of approach. Productivity bargaining might then be

seen as one way of providing joint control which also tries to link the money bargain with the effort bargain.

8.6 FLEXIBILITY AND CONTROL IN WAGE BARGAINS

Apart from their short term economic effects on wage costs, productivity and so on, productivity bargains may well have an important psychological effect on both parties. They necessarily impel each side to consider the objectives and motivation of the other to a much greater degree than is normal in traditional wage bargaining. For changes in working practices and methods to take place, workgroups need to understand why management desires to extend their area of control and what the economic consequences of making changes, or not making them, might be. Similarly, it is necessary for management to appreciate why workers seek certain forms of protection against arbitrary managerial actions and why they seek to establish their own forms of defence against fluctuations in earnings, or why they manipulate the effort-money relationship. There is a broadening of the areas of bargaining, which necessitates some appreciation of the other side's position even though, of course, this does not necessarily mean that either side will accept the basic premises of the other or that there will be a greater degree of commonly-accepted goals. Greater awareness of the motives of the other bargaining partner might not lead to greater acceptance of or agreement with their objectives but it does offer opportunities for more realistic bargaining with each side more able to obtain the things it really wants. It also allows each side to evaluate certain features of the existing situation, and decide whether or not some of these are really as objectionable as previously thought, and if so to decide what concessions it is worth making in order to remove them. It becomes possible, therefore, to detect obstacles which might appear to be less irksome than others, but which have a much more serious economic effect. For example, it might be irksome that only members of certain trade unions are "allowed" to give instructions to particular groups of workers, but this might have very little economic effect. Alternatively the degree of flexibility in the allocation of labour and the imposition of demarcation lines might seem less irksome because it has existed for longer and does not appear to challenge managerial authority in the same way, but might be much more important from an economic viewpoint.

Similarly the formalisation of procedural agreements and the establishment of jointly-agreed work rules can have important psychological effects which make a considerable difference to the atmosphere as well as the efficiency of the plant. It is possible to have formal procedural agreements at plant level which specify in detail not only the procedural steps to be taken in the event of a difference of opinion, but also the respective rights and duties of the various parties, in terms of decision-making as well as in terms of the money and effort bargains; yet such agreements do not have any specifically agreed wage structure or wage levels in detail. In other cases formalisation in procedure will be associated with a greater degree of formalisation in wage levels and structures, and the effort bargain may be brought in by means of job evaluation and job descriptions. In this case the question of flexibility of the wage structure will arise.

There are two broad schools of thought on this issue. One holds that, once a job evaluation exercise has been carried out and a mutually agreed wage structure established, that structure should be sacrosanct at least until the agreed review period comes round. The other view would argue that there must be some degree of flexibility in the wage structure - to allow for very short term changes in

278

work content, but also, and perhaps more importantly, to take account of the pressures of the local labour market. This debate raises once again the time-worn issue of rationality and control versus flexibility. In practice, however, discussion cannot continue for long merely by reference to these basic concepts. For control, although perhaps a desirable managerial objective, cannot be defended to the point where the continued application of some previously agreed wage structure or level, which is now inappropriate given changed conditions, seriously threatens the supply of labour to the firm. Equally, flexibility, which appears to have the attraction of permitting the firm to make immediate adjustments to changed conditions, cannot be defended if it means that the firm is continually altering some wages in response to external pressures but then finds that it has also to adjust the wages of other groups to maintain internal differentials, or if because of bargaining pressures it tries to alter its internal wage structure it then finds that other groups seek compensation.

Often the debate about control is really concerned about shifts in emphasis although it may be carried out in terms of some absolute principle. Control is necessary if excessive increases in wages are to be avoided, but similarly flexibility is necessary if adjustments to changing circumstances are to be possible. Both principles if carried too far can create undesirable conditions, as can their absence. In many cases the real problem is not whether there should be control, rationality or flexibility, but the question of who is to determine and apply them. Flexibility when exercised by management to change a wage structure may well be seen by workers as a loss of their control (perhaps jointly exercised) over wage differentials. Similarly, workers' pressures for the restoration of some previous differentials may be seen by management as a means whereby all groups are taking

advantage of particular circumstances affecting only
a small number of workers in order to obtain a general
wage increase. It may well be that ultimately the
crucial thing is not whether the system is defined as
one of controlled rationality with a predetermined wage
structure, or as one which contains a large amount of
flexibility, but whether or not the two sides basically
accept the same set of objectives for the wage system
and structure. If it is possible to obtain some agreement on the purpose of the system and structure, and
this will require agreement that the levels are 'fair',
then it may be possible to make changes in the structure
without generating a series of claims based on internal
differentials. It will also probably be necessary to
obtain general agreement about the effort bargains as
well, for many internal wage differentials claims are
based upon notions of equitable effort relationships.
It is usually easier to have views on these within the
plant than between plants.

It may also be desirable to have agreement that the
wage structure can be re-examined at intervals shorter
than a year if external pressures change in their
intensity or in their impact on various groups differ-
entially. This may mean, with job evaluation schemes,
that there has to be explicit acceptance of the implicit
assumptions governing all job evaluation schemes:
that external pressures as well as internal bargaining
pressures must be given some weight, even though
this may be disguised or hidden in the set of apparently
internally consistent 'objective' criteria or points
values for various jobs.

8.7 PRESSURES AND DIFFERENTIALS WITHIN
THE FIRM

With other types of wage payment systems the pressure
on the structure may come from pieceworkers. One of
the most difficult aspects of a wage structure is the
establishment of generally acceptable wage differentials

between different skills and occupations which have
different capacities to increase earnings through some
form of wage drift. This is often seen most clearly
in the widespread problem of the determination of the
pay for time-rated skilled craftsmen or maintenance
workers in relation to the earnings of semi-skilled
pieceworking process or production workers. Various
ways of trying to solve this problem have been
produced, e. g. lieu rates for time-workers, or a
periodic reassessment of their time rates in the light
of the development of piecework earnings. It is not
intended to discuss the most appropriate way of dealing
with this question; to a large extent this will vary from
plant to plant according to the particular conditions
existing there. There are two aspects which will be
referred to briefly.

Firstly, the question of wage drift. Increasing
attention has been given to wage drift and it has in
some ways appeared to be the villain of the piece.
Much of this comment has originated from consideration
of macro-level analysis connected with incomes policy
or with movements in aggregate wages. The concept
and indeed the measurement of wage drift has therefore
been concentrated on aggregate data; by wage drift we
mean something to do with the movement in actual
earnings (perhaps adjusted for changes in hours worked)
in relation to movements in wage rates as a result of
national or industry bargaining. While there are many
advantages in this approach to drift, it is not the way
in which most managers see it. They tend to regard
wage drift as some relationship between movements
in earnings (perhaps adjusted for hours worked) and
changes in productivity in the plant. They are therefore often thinking of "productivity drift." This is,
for them, a much more meaningful concept and one of
considerable concern to them. The fact that there is,
therefore, often a difference in the basic approach to
wage drift between managers and other commentators

281

is of interest and importance. For present purposes
it is more relevant that, from the viewpoint of most
managers, increases in wages at plant level which do
not exceed increases in productivity are not seen in
the same adverse light as wage increases which do
exceed productivity at plant level. We ought, perhaps,
to expect that, where pieceworking exists, some
increases at plant level will be an automatic consequence of increases in productivity. There will,
therefore, in a number of cases, necessarily be some
increase in the earnings of certain groups of workers.
In the absence of any predetermined mechanisms for
the maintenance of differentials within the plant, these
will lead to conditions where those differentials will
change and consequential claims for restoration of the
previous wage structure will occur. This is in some
cases inevitable, but, given the attitude to
"productivity drift" of many managers, not necessarily
undesirable.

Secondly, it may be that changing technology, which
leads to very different jobs and job contents, requires
a complete reassessment of traditional attitudes to
wage differentials. There is a strong feeling that
wage structures should reflect skill and training to a
high degree. In most cases we would expect, on a
priori grounds, that skilled workers would be at the
top of a wage structure with semi-skilled workers next,
followed by the unskilled. However, it may be that in
some cases the job contents have so changed as a result
of the requirements of modern productive methods,
that this traditional approach is no longer situated to
the conditions now existing inside some plants. For
example, in some engineering works there may be a
requirement for production workers to carry out
extremely monotonous, short-time manual operations
requiring some dexterity, but which contain practically
no job satisfaction whatever. In these circumstances
it may be necessary to pay these workers higher wages,

not because they have greater skill, but in order to induce them to put up with the extreme monotony. One solution could be to widen the job content so that there is greater satisfaction, but in some cases this is unlikely to happen in the near future, if only because the large capital outlay necessary to change production methods is unlikely to be forthcoming.

In these circumstances traditional differentials may be, or will have to be, reversed. We may have to reassess the factors rewarded in a wage structure and give far more weight to non-skill elements in certain cases, although not, of course, in all. Orthodox economic theory would express this by saying that the disadvantages of certain production jobs are such that they require very high monetary rewards in order to ensure that the net advantages are sufficiently attractive to ensure an appropriate supply of labour. This is not to suggest that all skilled and production workers' differentials are in need of revision, and far less in need of reversal. We suggest merely that in changing conditions it may be necessary to reassess traditional views on wage differentials.

8.8 LOCAL CIRCULATION OF WAGE DATA

As well as reassessing or examining their internal wage structure in response to changing conditions companies will also need to consider their external relativities. A number of local Engineering Employers' Associations already collect and circulate information about the relative standard hourly wages of certain occupations in various member firms. There are some conflicts in this activity: firms wish to know how earnings in their plants are moving relative to those in other plants, so that they can maintain some sort of competitive position in the local labour market, but it is not clear whether the circulation of such wage data is inflationary or not. If firms believe that they must maintain a certain position in the local wage league table, it is clear that in some situations an upward spiral can develop. This can happen if one or two companies increase their relative earnings levels, either because of some changes in the internal labour market (such as a productivity bargain), or because of changes in internal bargaining pressures, or because they are actively trying to expand the numbers employed in that particular occupation. If other firms are unaware of the changes in the effort bargain, or because of the force of coercive comparability claims, or because they fear a loss of labour, they may grant similar increases even though there may be no strong economic reason why they should do so. The reasons behind the wage increases in other plants can be more important than the mere fact that they have occurred, yet this can be an area where the common interests of the various firms is regarded as less important than the individual competitive position of each of them in a tight labour market.

Even if information is shared it may be that the use of a single figure - averages for manual workers and perhaps medians for staff workers - presents a misleading picture. In a number of firms there is a considerable spread of standard hourly wages for members of the same occupation, and, while there may be good reasons for this, it does mean that comparison of the single figure for each plant can be misleading, especially from a labour recruitment and retention viewpoint. If new recruits cannot reasonably hope to receive something like the average wage level it can be a very bad guide to the firm's competitive position on the external labour market. If the worker's expectations are much higher than the possibilities actually open to him in a particular internal labour market, there may be a rate of high labour turnover which is more strongly marked than normal even among employees with relatively short service. This is why there may be correlation between average wage levels and turnover in some situations and not in others; in some cases it is the earnings of the individuals who leave that are important, not the average level of earnings. In other cases, of course, there may be no correlation between earnings and turnover as non-wage factors might be the dominant ones.

This is not to imply that circulation of average wages of certain occupations has no beneficial effects but rather to emphasise the dangers that there might also be. Essentially the crucial point is the view adopted by the firm about the importance of external labour market pressures and the interpretation it places on such indicators of these as are available to it. These indicators include non-wage factors such as the number of vacancies and unemployed. One of the major themes of these papers has been that it is very difficult indeed to interpret these external economic indicators and that in many cases a simple interpretation is likely to be wrong. The economic indicators may be signalling institutional pressures, as there is no other easy way in which they can express themselves to others except by changing economic variables such as wages. Unless one believes that all institutional pressures are merely reflections of existing economic conditions, some room must be left for the result of those forces that are not purely economic in their source or impact. It is the interrelationship of the various forces and pressures that cause differences in and changes in wage levels and structures, and it is unlikely that such forces will be uniform throughout even a single industry in a local labour market.

Index

other attractions 31, 64; package of attractions 31–3;
rate for the job   30

Infrastructures: conflict resolution mechanisms 178-80;
primary 176-88, 198; secondary 176-8, 180, 198; use
of concept 178
Internal labour markets 17-18, 22-5, 51, 54-63; and
external labour markets 54, 62-3, 267-70; and wage
structures 215-60; apprenticeship of skilled workers
58-60; conditions within market 66; dilution 24;
efficiency earnings 60; manpower effort and its supply 23;
paid breaks for fitters 61-2; piecework systems 24;
pressures 65-6; producticity bargaining 23-4; 62-3;
types of market 54-7
International Labour Office, survey of payment by
results 108-9
Inter-plant wages structures 75-85: competitive theory of
labour markets 75; differentials in Birmingham and
Glasgow plants 76-80; measures of dispersion 76;
overtime working 83-4; ranking of plants by standard
weekly earnings 80-5; stability of structure 83-5;
substantial differences in plant earnings 76, 79-80, 84-5
Intra-plant wage structures 127-67: and inter-plant wage
structures 127; changes in occupational earnings 156-64;
earnings structures 150-6; wage differentials 128, 130;
wage negotiation machinery 130-8; wage payment methods
138-50; wage settlements 129-30

Jaques, Elliot 101, 177
Job requirements, changes in 189-91

Kerr, Professor Clark, 48, 54
Keynes, J M (Lord Keynes) 20-1
Knowles, K G J C 129, 132, 135, 146

Labour market analysis 16-22 approaches 17-22
classis economic theories 18-21; comparability claims
21-2; concept of labour market 17, 28; external labour
market 17-18; internal labour market 17-18; operation
of local labour markets 20; reason for analysis 16-17

T

Labour turnover and wages 68–99: barriers to labour
  mobility 68–9; competitive pressures 69, 75, 94,
  96–7; difficulty of applied research 70–1; disparities
  in plant wage levels 69–70; traditional theory of labour
  market behaviour 68–70; method of inquiry, 71–4; plant
  earnings and labour turnover 71; wage earnings in different
  plants 71; "anti–competitive" and "impeditive" forces
  96–7; computer analysis of personnel records 72–3;
  concept of equilibrium 96–7; earnings returns to DEP
  and EEF 73; equilibrium of net advantages 85–6; inter-
  plant wages structures, see separate entry; labour
  turnover and earnings variables 86; measurement of
  labour turnover 86–93; non–pecuniary factors 95–6;
  study of engineering plants (1959–66). 72–4; variations
  in work requirements and living standards 94–5
Labour wastage 202–11; bimodal age structures 205–8;
Labourers, key wage rates for 130
Lanarkshire, North, study of engineering plants in, 72,
  149–50
Legge, Karen 9–10, 113, 124: "The wage payment system:
  a primary infrastructure" 168–214
Length of service awards 149
Lerner, S W 127, 132, 134–7, 143, 147
Lester, R A 70, 95, 96
Lieu bonuses 144–5, 147, 227
Local circulation of wage data 283–5
Local labour market surveys 36–49; details of standard
  hourly earnings 37–47; differences in wages for same
  occupation 48; reservations 37–8
Local labour markets and plant wage structures 15–27;
  definition of local labour markets 16, 29–30; internal
  labour markets 17–18, 22–5; labour market analysis 16–22;
  work place behaviour 24–7
Long, J R 69
Lupton, Professor Tom 101, 102, 110, 115, 120, 124, 168
  180, 191, 238

Productivity: and supervisory leadership 111; "drift" 281-2; earnings and changes in productivity 136; increases and wage drift 135-7; relationship with wages 263-7;

Productivity bargaining 23-4, 62-3; economic effects 273-7

Pugh, D 120, 121

Rate for the job 30

Reciprocal and non-reciprocal wage payment schemes 110

Reciprocity, principle of 112-20

Recruitment rate 86-7 93-4

Reddaway, W B 87

Redeployment of labour 191-6, 210-12: through overtime 199-202

Regression spiral, the 168, 170, 171, 173, 175, 188-91, 202, 211: changes in job requirements 189-94; changes in manpower requirements 188-9; changes in product market 188; 198-9; redeployment of labour 191-6, 199, 202; vicious circle of bureaucracy 198

Rehn, G 133, 134

Reynolds, L G 68, 70, 95

Robertson E J 10-11: "Local labour markets and plant wage structures" 15-27

Robinson, Derek 11, 70, 127, 135, 146, 150: "External and internal labour markets" 28-67; "Wage structures and internal labour markets" 215-60

Role-activation conflict 120

Role-legitimation conflict 121

Ross, A M 128

Sayles, L R 113

Secondary infrastructures 176-8, 180, 198,

Shimmin, S 101

Shop stewards 65, 252

Skill groups: and measurement of pay 219-24; average hourly piecework earnings 231-3; changes in measurements

175-6; further implications of labour wastage 202-11; market structures and organisational infrastructures 175-80; model of inter-relationships between important factors 169-76; moderating functions 180; "open system" concept 173; primacy of product market 174-5; regressive spiral 168, 170, 171, 173, 175, 188-91; wage packets 184-8;

Wage payment systems 100-2, 105-6, 108-10; 138-50; definition 109-10; in Glasgow and Birmingham plants 138-50; pieceworkers and timeworkers 138-50; reciprocal and non-reciprocal schemes 110; tradition of individualism 115

Wge/productivity relationship 263-7; differences in effort bargain 264-5; wage claims 267

Wage settlements 129-30; comparability 129; "fair relativities" 129-30; patterns 129; social pressures at national and plant level 129-30

Wage structures and internal labour markets 215-60: components of pay 227-38; distribution of earnings 245-60; measurement of pay-by-skill groups 219-24; method of pay 221-4, methods of measuring wage levels 217-20; national bargaining 216; occupational wage structures 238-45; wage structures of skill groups through time 224-7

Wages and labour turnover 68-69

"Wealth of Nations (Adam Smith) 18-19, 68

Wedderburn, D 74

Wilcock, R C 74

Wilkinson, R 80, 87

Wilson, Shirley 116, 124

Woodward, Joan 111

Wootton, B 129

Work measurement 143

See also Measured day work systems

Work place behaviour 24-7; plant bargaining 26-7

Work requirements, variations in 94-5